Leveled Reading, Leveled Lives

Leveled Reading, Leveled Lives

How Students' Reading Achievement Has Been Held Back and What We Can Do About It

TIMOTHY SHANAHAN

HARVARD EDUCATION PRESS
CAMBRIDGE, MASSACHUSETTS

Paperback ISBN 9798895570036

Library of Congress Cataloging-in-Publication Data

Names: Shanahan, Timothy, author.
Title: Leveled reading, leveled lives : how students' reading achievement has been held back and what we can do about it / Timothy Shanahan.
Description: Cambridge, Massachusetts : Harvard Education Press, [2025] | Includes bibliographical references and index.
Identifiers: LCCN 2025013538 | ISBN 9798895570036 (paperback)
Subjects: LCSH: Reading—United States. | Reading—History—20th century. | Reading—Research—United States. | Reading—United States—Code emphasis approaches. | Reading comprehension—Study and teaching—United States.
Classification: LCC LB1050.2 .S435 2025 | DDC 418/.40973—dc23/eng/20250519
LC record available at https://lccn.loc.gov/2025013538

Published by Harvard Education Press,
an imprint of the Harvard Education Publishing Group

Harvard Education Press
8 Story Street
Cambridge, MA 02138

Cover Design: Eric Wilder
Cover Image: books by Kitsada Wetchasart via iStock, brush font by Anastasila Hevko via iStock

The typefaces used in this book are Sabon and Myriad Pro.

For Cyndie with love

Contents

Preface

I've been studying reading and the teaching of reading since I was eighteen years old. Now, as I ready myself to leave the room more than fifty years later, I've written a book that challenges a great deal of what I thought I knew for so much of that long career.

I've gone on this authoring journey, not like Ishmael going to sea to fight off "a damp drizzly November in my soul," but to explain to those who follow why this generation of educators has failed and how they might avoid letting down the children whom they teach. When I left high school in the late 1960s, American literacy levels had nearly peaked. What no one knew then was that the two centuries of steady improvement in American literacy was about to come to a screeching halt.

Since then, literacy levels have languished.

- They have languished through several so-called "reading wars," generational arguments about the role of phonics in the teaching of reading, including our current "science of reading" set-to.
- They have flagged despite billions of dollars invested in hopeful national education reforms (e.g., Right to Read, Reading Excellence Act, Head Start, Reading First, Early Reading First, Striving Readers, Common Core State Standards), and many state initiatives as well.
- They have stayed stuck to the post in the face of unprecedented generous efforts to distribute hundreds of millions of books to kids (e.g., Reading is Fundamental, First Book, Book Trust, Dolly Parton's Imagination Library).
- They have been running in place for fifty years notwithstanding the efforts of national research centers dedicated to increasing our knowledge about how best to teach reading.
- They have been in steady state despite media efforts (e.g., *Sesame Street*, *Electric Company*, *Between the Lions*, *Reading Rainbow*), commitments by celebrities (e.g., Laura Bush, Henry Winkler, LeVar Burton, Taylor

Swift), and the involvement of enterprises certain to motivate young readers (e.g., Pizza Hut, National Basketball Association, National Football League).

This book explains why that is and what we can do about it.

When I became a teacher in the late 1960s, the idea of teaching students "at their reading levels" was widely accepted. Fifty years later, it is even more popular.

As a young teacher, I bought into the idea that the surest way to success was to teach students to read with books they could already read reasonably well—without many unknown words or much content challenge.

It made so much sense to me. I thought it worked in my own classrooms where I had tested students to determine their reading levels, placed them in texts at different levels of difficulty, and grouped them for instruction around these "just right" books. Later, like thousands of other university professors, I taught teachers about readability and book leveling to maximize literacy learning for all.

Then I read the research that had been the basis of the "instructional reading level" idea, an unpublished doctoral dissertation from the 1940s. I read it, and was gobsmacked. I realized that my strongly held pedagogical beliefs had been based on a "naked Emperor" study, a study that provided a decidedly soupy foundation for teaching reading. I wrote a chapter about that unnerving experience and quickly filed it away. I recognized that the "instructional level" was a fiction, but I had no alternative. If matching kids to books offered no real learning benefit, then what would? Without an answer, I thought it better not to rock that boat.

Occasionally, scholars would argue about whether textbooks were too easy. I ignored those debates with a wave of my hand. What did it matter? We weren't teaching kids with grade level textbooks anyway—something never acknowledged by either side in those arguments.

That's where things stood until the Common Core State Standards (CCSS) came along. Although I helped write those standards, I was not involved in what turned out to be their most revolutionary contribution to reading pedagogy. These standards, unlike all that preceded them, established text levels that students had to be able to read if they were to meet the grade level requirements. Previous state educational standards always avoided this. The fear was that if fourth graders were required to learn to read fourth-grade texts, then teachers might try to teach with fourth-grade texts. For reading educators who had insisted that children learn best from books matched to their reading levels, this heresy was the equivalent of melting the polar ice caps to reduce global warming.

As it turns out, no one need have worried. As textbook publishers increased text difficulty to meet the CCSS requirements, teachers just taught more children with below grade texts, undermining any benefits that may have resulted from the standard.

Over recent years, an accumulation of research has revealed that teaching students with books at their supposed "instructional levels" offers little if any advantage. In fact, under some circumstances, teaching reading with more difficult texts—texts teachers long have been advised to shun—can boost reading achievement.

This book details how and why an instructional approach so out of accord with research could dominate American schools for so long. It provides the most comprehensive analysis of relevant research and explains why this popular approach could never work. Finally, and most importantly, it offers an alternative vision to reading instruction more likely to increase American literacy attainment, providing research-based guidance on how to teach reading with challenging texts. This guidance is also relevant to those who teach content subjects like history or science, subjects that should require text reading.

The title of this book is a paraphrase of something Alfred Tatum, provost and executive vice president for Academic Affairs at Metropolitan State University of Denver, once said: "Leveled texts lead to leveled lives." Alfred was a student of mine, and then a colleague and friend. He came to this issue through his efforts to identify how best to school African American boys, whose literacy levels have long lagged national averages. He recognized that limiting these young men to high interest, low readability texts could only "slow walk" their educations, postponing the intellectual development that socially significant texts could foster. Alfred espouses the idea of teaching with what he calls "enabling texts," texts that "move beyond a solely cognitive focus . . . to include a social, cultural, political, spiritual or economic focus." He argued that "lower readability begats lower readability," recognizing that protecting students from difficult texts would put them on a treadmill with no exit.

For nearly a century, American educators—including me—have sought to keep children on that well-intentioned treadmill. This book explains why it's time to take them out for a real cross country run, and details how we can do that successfully.

Given the extensive use of scholarly resources, it was impossible to include complete references for each chapter in this volume. Accordingly, a complete bibliography for each chapter or chapter section is provided online at: https://hep.gse.harvard.edu/9798895570036/leveled-reading-leveled-lives/.

I would like to thank Chris Condon and the other librarians at the Richard J. Daley Library at the University of Illinois at Chicago for their unstinting efforts to secure all the relevant sources, no matter how rare and obscure, needed to write this book. I would also like to thank Dahlia Mills, librarian and workspace coordinator at the University Club of Chicago where I wrote this book. Dahlia always welcomed me with an encouraging smile and kind words, making it a pleasure to get down to work. Karen Adler, acquisitions editor at Harvard Education Press, was the perfect editor for me, giving me just the right balance of cheerleading, sober advice, and sufficient rope to hang myself. Of course, in a lifetime of teaching, administering, and researching, one gains untold knowledge and direction from an ever-changing cast of mentors, colleagues, editors, and students both too numerous to note and too diffuse in their impacts to either credit or blame them for something as specific as a book. My gratitude goes out to all those whose wisdom, generosity and patience enabled me to write this book. They deserve my thanks. Any criticism this work may attract is mine alone.

Protecting Children from Complex Text

During the 1930s, A. J. Liebling was Paris correspondent for the *New Yorker.* His affectionate passages on cassoulet and Chablis showed his veneration of French culture. He grieved when forced to flee the Nazi occupation, and as soon as possible he returned, cruising in on a landing craft with the invasion troops on D-Day. Liebling wrote about the moment he realized the Allies were sure to win the war: "The factories would furnish the planes, the American system of public education would furnish the crews; it couldn't be anything but a win."[1] The defeat of evil was a certainty, in Liebling's mind, when the best educated kids in the world mounted up. After a lifetime devoted to America's public school kids, I am ashamed to realize that no modern-day Liebling would today utter such a brag.

Our kids do not read well.

According to the National Assessment of Educational Progress (NAEP), America's reading report card, approximately 30 percent of students read well below their grade levels—it varies a bit by age—and another 30 percent can only demonstrate "partial mastery of the knowledge and skill that are fundamental for proficient work at a grade level."[2]

I do not want to mislead. Almost all our kids are learning to read. They are not, however, learning to read well enough to safeguard their full participation in American society or access to opportunity in twenty-first century America. How well they read will determine their eventual educational attainment,[3] family income levels,[4] employment,[5] health status,[6] degree of social participation and civic involvement,[7] and their ability to avoid or prevent a plethora of social ills.[8] Reading scores tick up or down a bit from time to time (the COVID disaster has had a depressing impact). However, the most accurate characterization would be that achievement has languished for more than a half century. Generation Alpha reads neither appreciably better nor worse than the Baby Boomers to which I belong.

Obtaining 1970 reading scores in 2024 is a bum deal, sort of like being paid 1970s wages. Inflation makes that unthinkable. Average salaries in the '70s (about $8,000) fall far short of today's poverty line. Globalization and technology—along with a plethora of social changes—have raised the literacy ante. We may not read for pleasure as much as we once did, but daily reliance on text has climbed considerably—think how often you glance at your smartphone. Manufacturing provides another apt example. In the 1970s, I worked in a tool and die shop, cutting machine parts on a turret lathe, a job requiring no reading. Workers today still cut metal parts, they just do it with computer-driven lathes. Blue collar-work is now reading-centric. With America's reading achievement stuck in neutral, those educational advantages that Liebling vaunted have diminished on the international stage.[9] Our position in world literacy standings has melted like an ice statue in the sun. This slippage in the world reading rankings is attributable to improvements elsewhere, not to any deterioration in American reading levels. But slippage there has been.

There is no shortage of explanations for our educational slump: inattention to the science of reading, socioeconomic inequality, racism, immigration, inattentive parents, broken families, lousy schools, the proliferation of screens, "kids are different now," and so on. This book, too, explains our seeming inability to improve reading, along with a detailed description of a solution.

Rather than remaking society or touting panaceas incommensurate with the state of things, this book exposes a problem hidden in plain sight. Our failure is not one of lassitude or neglect. We are undermined by our fealty to educational theories and pedagogical practices that no longer serve us well. Instructional methods well-meaningly formulated to support learning impose an intractable ceiling on our progress. Years ago, the economist John Kenneth Galbraith wrote about the dangers of what he called "conventional wisdom," the accepted beliefs, theories, and practices that hinder progress and limit potential. For the past fifty years, with reading scores seemingly frozen in amber, reading educators have gripped tight to instructional practices that are more problem than solution.

THE PROBLEM AND ITS SOURCE

This book contends that American children are being *prevented* from doing better in reading by a longstanding commitment to a pedagogical theory that insists students are best taught with books they can already read. This approach was readily accepted for its consistency with popular beliefs. Over time, empirical data has gradually accumulated, exposing the stifling constraints inherent in that easy reading approach and divulging its failures. But to no avail. This practice dominates American pedagogy. University teacher preparation programs continue to advocate it. State education policies often promote it, as do local school district dictums. Publishing companies dutifully design their programs based on it. Maddeningly, again and again, reading reform efforts have been strangled by the oppressive strictures of this unfortunate dogma. Teachers, administrators, professors, and publishers either ignore or resist reforms inconsistent with their faith in the notion that success depends on teaching students to read with books they can already easily read on their own with little or no assistance.

Before getting too far into the argument, it might help to clarify terminology central to these issues. "Grade level" refers to the book placements provided by various publishers. Historically, these were subjective designations, but more recently state educational standards indicate how difficult the books should be for each grade level. If students learn to read the books assigned to each grade level, they should eventually graduate from high school with a sufficient level of literacy. By contrast, "reading level" refers to how well students can read. Fourth graders may not be able to read a fourth-grade book well because their reading levels are insufficient. Finally, the "instructional level" or "instructional reading level" is a theoretical construct meant to describe the appropriate student-text match that teachers should aim for so that learning will be maximized. The claim is that if students are taught with books at their "instructional level," then they will make the greatest learning progress. It is my contention that this instructional level construct is a harmful fiction that holds students back. Teachers should teach most students with grade level texts rather than trying to match instructional books to the students' current reading levels.

I am not the first to recognize the stultifying effects of books that are too easy. Such complaints, however, have usually focused on the books themselves rather than the pedagogy—spawning distracting arguments over whether today's schoolbooks really are easier than their historical forerunners.[10] Arguments that would matter only if students were taught from these books. The instructional level doctrine advises a strategic end run around whatever textual difficulty the books may present. Higher levels of challenge can do nothing to improve achievement if offset by teachers shifting kids to easier reads. Grade level challenge is irrelevant if fifth graders are taught from third-grade books. When will they have a chance to take on fifth-grade reading fare? Perhaps in seventh grade. The inexorable conclusion to this sequence should be obvious: high school students graduating years behind grade level in literacy.

Why would experts condone and promote such a seemingly goofy pedagogy? Because of reliance on axiom. An axiom is an idea regarded as self-evidently true, requiring no empirical evidence. At one point in American history, the twig was bent towards making schooling easy so children would like it. That axiom encouraged text simplification and led to the creation of textbooks leveled from easy to difficult. At a later historical juncture, it became abundantly clear that individual differences in reading were extensive within graded classrooms. This led to another axiom, this one proposing that reading instruction would be more successful if each student was taught with "just the right" text.

These seemingly reasonable notions raise an important question: Which texts are "just right" to increase learning? It is one thing to tell teachers to individualize instruction to optimize learning and prevent frustration and avoidance. It is quite another to prescribe valid systems of testing (to determine how well the kids can read), readability (for leveling the books reliably and appropriately), and organizational plans to facilitate the delivery of such instruction.

Three sets of criteria have been proposed for making book-match determinations. Emmett Betts originated the theory of an instructional reading level in the 1940s and provided the most complete explanation of its purpose and operationalizing criteria.[11] His approach has been widely embraced by reading educators. Edward E. Gickling, in the 1970s, acknowledged Betts's contribution and suggested two different instructional levels for special education students—one for text reading that he based on Betts's work and another for seatwork, assignments that students are expected to complete on their own at their seats, away from the teacher.[12] Around the same time, Marie M. Clay included instructional level criteria for her Reading Recovery program aimed at first graders who were struggling to read.[13] As will be explained in greater detail in chapter 6, it is a bad idea to ramp up text difficulty on beginning readers, which would put Clay's criteria beyond this book's scope. However, professors at Ohio State University, Irene Fountas and Gay Su Pinnell, developed a very popular classroom reading program inspired by Reading Recovery which implements Clay's criteria through the grades.[14] These three approaches may differ a bit in their theories and criteria, but they all suffer the same theoretical and technical limitations and are just variations on the same bad idea.

Since its introduction, the instructional level approach has proliferated in American schools. What began with a book for each grade level, now has metastasized into twenty-six supposedly distinct text levels. The presence of informal reading inventories, timed oral readings, running records, and computer-driven testing schemes have all burgeoned in this ardor to teach reading with the right book. Students must be tested repeatedly, to avoid the supposed disaster of reading the wrong text. Classrooms—and school libraries—are replete with level-labeled book bins, books branded with color-coded dots, and shelving systems aimed at ensuring that no child strays into books beyond their prescribed challenge level.[15] One wonders how many students eschew reading when their choices are constrained to a universe of books they can already read with ease. Children chafe at the restrictions, and parents are often chagrined to find their kids cannot be credited with reading books lacking appropriately colored dots.[16]

These complaints are legitimate, but independent reading is not the major focus of this book. My concerns are more with the limitations on what students are allowed to learn *within* instruction. Texts students can already read well—books at the students' supposed "instructional levels"—have become an almost universal platform for American reading instruction. Reading is so often taught in small groups—not so teachers can guide efforts to negotiate difficult books, but to ensure that the books be easy enough that not much guidance is needed. No wonder so many children dislike their reading instruction![17]

Teachers have been led to believe that this easy book approach is research-based and that challenging students with harder books will be damaging: stultifying learning, imposing disfluency, and requiring word guessing rather than reading.[18] These cautions have become so commonplace that most teachers are shocked to discover their flimsy evidentiary base. Recent research attributes no clear benefits to instructional level teaching and suggests that more demanding texts can mean more learning.

Reading levels in the US would be higher if students were taught with grade level texts instead of instructional level ones. This is not a "you have nothing to lose but your chains" kind of argument. I am not proposing a magic trick in which harder books automatically translate into improved reading scores. Such prestidigitation is best left to instructional level proponents. The idea here is not to just throw kids in the deep end and hope they'll swim. Teaching with grade level texts requires thoughtful instruction. My proposal is to replace the student-book matching fetish with instruction aimed at enabling kids to read harder books successfully.

One might respond to this with resignation: "Let's face it, we can't get everyone up to grade level." That may or may not be true. Nevertheless, it is repugnant to endorse a pedagogy that not only accepts this lag but *enforces* it. The instructional level, rather than maximizing learning, imposes upper-bound limits on how much progress students will be permitted. The notion was originally espoused to ensure that everyone learned, despite their individual differences. It does seem to do this; that is, most kids learn something when taught at their instructional level. But greater progress is possible with more challenging texts. For instance, a recent analysis of 27,814 American schools whose students enter below grade level reported that of these, only 1,345 schools managed to accomplish better than average learning gains. One of the distinguishing features of these champions? They teach English and math at grade level, rather than trying to reduce the curriculum to the students' already low performance levels![19]

READING ACHIEVEMENT AND EDUCATIONAL REFORM

Over the past half century, there have been three major waves of reading reform (the "reading wars"). Each focused on the need for explicit phonics instruction in the primary grades. The first of these waves was in the late 1960s, the second in the 90s, and we are currently tangled in the third. The earlier efforts witnessed subsequent gains in fourth-grade reading scores.[20] Perhaps the current effort will too. No matter. Ultimately, these reforms have failed. Any early reading advantages they have accomplished have been thoroughly cannibalized before students reach middle school. Seemingly, fourth graders with improved reading never reach eighth grade. Our goal should be to graduate kids from high school with reading abilities commensurate with their personal, social, civic, and economic goals. How well someone reads at age nine is much less consequential than how well they read at eighteen. Improving early reading achievement is laudatory, but it has not led to gains in later achievement.[21]

The easy-book approach has helped undermine public policies and initiatives aimed at higher reading achievement. In the twenty-first century, the federal government and many states have expended billions of dollars on impressive efforts to improve reading. None have made a dent in how well our older students can read.

The Common Core State Standards (CCSS) is an interesting case in point. These goals were quite innovative regarding reading. Unlike the educational standards they replaced, CCSS established how well students needed to be able to read at the various grades if they were to read well enough by high school graduation. This had always been ducked by standard makers in fear that it might encourage teachers to teach with grade level books instead of instructional level ones—a criticism oft expressed about the CCSS standards.[22] From the 1980s until 2010, educational standards inventoried the reading skills students were to be proficient in, but they were assiduously silent about the kinds of texts in which these skills had to be implemented. Most of us can draw inferences or identify a main idea in books like *Fun with Dick and Jane*; fewer of us can do so with *Finnegan's Wake*. Common Core challenged the instructional level idea by indicating that applying fourth grade skills to a third-grade book would be below standards.

CCSS set those requirements for grades 2–12 (not beginning readers) and included operational definitions of these levels. Major textbook publishers promptly complied with those requirements; a policy change that should have provided a clear test of what is proposed here. But that is not what happened. According to two national surveys, as the reading books increased in difficulty, more teachers than ever before embraced the idea that children must be taught from texts at their "reading levels."[23] As grade level books increased in difficulty, teachers undercut the requirements by teaching with below grade level texts. Resistance was so strong that some states backed down. New York is a good example. It dumped its requirement that students learn to read grade level text, replacing the learning goal with an instructional prescription: "Students should have authentic opportunities to engage with texts that specifically correlate to their individual levels of their word reading skills."[24]

This kind of policy failure is not unusual. It is often described as "risk compensation." Laws requiring automobile seatbelts should have saved lots of lives. The actual benefits were surprisingly modest. Seatbelts made drivers feel safer, encouraging faster and more reckless driving. In reading education, policymakers set requirements to ensure all students have an opportunity to learn to read well enough for higher education, workplace participation, or military service. The plan fails when teachers protect kids from the new requirements rather than trying to meet them.

I am not describing resistance or insubordination. Teachers who are teaching their students with below grade books are usually not rebels with a cause. Surveys indicate that they believe their actions to be consistent with state policies and supported by research. According to the RAND survey cited in note 23, teachers who knew their state standards were less likely to adopt these contradictory practices. Given the marketing efforts of some publishing companies and the sincere but misleading claims of some educators, it should not be surprising that teachers are confused. Good intentions aside, demoting children to below grade level books is inconsistent with the policies of most states.

The states themselves certainly could do a better job. Mandating that students be taught with harder texts is reform on the cheap. Such mandates should be bolstered by professional development efforts aimed at providing teachers with the tools needed to carry out those mandates.

University-based teacher education programs could readily address these contradictions, preparing teachers to teach reading with more challenging texts. For the most part, that has not happened. In fact, the most vociferous arguments against these policies have come from professors. Much of this opposition is based on faulty premises (e.g., it is better to teach reading with easier books because children can read those better; it is a bad idea to teach beginners with harder books so no one should be so taught; text readability measures are too unreliable for use in standard setting, but they can be used much more precisely to make instructional decisions). I suspect that not one in one hundred reading professors has ever read any of the studies used to set the instructional level criteria, despite espousing their use. Not surprisingly, most of the research reviewed here has been ignored by these critics.

Parents could set things right for their kids, complaining about these instructional practices. Perhaps, but often they have no idea that their children are locked into below grade level texts. They presume their third grader is learning to read third-grade books, just as they suppose a regimen of grade level science, social studies, and math. It has been documented that school grading policies confuse and misinform parents.[25] A staggering ninety percent think that their children are reading at or above grade levels—a belief in stark contrast with achievement data. School policies differ as to what parents must be told. Some schools confer reading grades based on improvement or effort. Children may receive an “A” in reading for progress, while performing far below grade level. A fourth grader working in second-grade texts may get high grades, with parents none the wiser.[26] Even when accurate information is given, it is all too rare that parents are told that their children’s reading instruction will be focused on books far below grade, leaving parents in no position to ask how their youngster is supposed to catch up with their classmates.

Some “easy reading” authorities advise teachers to be honest about how well a child is doing. For example, Irene Fountas and Gay Sue Pinnell recommend that “rather than reporting levels to parents, use language like:

reading at, reading above, or not yet reading at grade-level expectations."[27] But then they discourage sharing specific information about what the kids are to be taught. A parent of a fourth grader, for instance, may be told that their child is in Level J. What they do not know is that Level J books are for Grade 2 children. The recommended language camouflages how far behind a student is and what the remedy is to be—up to a year of reading second grade books, with little or no instruction in how to handle stymieing fourth-grade text demands. The most widely used commercial reading programs in America's schools are based on this "easy book" pedagogy.[28]

It is not just that children are placed in books that are too easy. For the most part, they are not taught how to read books at all. The point of such "instruction" is more to provide practice reading texts at the students' reading levels rather than to tutor kids in the last iota of skills that should enable them to read these easy books perfectly. Instruction is rarely aimed in any specific way to increase the ability to meet the demands of grade level texts. Rather than striving to empower kids to scale the heights of texts they cannot yet read well, instruction perseverates on the hopes that practicing easy reading will magically result in more advanced reading abilities.

The lowest performing students may manage to escape the mind-numbing focus on easy reading. This is not because teachers recognize the value of harder text, only that many of them are unwilling to lower instruction as much as might be necessary to accommodate these students. A fifth-grade teacher may be willing to teach with a fourth-grade book, but not a second-grade one. Again, this should be an opportunity to evaluate the claims made here, but again it is not. Those low readers placed in frustration level texts are offered little relevant guidance or support. It would be rare for teachers to have professional preparation in how to facilitate learning from challenging texts, and foolhardy to seek such guidance, since the practice is discouraged by the educational establishment and may be viewed as malpractice. Children are to stay to the shallow water, and if for some reason they end up in the deep end, they are to do so sans water wings.

Basically, instructional level theory minimizes teaching. The idea is that if kids practice their reading with texts that they can read well—though not perfectly—they will be able to improve with minimum help. That this progress will be glacial for most students, impeding growth more than impelling it, is ignored. Hearing the criticism that many students languish at level for extended periods of time, Fountas and Pinnell, in the second edition of their book, advise advancing those students to the next level despite the lack of improvement.[29] That sounds like great counsel to me, but raises the question, If those students can learn from harder texts, then why can't the others?

WHO IS HARMED?

I have taught elementary school, been a director of reading in a large urban school district, and have spent literally thousands of hours in classrooms. I am aware of how unpleasant and uncomfortable classroom life can be when students struggle with a text. I appreciate the desire to minimize any embarrassment or classroom disorder that may stem from such struggle. However, it would be better to scaffold success with more challenging books, than to try to avoid these unfortunate situations by teaching with books the students can already read—books that by design minimize learning. Teaching with books students can read reasonably well slows progress and dampens pride by making learning so subtle as to be obscure.

Instructional level theory is meant to facilitate learning. In its defense, it is often pointed out that students can read instructional level books better than grade level ones—in terms of fluency and comprehension.[30] But such data prove nothing about the supposed *learning* advantages attributable to the practice. Despite good intentions, the instructional level needlessly prevents students from engaging with grade level curriculum, a practice more akin to retention or segregation than school improvement.

Sadly, students from the least advantaged demographic groups are most likely to be placed in below grade books. Which means, of course, that hopes for future social equality are to be nipped in the bud early in these children's educational lives. The fourth graders incarcerated in second-grade reading books will later be expected to compete as equals with their more advantaged peers who will spend fourth grade dealing with sophisticated fourth-grade language and content. Talk about separate but unequal. No wonder the use of within-class reading groups has been found to hinder the educational progress of African American students;[31] a problem long dismissed out of hand, since reading level teaching was meant to maximize success. Nevertheless, as evidence has accumulated revealing its failure, the practice continues unabated despite its unfortunate social consequences.

Most school districts have clearly formulated retention policies. If students are to be flunked—that is, kept for another year at current grade level—parents must be informed early; students may be enrolled in Tier 2 interventions or summer school programs to head off the impending retention or to make it effective. There may be requirements for multiple sources of evidence, and these decisions are monitored individually and districtwide to ensure value and fairness. Instructional level placement requires none of these protections, though it just as successfully blocks access to grade level curriculum. As such, it serves as a kind of ghost retention, retention with little chance of success.

Almost everyone in grades 2 through 12 who are taught to read with below grade level texts may be harmed by the practice. Research evidence shows that students exposed to grade level curriculum do as well as or better than those taught at their instructional levels. Even when grade level teaching is not an improvement on the instructional level version—in terms of reading gains—it has the advantage of neither segregating these students, nor labeling them as low or slow.

PREVIEW OF WHAT IS TO COME

The purpose of this book is to challenge the idea that students need be taught to read at their instructional levels. As noted, I am not the first to emphasize the value of teaching with more challenging texts. These days it seems fashionable for scholars and teachers to note potential benefits for challenge or struggle. There is a growing body of empirical studies addressing the issue, too. What is missing is a single work that makes the case for replacing instructional level theory with a challenging text theory. This book is meant to provide a comprehensive, critical and purposeful analysis of instructional level theory and its implications, as well as providing an evidence-based consideration of how we can effectively replace this theory.

Chapter 1 considers the historical sources of the instructional level, explaining why it has been so persuasive to teachers. Chapter 2 explores how various psychological theories and intellectual movements have been mischaracterized to support instructional level reading. Chapter 3 synthesizes an extensive collection of research studies that overwhelmingly contradict the instructional level theory. Chapter 4 shows why the instructional level idea is too simplistic to support maximum learning gains by analyzing the validity and reliability of the assessment and instructional approaches it depends upon. Chapter 5 describes an alternative theory of instruction explaining why teaching students to read challenging texts is a better idea. Chapters 6, 7, and 8 provide detailed descriptions of the types of instruction and scaffolding needed to support learning from grade level texts, including word reading and decoding, reading comprehension, and motivation, respectively. Chapter 9 summarizes the book and provides additional practical implementation advice. We have a sacred duty to educate our children in ways that will assure their future success. As such, this volume should offer educators, policymakers, and parents a clear idea of why current instructional approaches are failing to meet both societal and individual literacy needs as well as providing a coherent blueprint for reform.

The History of an Instructional Approach

Reading education is a contentious field, its disagreements long characterized as "reading wars." The role of phonics has been a matter of dispute for centuries, and disagreements over what students should read stretch back as far. Nevertheless, that children should learn to read with relatively easy texts has been widely accepted.

This chapter explores the history of instructional level theory, and why it has been so readily and persistently accepted. This chapter revisits the events that laid the groundwork for matching students to texts to promote learning. Long before there were text-matching methods, American educators thought that learning should be easy and that instructional demands would alienate students. Likewise, educators came up with the idea that different learners needed different books long before this instructional regime became popular.

ABRUPT LEARNING PROGRESSIONS, 1620–1776

For many, American education starts with the Mayflower.[1] Escaping persecution, English Protestants chartered a boat, gathered their belongings, and fled to the New World. The oft-told story of this adventure usually emphasizes the "dying time" of that first winter, their loyalty to faith, their thanksgiving under dire circumstances, and the selfless kindness of the Wampanoags.

Whatever the shortcomings of those historical claims, our concerns are only with the reading and reading instruction that rode with them across the seas. The England the Pilgrims knew was not especially literate. Fewer than half the men of that period could read, with literacy even rarer among women.[2] Schools, tutors, and the like were not readily available. There were few books attuned to the teaching of reading.

The religious ideology of the Pilgrims required men and women be able to read, and many could.[3] The Mayflower Compact and other Pilgrim documents support this conclusion. The Pilgrims rejected the idea that any human being—pope or queen—could prescribe religious beliefs or practices. They wanted no authority between them and their God. An ability to read and interpret the Bible for oneself was an essential religious duty.

They brought along a remarkable amount of furniture and accoutrements of European life. However, it is doubtful they or those who soon followed possessed books for reading instruction. The Bible could be used for this purpose, and there were also hornbooks, pieces of wood onto which were affixed instructional pages—the alphabet, letter sounds, lists of syllables, prayers, brief biblical passages, moral maxims, catechism pages, and the like.

Their educational goals were not especially ambitious either. They wanted children to master the texts taught. Memorization was as acceptable as reading ability.[4] The purpose of learning to read the Bible was not to enable the reading of other texts. They were learning to read the Bible to read the Bible.

Within a century, books for reading instruction emerged. The *New England Primer* was the first notable example.[5] It was widely available in many editions throughout the colonies, and it was widely used for one hundred years, eventually selling millions of copies. Its opening pages were reminiscent of the scraps that had been stuck to the hornbooks—starting with the alphabet, nursery rhymes that paired letters and sounds, and various pedagogical devices like lists of vowels and syllables. It then quickly devolved from brief, simple texts (e.g., The Lord's Prayer) to more expansive moral lessons. Over about one hundred pages the *Primer* took students from the ABCs to college level fare; progressing not very gradually from simple to complex.

Reading development, with such books, was a sprint. What today takes a youngster from kindergarten to college to accomplish, was then supposed to be completed in a year. With that, literacy levels remained low—most students not exceeding simple prayers. The books were hard, and the teachers poorly prepared to smooth the students' paths.[6]

LAYING THE GROUNDWORK, 1776–1840

Throughout the 1700s, printers published spellers and grammars for reading instruction, but none could dethrone the *New England Primer.* That changed in 1783, when Noah Webster, of later dictionary fame, issued his *American Speller* or "Blue-Back Speller."[7]

Webster had briefly been a schoolteacher and knew the limitations of the reading books.[8] He believed the new nation required a better guide to reading and spelling. Accordingly, he revised and improved Reverend Thomas Dilworth's *A New Guide to the English Tongue* (1740), then the most popular spelling book.[9]

Webster's books were special due to their emphasis on educating American citizens and their standardization of American dialect. Our interest, however, is in their more gradual introduction of reading instruction. Webster reworked Dilworth's books into three volumes,[10] making this multi-book series the first of its kind in America.

The first in the series, the speller, emphasized individual words, beginning with the ABCs and letter sounds, along with lists of two, three, and four syllable words and spelling patterns. Initially, the speller was little more than lists, but with each edition, more brief easy reading passages were included. The second book, *An Introduction to English Grammar* (1784), never sold well and was soon discontinued.[11] The third was a reader and oratory, *Necessary Rules of Reading and Spelling*.[12] It was precursor to today's reading textbooks, an anthology of selections including speeches and other texts thought indispensable to a Republic. These selections were markedly more challenging than those in the earlier books. These volumes went through many printings over their 50-year publishing span. Not only was the speller supplemented with reading text, but harder selections were swapped out, too. According to Rudolph R. Reeder's historical investigation of American schoolbooks, "gradually the material which was in no way adapted to the comprehension of children was eliminated."[13] Such revisions increased the program's appeal to children's interests and reduced reading difficulty.

From the 1790s through the 1830s, several multi-book competitors to Webster's *Institute* appeared, none achieving the popularity of his speller.[14] All these programs aspired to "systematic gradation" of books for reading instruction. They varied greatly in how well they did this. Some series did not number the books, or provide guidance to proper sequence. As with Webster's program, the texts were published one at time, accumulating into a series. Though the texts varied in difficulty, they frequently were more like an overlapping patchwork than a well-defined series of stairsteps.

Multi-book series became the standard in design, if not always in practice. Webster's *Speller* far outsold his other books (more than 100 million copies), probably because few children were in school for extended periods, obviating the need for the harder books. That also meant that book sequencing was not necessarily honored in practice. Many schools that employed

Webster's speller followed up with his competitors' more advanced books. Without a well-organized system of public schools there was no way to align these books with schooling.[15]

Nevertheless, these multi-book programs were a silent acknowledgement that reading ability develops best over an extended period, that the accomplishment of higher levels of literacy require exposure to greater amounts of text, and that texts should be arranged to lead gradually from simple texts to more challenging ones. Webster's books went through a remarkable 385 editions, and over time he weeded out texts thought to hold little interest for children and simplified the reading demands. What was true for Webster, was true for his competitors: "By the end of the 1820s, primers began to reduce dramatically the total number of words they introduced."[16]

There are two relevant pedagogical issues here—how much difficulty learners should confront and the need for differentiation. It was the first of these that dominated pedagogical thought throughout the eighteenth century.

LEVELED READERS, 1840–1890

During the first half century of the American republic, there was no organized universal program of public education. That began to be remedied in the 1840s. Horace Mann, Secretary of the Massachusetts Board of Education, wrote persuasively about the need for a system of American schooling, and proposed key features for such a system.[17] Mann's educational philosophy was based upon his observations of Prussian schools and his reading of the works of Johann Pestalozzi, a Swiss educator. Mann's efforts ushered in the so-called "Common School Era," a watershed in American educational history. These reforms altered both who was educated and how they were taught, changes still evident today.

Those reforms significantly impacted how students were matched to texts. First, public schools were open to all (except enslaved people) free of charge, which increased attendance and duration of schooling. This increase enhanced the potential profit authors and publishers might anticipate and encouraged the development of more expensive-to-produce textbook programs.

Second, children were classified into grade levels by ages. This provided a common plan of school management with more concrete goals. Students taught specific things in third grade expected something more challenging and sophisticated in grade four, and so on. This required a more progressive approach to teaching.

Third, in response to the graded school, textbook publishers revolutionized reading books by fitting them to this organization. This meant providing "leveled readers," books for each grade. This led to replacing the patchwork quilt of text levels with series that were truly sequential. The correspondence of these programs with the graded organization of the schools made the books a practical necessity for teachers.

Textbooks were so influential because "teachers were meagerly educated."[18] Initially there was little opportunity for teacher preparation. New textbooks offered powerful supports for teachers, along with homely advice on teaching. Education journals also began to proliferate, offering school leaders philosophy and practical advice, and eventually a loose network of two-year colleges emerged—"normal schools"—for teacher preparation.

One theme of this movement emphasized the idea that learning should be easy. Students were to be led through relatively simple lessons that would progress gradually. The importance of "going slow" and "making it easy" was repeatedly emphasized throughout this entire historical period.

Via Horace Mann, Pestalozzi's pedagogy was widely circulated. Pestalozzi championed the ideas that teaching should follow a sequence from simple to complex, easy to difficult, and concrete to abstract. Mann wrote, "It is the duty of the teacher to bring knowledge within arm's length of the learner; and he must break down its masses into portions so minute, that they can be taken up and appropriated, one by one."[19] This theory nourished the idea that education should "reduce every subject to its elements, and present one difficulty at a time."[20] Well-known educators like Branson Alcott espoused teaching that "moved from the simple to the difficult, from the known to the unknown, and from the concrete to the abstract, stressing always short steps, plain language, and allusion to familiar objects and occurrences."[21] They were promoting easier, more child-centered, gradually progressive reading programs.

Remarkably, early in this period, these notions were controversial and generated some pushback. According to the *Common School Journal*, "What sort of books . . . should instructors use in teaching children to read? It is too commonly supposed that this question is satisfactorily answered by saying, that children should be required to read nothing which they do not understand."[22] This uncharacteristic position decried the more popular notion of limiting textbooks only to "easy pieces, as they are called, for children to read."[23]

"Easy pieces" eventually came to characterize American reading instruction, but at this time finding how best to reduce reading difficulty was a dominant concern. As one unnamed author noted, "In the mixed schools of this country, a large majority of the children read in books entirely beyond their comprehension. This is a great misfortune. It checks all real progress. . . . The reading matter for children should be nearly on a level with their reading comprehension of the subject."[24] This article went on to complain about the vocabulary and decoding demands of texts used to teach reading—a complaint made despite four decades of progress in difficulty reduction.

One motive for easier texts had to do with teachers' major concern of the time. An examination of educational journals, teachers' diaries,[25] contemporary fiction centered on teaching,[26] and histories of the period all point to student discipline as the issue that kept teachers up at night. Teachers reasoned that greater instructional demands might anger students, leading to truancy and misbehavior. Proceeding from simple to complex was a commonsense insight of the educational philosophers, but for teachers it was appealing mainly in the hope it would palliate the unruly.

The graded textbook programs represented the first true realization of the notion that reading could be taught successfully by leading students through a sequential series of texts gradually increasing in difficulty. This idea spread as much due to its pedagogical practicality as to the potential financial benefits it promised (selling six or seven books to a school rather than one or two was a lucrative windfall). This invention was as much about profit as pedagogy.

Notions of easing difficulty, making progress gradual, and linking educational demands and student behavior were consonant with a changing perception of childhood. In the seventeenth and eighteenth centuries, children were viewed as smaller adults, expected to work, wear the same clothes, and read the same books as their elders. This began to change by the end of the eighteenth century (hence the revisions of Webster's books), and during this period the realization of childhood as a distinct period of life became pronounced. "Reformers like Henry Barnard and Horace Mann led the attack against arcane and unchildlike reading in the second quarter of the nineteenth century."[27]

Children's literature continued to emerge during this period, and this development was gradually folded into textbook programs too. As one program bragged, its content aimed at being "within the range of [children's] experience, pleasing to the imagination, and chaste and progressive in style and matter."[28]

This effort to simplify and ease the way for young readers impelled reductions in selection lengths and vocabulary variability, and emphasized content aligned with children's tastes. It encouraged various instructional innovations—such as the teaching of new vocabulary words prior to the reading of a selection. Students were expected to read more than in previous instructional texts, but the selections were easier and increases in difficulty were less steep and were bolstered with greater pedagogical support.

There were dozens of competing reading series produced from the 1830s on.[29] One with a particularly apt title—Tower's *Gradual Readers*—emphasized what initially was little more than aspiration, but by the 1860s had become a true hallmark.[30] The 1830s witnessed the first programs with grade level designations. It was not until the late 1860s that the content of the programs fully reflected this grade level linkage.

It was *McGuffey's Readers* that achieved "bestseller" status during this era.[31] *McGuffey's* did not predominate due to superior design but because its publisher had the foresight to smuggle printing plates into the South prior to the outbreak of the US Civil War.[32] McGuffey's books depended on short simple stories in the first three grades, with more literary selections beyond that. "In the nineteenth century, educators discovered the simpler style was better for teaching students to read. They began separating students and textbooks into different grades."[33] The basic premise of those programs became the conventional wisdom of reading educators then and now.

According to Richard L. Venezky, "vocabulary control and the need for repeated exposure to new words slowly entered most textbook series through the middle of the nineteenth century."[34] As the vocabulary demands of the texts were increasingly controlled—reducing the variability and increasing the amounts of word repetition—the programs began to reduce their attention to spelling or phonics. Instead of trying to teach students "how words work," they shifted to memorization.

The pedagogical recommendations of prominent educators and the easy availability of graded reading materials provide important backdrops to what would eventually become an almost universally accepted wisdom about how best to teach reading. The idea that reading lessons should be easy and that learning progress should be gradual were conventional by the 1890s.

THE NEED FOR DIFFERENTIATION, 1890–1950

This era preserved the earlier commitments to simplification and gradualism but also emphasized greater scientific precision in making these determinations and explored the more substantial differentiation of instruction. By the beginning of this period, it was evident that assigning students to graded classes was insufficient to fully address student variation. Grade levels and reading attainment were not always in close accord.

Classrooms often served forty to seventy students, so teachers were forced to reorganize—focusing lessons on one group of students while others waited. "Through an informal method of grouping different levels, the teacher attempts to keep the youngster at work on various tasks."[35] Unfortunately, large class sizes boosted variability, while simultaneously complicating the formation of smaller, homogeneous within-class groups. There was little support for such differentiation, in terms of text availability and supplies, methods for determining group membership, or means for keeping everyone engaged while the teacher instructed others.

What had earlier been unspoken concerns now burst forth as the major pedagogical challenge. There were many reasons for this shift—economic, political, social, intellectual, and technological. The early years of this era witnessed major economic depressions and social dislocations. The economic panics of the 1890s pushed families from their farms and into cities and towns, swelling school enrollment. This dislocation coincided with major immigrations from southern and eastern Europe which diversified the student population. Soon, the Great Migration of African Americans from the South to northern cities further complicated matters.

This period encompasses the Progressive Era, a political movement aimed at accomplishing sweeping improvements in American society through the expansion of labor rights, women's suffrage, economic reform, environmental protections, and the welfare of the poor. Pertinent to text matching issues were the child labor laws that banned children from the factories and mills. Coinciding with this national legislation was the state-by-state adoption of compulsory education laws. Children could no longer work and had to attend school.

Enrollments increased and student differences widened. No wonder the urgent desire for ways to effectively differentiate teaching. Unlike in previous eras, these teachers could depend on a substantial educational infrastructure. The common school had become a universal, and teachers could now avail themselves of normal schools, textbooks, and journals. Even more exciting were the possibilities of the new departments of psychology and education that had sprung up at the universities (e.g., Columbia, Clark, Chicago). They provided new research and professional development opportunities. The universities promoted concepts of *readiness* and the *measurement movement.*

The theory of readiness held that learning only results from instruction if students are adequately prepared to learn. If a lesson fails to match a student's level of cognitive development, then there would be no learning, no matter the quality of teaching. Some versions of the theory held that teaching students something they were not yet ready for was potentially harmful. This shifted the pedagogical gaze from teaching to predicting. The critical element was the identification of students' readiness. That is a prime reason why pedagogical thought focused so heavily on placing students in *appropriate* text—texts the students would be ready to learn—rather than on formulating methods for teaching students how to read harder books successfully.

Another influence came from the measurement or testing movement. Psychology had been pioneered in the 1860s by the field of psychophysics, focusing on the measurement of sensation and reaction times. Those emphases morphed into the insight that other phenomena such as cognitive skills and academic abilities could be measured too, leading to the invention of a great variety of tests.[36]

The idea of measuring individual differences was not limited to people and their abilities. Since Aristotle, it had been recognized that texts varied in comprehensibility. Some texts are more difficult to understand than others. Difficulty was long accepted as a general property of text, not necessarily something open to scientific measurement. During the nineteenth century, authors and publishers graduated the difficulty of texts by controlling the numbers of syllables or the vocabulary choices, methods without validation. By the 1920s, there were efforts underway to identify the properties of texts for the different grade levels[37] and to develop objective methods for estimating text difficulty.[38]

It was these basic ideas—that students could not learn what they were not ready to learn, that tests could determine readiness, and that text difficulty could be measured scientifically—that distinguishes this period from the previous one. Coupling these "modern" theories with the accomplishments of the previous era led to efforts to identify students' reading levels and to regroup children within and across classes to facilitate matching them with just the right books. Student grouping was no longer to be left to the machinations of individual teachers working from intuition. Now they would be accomplished through widely shared, structured approaches of testing.

Early efforts to match students to text and to place them in texts thought to be easy enough to nurture learning tended to be idiosyncratic; that changed. In Boston first grade classes, for instance, "several primers and first readers [were] available, and lessons [were] selected according to the children's ability and need."[39] Meanwhile, in Chicago, students could not start those beginning readers until they had mastered a reading vocabulary of two hundred words, to protect against overly challenging books. That evidently was not an issue in Cleveland or New Haven, where all students moved directly into such texts. By 1920, a survey in Wisconsin showed that 58 percent of primary-grade teachers were already focusing their instruction on small reading ability-based groups and 42 percent were adjusting the levels of the texts.[40]

Few specifics about these early pedagogical moves are available. We know not how they determined levels or matched kids to books. We can, however, examine some of the advice that was provided to teachers. Here is a characteristic example from a textbook of the time, which after emphasizing repeatedly the importance of ease and simplicity in lessons, offered the advice that reading books should consist of the following:

> selections that are well suited to the pupils in degree of difficulty. . . . In order to be suited in degree of difficulty, the subject-matter should be within the understanding and experience of those who are to read it, and the language should be within or but slightly beyond the vocabulary of the class. This kind of material . . . should not contain too many difficulties, otherwise it will lead to discouragement. There should be but few unfamiliar words, and these should be explained and pronounced before the recitation begins, or before the paragraph is read aloud, so that the pupil will be able to use them unconsciously in giving expression to the thought.[41]

The idea was still one of motivation (focusing on topic familiarity) and ease of reading—(there should not be many unknown words, and frustration, discouragement, and fatigue must be avoided). Recognition of the need for some degree of difficulty was occasionally noted. There "should be such a grade of difficulty that the pupil has some work to do, some effort to make . . . Otherwise, there is no educative activity involved in his reading."[42] These beliefs were transformed from glittering generalities or aspirations into assessment formulas, textbook designs, and grouping strategies, purportedly with a firm scientific basis.

An early example of this described a scheme for evaluating reading levels and dividing classes for instruction.[43] This idea—that testing and instructional grouping could be used to match students to reading instruction—exploded, and with more of a focus on book matching than on developing the skills to read the books.[44] What ensued over the next few decades was nothing less than a nationwide search for the holy grail, the one true way to match students to books for reading instruction.

Research identified word frequencies as a factor in text complexity[45] and provided insights about sentence lengths, too.[46] Later research would revise and refine these ideas. Even early on, however, they contributed to how adroitly publishers had built gradualism into their reading books, objectively controlling vocabulary introduction, repetition, and the distribution of grammatical complexity. The numbers of texts in reading programs increased again,[47]–adding two to three brief beginning books called "preprimers" and dividing some grade level books into semester volumes. All this increased the flexibility with which students could be matched to texts.

New reading and intelligence tests became available. With experience, educators found that standardized tests usually lacked the flexibility needed for use as practical tools for placing students in books. Standard test scores and percentiles did not correspond well to how schoolbooks were graded. Accordingly, the testing movement produced informal classroom assessments such as the informal reading inventory (IRI), which identified the books that could be used for teaching. Students read graded passages aloud and answered comprehension questions to determine the right level. We now know books vary greatly in difficulty, meaning that a single passage cannot provide a reliable prediction of how well students will do with the rest of the book.[48] Nevertheless, testing students with the texts to be taught had a face validity persuasive to teachers and principals.

From 1920 to 1950, school systems experimented with how to make sure that students were taught from books at scientifically determined levels. The Albany Plan, for instance, employed a formula that combined school entrance age and achievement test results to assign students to textbooks.[49] The Elmwood City Plan combined the results of an IQ test and a reading readiness test for this.[50] Another scheme monitored student progress against a collection of word cards, not allowing students to precede until those were mastered.[51] In Joplin, Missouri, Mankato, Minnesota,[52] and Berkeley, California, students were regrouped across grade levels so students with the same reading level could be taught together, no matter their ages.[53]

These schemes—and several others—aimed to disconnect reading lessons from grade levels. There was wide agreement that this would be beneficial—with virtually every reading guru of the time cheering it on (e.g., Edward Dolch, Donald Durrell, Arthur Gates, William S. Gray, Albert J. Harris, Marion Monroe, Paul Witty). But there was great uncertainty about how to go about it.

E. L. Thorndike's approach served as an influential model, though more honored in the breach. "Words unknown to the reader should occur only rarely. A reasonable standard is not over 1 in 200."[54] Others focused on word reading accuracy, not word meanings. The pervasiveness of these schemes reveals the strong professional desire to address student variability, and a strong commitment to accomplishing that through proper text placement. A survey showed that teachers preferred within-class homogeneous grouping because of its effectiveness, motivational value, and positive impact on discipline—cherished beliefs not necessarily supported with empirical evidence.[55]

In 1946, Emmett Betts published the most influential reading textbook of its era, *Foundations of Reading Instruction*.[56] Dr. Betts had a long and illustrious career in education, serving many roles (e.g., principal, school superintendent, professor), publishing more than 1,300 papers and articles, and being one of the founders of the International Literacy Association. He was especially known for his opposition to what he called "the vicious tendency in the schools to do little about individual differences," and the procedures and tools that he created to support the differentiation or individualization of reading instruction.[57]

In his textbook, Betts claimed that all students have independent, instructional, and frustration reading levels. An independent level indicates the level of difficulty of the texts that can be read effectively without assistance. The instructional level indicates the best level of texts to use for reading instruction, and frustration level texts are to be avoided since these would be too difficult to foster learning. Betts offered a plan for constructing, administering, and scoring "informal reading inventories," tests that would allow teachers to identify children's reading levels. According to Betts, a text would be beneficial for instruction if students could read the words with 95 to 98 percent accuracy and 75 to 89 percent comprehension of the text, meaning students would have little to learn from the texts used to teach. Betts even referred to empirical research that supported his claims. For a century, teachers had been admonished to avoid difficult texts. Now there was a scientific plan that would ensure ease of reading and superior learning.

For whatever reason—the reasonableness of the argument, its consistency with past claims, the plan's practicality, or its purported scientific basis—this scheme became the basis of today's reading instruction. There have been occasional minor efforts to refine Betts's criteria—and a couple of major alternatives to it. Nevertheless, this scheme and its offshoots continue to dominate the teaching of reading in America.

During this era, texts for reading instruction continued to grow easier and the learning progressions more gradual. There was little if any pushback against these changes. Sometimes there were arguments over how best to match kids to books, but no opposition. It should be noted that this period witnessed the greatest literacy increase in US history.[58] This success may be one reason why the approach holds so many in thrall. The conclusion that this approach was the source of those big literacy gains is tempting, but there are many other more likely reasons for it, including major increases in school enrollments, lengthening of school years, and a more highly educated and professionalized teaching force. Text matching may have contributed to the improvement, though it is unlikely that it was a major cause.

DOMINANCE OF INSTRUCTIONAL LEVEL THEORY, 1951–2023

This final historical section can be brief. For the most part, much has been done to increase the implementation of the instructional level idea, with little additional innovation. It is the rare school today that does not group elementary readers based on text levels. Teacher surveys suggest that this approach is used more widely than ever.[59]

Textbook vocabulary controls reached a pinnacle of rigidity and systematicity in the 1950s. One program, for example, limited the introduction of new words to one to two per page, with each repeated fifteen times or more in the ensuing pages.[60] Other programs adopted similar design rules. Some early readers included no more than eighty words. This gradual and systematic introduction of words required texts written for reading instruction and precluded the use of literature. In the lower grades, it rendered the language of the texts wooden and unnatural: "See Dick run. Run, run, run. Run, Dick, run."[61]

Artificial language, emphasis on word repetition, and limited content raised concerns and elicited public scorn.[62] There was a backlash against these rigid vocabulary controls so that, by the 1970s, publishers replaced these controls with readability estimates. This allowed "basal readers" to become the anthologies they are today. Up to then, assessments and instructional texts were constructed using the same difficulty algorithms which had facilitated a closer match between placement decisions and instructional demands.[63]

Despite this reform, these textbooks continued to elicit criticism, particularly from the "whole language" movement of the 1980s.[64] Whole language advocates championed the idea that instructional texts needed to be "authentic." They believed that ease and gradualism mattered less than the richness, depth, and quality of literature.[65] Authenticity was supposed to promote learning through motivation. Students would so want to read that they would somehow conquer the demanding language of books with little explicit teaching or support.

This idea was institutionalized by the state of California.[66] It adopted an instructional framework and banned the purchase of textbooks that included selections written for the purpose of teaching reading. Complicating matters, California prohibited publishers from simplifying these texts in any way. Beginning reading books increased in difficulty while phonics and spelling instruction were eschewed. The importance of the lucrative California market to the publishing industry made this approach the *de facto* educational policy of the nation.

These whole language textbooks raised the bar the most for beginning readers.[67] Publishers were able to find acceptable texts for older kids—appropriate literary texts at grade level. It was different with beginning reading books. There were not enough trade books or children's magazine articles easy enough for first grade reading. Most texts that met the requirements were written for reading to children, and these were too hard for beginning readers to take on themselves. Elfrieda H. Hiebert has documented the increases in difficulty this imposed on reading novices by showing the formidable increases in vocabulary demand that these new textbooks presented.[68] Making matters worse, teachers were provided no guidance as to how to facilitate reading with the harder books. In too many classrooms, beginning reading instruction devolved into nothing more than teachers reading textbook selections aloud—with kids scrambling to memorize what they heard so they could "read" it themselves. Not surprisingly, this brief flirtation with higher text levels with limited instructional support coincided with a precipitous decline in reading achievement.[69] This led to the "reading wars" of the 1990s.[70] California soon after dumped its whole language framework and publishers returned to more traditional fare.

During this morass—with frustrated teachers, parents, and beginning readers—Fountas and Pinnell published their landmark text, *Guided Reading*.[71] It argued for an approach well aligned with Betts's instructional ideas—though adjusted to Clay's Reading Recovery criteria—90 percent word reading accuracy as opposed to 95 percent. Some modifications and modernizations accompanied this renewed embrace of the instructional level. Instead of textbooks, their text leveling systems allowed instruction with trade books. Readability assessments were not well attuned to beginning text levels, so Fountas and Pinnell developed their own qualitative scheme for sorting books on an A-to-Z continuum.[72] Children's publishing had exploded since Betts, so there were now large numbers of inexpensive paperbacks written for children that could be placed on the continuum. The term "leveled books" does not mean that these books were revised somehow, only that they have been assigned a level based on relative difficulty. Schools organized book rooms, stocked with multiple copies of books the teachers could match to the children's reading levels. IRIs were replaced with running records—an analogous oral reading test. There are important differences in these instruments, but when it comes to matching books to students, they are essentially the same.

The introduction explained how the Common Core Standards tried to increase the levels of books used for instruction in grades 2 through 12, and the resistance that generated. It set performance goals for kids that if accomplished would guarantee their ability to participate fully in American society. As noted, this plan was undermined by teachers who believed that no matter the goals, students would be best taught with books they could already read reasonably well. Textbooks increased in difficulty, but, as with the whole language debacle, with no professional preparation provided for the teachers. With harder texts, comprehension is more difficult, so student success depends on appropriately supportive teaching—teaching not as necessary when the students can read the books successfully on their own. The introduction of more demanding texts without guidance in how to teach these texts impels teachers to move students to more readable texts (or, in the whole language instance, to reading the books to the students). Teachers responded to these new policies by avoiding the demanding texts, rather than teaching students how to read them.

CONCLUSIONS

Each generation faces social challenges and shapes and reshapes education to meet those challenges. Some strategies become permanent features of the education landscape, while others are superseded, reformulated, or forgotten. Over four hundred years, the United States has been transformed from a colonial theocracy with little need for universal or manifold literacy to a mighty nation highly dependent on reading and writing for its governance, security, economic well-being, and full social participation. Correspondingly, education has adjusted again and again to expanding the literacy franchise to accommodate these changes.

Initially, education reforms were aimed at making literacy learning easier and more gradual, spreading it out over longer time periods. Easier texts were introduced, and the progression of text difficulty was made more gradual. Accompanying reforms—shifting to subject matter more aligned with children's interests and adding illustrations—also helped make reading education more appealing. Over time, these alterations were institutionalized with the creation of the graded common school and the multi-grade reading series.

The success of the changes led to new challenges. With larger and more diverse school enrollments, students with wide ranging reading abilities populated grade level classrooms. Educators tried to differentiate instruction by organizing reading less by grade level, and more by reading level—trying to match students, whatever their ages, to the reading demands of the schoolbooks. That approach seemed to facilitate greater learning.

For more than fifty years, American reading attainment has been stagnant. Whatever gains were to be derived from matching kids to books seem to be baked in the cake. If anything, limiting instruction to books the students can already read and providing little instruction aimed specifically at increasing the levels of books that student can read seems to be holding students back more than propelling them forward. It is time that we, like past generations of educators, rethink literacy instruction to meet the educational needs of our society.

The Misuse of Theory

A theory is supposed to be a sound basis for rational action. A theory of academic learning would explain an education phenomenon and include a framework to help us understand key variables and anticipate what may happen in the future. Ideally, such a theory would be the basis of instructional planning. In the real world, the relationship between theory and practice is more complicated and nuanced than that.

The concern here is not with the translation of theory to practice, but in how we use theories to defend or explain our choices. We suppose ourselves to be rational actors, particularly in our professional endeavors.[1] Attributing our actions to an authoritative theory delivers comforting reassurance. Explaining our choices in terms of well-respected theories protects us from criticism.

The idea of teaching reading with easily read texts is without that kind of authoritative theoretical imprimatur. Its basis is more in a set of commonsensical notions—people like things they can do easily, learning is best accomplished gradually, people have reading levels, and so on. Not surprisingly, each generation of educators, though subscribing to these homely beliefs, has sought the comfort of well-regarded theories. Rationalizing one's actions with the tenets of the theory *du jour* is more intellectually defensible than admitting that these unstudied notions just seemed right. Educators, when explaining the instructional level, have oft tried to cloak their beliefs in the intellectual garments of the time, though ill-fitting.

This is common and natural. Psychologists have derived various explanations of such behavior. Human beings are hard wired see connections among things, even when none exist. Psychologists refer to this as "illusory correlation," our ability to see associations that are not there.[2] Another explanation is that when someone acts, they will seek to justify their choices. This is the process of cognitive dissonance.[3] Once an action is taken, individuals are energetic in seeking evidence for why they did so. People read more articles that tout the quality of their new car *after* the purchase than before. Logically, one would want this information to help make the decision, and yet it is sought when its only purpose can be to provide reassurance of the soundness of the choice. Accordingly, the instructional level has been explained and defended with four psychological theories—readiness, frustration, high accuracy learning, zone of proximal development—different theories for different eras. Nevertheless, for the most part, the use of these theories to defend the instructional level are irrelevant, misleading, and sometimes outright false. This chapter will explore each of these theories and their irrelevance.

READINESS THEORY

Developmental psychology has its roots in Charles Darwin's theory of evolution. Developmental psychology considers how we grow, change, and adapt across the course of our lives—biologically, genetically, neurologically, psychosocially, and culturally. Darwin studied how species came to be, and the changes they must have undergone in response to their environments. From this, it was a minor shift to considering the changes that individuals within a species may undergo. The chicks of most bird species cannot fly at birth, but later physical abilities emerge enabling them to learn to fly. Generalizing these concepts to human growth was an obvious step.

Psychologists have often focused on two kinds of change that individuals undergo in a lifetime—development and learning. *Development* refers to changes of structure, function, or behavior that occur naturally; changes that take place in all or most members of a species in a similar time sequence, no matter the individual experience. "This growth is inherent and lawful; it reflects maturational patterns that are the product of evolution."[4] We may think of these developmental changes as resulting mainly from aging or maturation. *Learning*, on the other hand, refers to changes due specifically to the environment. We all might go through a similar sequence of development, but what we learn will differ based on environments and experiences. According to this view, development and learning are somewhat independent, though development may limit (or enable) what can be learned at any given point in time—those chicks were not going to successfully learn to fly until they had sufficiently strong wings.

Language development and language learning provide a good illustration of this relationship. Children usually begin gaining new vocabulary slowly when they are six to twelve months of age, and then from that point until they are about five years old, vocabulary growth is prodigious, enabling the mastery of thousands of words. Neurological study has identified changes in the brain that enable rapid language development,[5] and these patterns of growth seem to exist universally in our species, no matter the culture.[6] Physiological precursors and commonality across cultural boundaries are hallmarks of a developmental factor. Without those early neurological changes, language learning will be severely limited. But once those developmental changes occur, then language learning becomes possible. And, because learning is different than development, what is learned will be shaped by experience. Almost all toddlers will learn language during that period, but the language they learn and how they use it will be determined by their environment. It is no accident—though it is certainly convenient—that kids learn the language spoken by their parents or caregivers.

G. Stanley Hall, the "father of American psychology," was the first to identify adolescence as a discrete stage of human development.[7] Another authority in the first decades of the twentieth century, Arthur Gesell, one of Hall's students, conducted descriptive studies of infant development, detailing—based on careful observation—the normative ages of behaviors (e.g., first words, spoon holding, toilet habits). Gesell believed that behavioral patterns emerged naturally and in a standard sequence due to physical maturation—with little regard for learning.

The idea that human behaviors were enabled by physiological and cognitive growth placed an upper-bound limit on what could be learned at any point. Gesell's work was not just recognized in the fields of psychology and education but was well known to parents across the nation into the 1950s. Theories emerged claiming that teaching children what they were not developmentally prepared for—such as potty training prior to the onset of the physiological ability to control bladders or bowels—would damage a child's psyche, leading to neurosis or mental illness. This, in a nutshell, is the idea of "readiness."

The educational question raised by developmental psychology was whether students were ready for what we intended to teach. The most obvious application of this theory to reading education was the notion of "reading readiness." First grade failure due to a lack of progress in learning to read was a major concern in the 1920s and 1930s. Many six-year-olds were being retained for an additional year of first grade at a great economic and social cost. Scholarly attention to this problem was aimed at identifying the earliest point at which students could begin to learn to read successfully. For example, there was the then-famous "Winnetka plan."[8] This research found that students who failed grade 1 tended to start the school year with mental ages lower than 6.5—their scores on an IQ test were lower than what would be average for a six-and-a-half-year-old child. Accordingly, the schools in Winnetka, Illinois delayed the onset of reading instruction for children who fell below that benchmark. If the kids were not ready, they would wait until they were. "Readiness programs" were developed not so much to prepare students for learning to read, as much as to ensure that no damaging reading instruction crept in too early. Such prudence was thought to reduce retention rates and avoid the psychic damage that premature teaching would cause.

These days, most school districts start reading instruction in kindergarten, and programs like Head Start introduce reading lessons even earlier. Nevertheless, when I was in kindergarten during the 1950s, my mother was cautioned not to introduce reading to me because of the potential damage. When I became a teacher in the early 1970s, the idea that such instruction must be delayed until January of Grade 1 was still widely honored.

What changed?

By the 1960s, enough research had accumulated to suggest that adjusting instruction to students' learning needs rather than waiting for development to catch up was a better way to go. Famously and influentially, Jerome Bruner asserted, "We begin with the hypothesis that any subject can be taught effectively in some intellectually honest form to any child at any stage of development. It is a bold hypothesis and an essential one in thinking about the nature of a curriculum. No evidence exists to contradict it; considerable evidence is being amassed that supports it."[9]

This statement assuaged the fears of American parents shaken by the Soviet Union's launch of Sputnik. Everyone wanted to believe that American children could do better in the sciences. Waiting for readiness no longer was socially acceptable. Since then, readiness to learn has been thought to be more under the control of learning than development. Although the readiness concept continues to be important in psychology, it is the rare expert who would argue for delaying teaching in the hopes that would better prepare students for eventual success.

Frankly, it is surprising that the "delay-don't-teach" approach to reading was such an influential idea. Most research in the first decades of the twentieth century emphasized readiness, but some studies of the time took a different tack. Arthur Gates found that it was possible to teach reading successfully to children with mental ages of 3.5, by adjusting the instruction to fit the youngster's needs.[10] Simple modifications to instructional routines (e.g., shorter lessons, more opportunity for movement, greater emphasis on guiding attention, responding to what the child already knew) were remarkably effective. Nevertheless, the zeitgeist of the times was to focus on waiting for readiness—not on how to make lessons effective for all.

The testing movement was getting underway during this period. Test developers sought tools that could determine who was ready.[11] Cattell noted that researchers were "collecting large masses of observation and organizing them into descriptive patterns at ascending stages of the age cycle,"[12] and that the measurement movement was designing instruments that could efficiently identify where students were on the cycle.

Readiness was so widely espoused and strongly held from 1890 to 1950 that it is not surprising that the concept was stretched beyond its initial focus. No longer was the concern solely with what was developmentally possible, but with circumventing anything that may interfere with learning—such as avoiding challenging text because of its potential for discouragement.[13] No one bothered with empirical evidence to support such claims, given the wide acceptance of the idea that students could only learn what they were ready for. Accordingly, readiness theory was used to explain the instructional level. Students with second-grade reading levels could not be taught to read a third-grade book because they would not yet be ready for that. Spending additional time practicing with a second-grade book until students were ready for the harder text was the only sure avenue to success. These notions continue to be rigidly adhered to in some schools, as if reading certain books were a matter of development rather than the province of teaching and learning.

FRUSTRATION THEORY

Frustration theory was another influential intellectual focus throughout much of the mid-twentieth century. Sigmund Freud and psychoanalytic theory placed frustration at the center of a plethora of psychological phenomena (e.g., sexual development, learning, aggression, and criminal behavior).[14] Behavioral psychologists focused on frustration as well. It was a phenomenon particularly amenable to study using their paradigm; one could easily prevent rats from reaching a goal and observe the impact on learning or other behavior. The basic premise of much of the early thinking on frustration was straightforward: if students were blocked from accomplishing a goal (e.g., learning), then they would become frustrated and would stop trying to attain the goal. There also may be other unfortunate implications such as increases in aggression.

If assigned a text that was too difficult, it was assumed students would be frustrated. Readiness focused on the importance of appropriate conditions for learning, while frustration theory emphasized the potential impacts of failure to learn. Readiness was used to endorse the claim that certain levels of text placement would optimize learning, while frustration theory seemed to support the idea that hard text would have negative consequences. That these theories were inappropriate to the reading phenomena they were applied to was something few educators noticed.

Texts beyond students' instructional reading levels were labeled as "frustration." The idea was that if students were to make more than five to ten errors per hundred words on a first reading (it differs a bit from theory to theory), then they would not only fail to learn, but would be frustrated, with all the emotional implications of that. The original idea was that teachers had to do more than count errors. They were cautioned to be on the lookout for physiological signs of frustration, too. Later authorities took this further by hooking readers up to polygraph machines—lie detectors—to tease out more subtle physiological signs of tension and frustration by measuring blood pressure, pulse, and skin conductivity.[15]

The use of the term "frustration" to describe texts' level of difficulty would have reached a susceptible audience in the 1940s. The volume of frustration research was high, and such studies had wide exposure in the popular media. Everybody "knew" that frustration causes aggression. Teachers came to see the instructional level as a tool to prevent misbehavior.

At some point, the results of frustration research and popular conceptions of frustration diverged. Frustration turned out to be a much more nuanced and complex phenomenon than had been supposed. It turns out that frustration is mediated by student perceptions, degree of task complexity, explicitness of the goals, internal and external motivation, duration, frustration tolerance, degree of frustration, and other individual and contextual variables.[16] The nice neat linear theory that instructional leveling champions—read a hard book, get frustrated, fail to learn, misbehave—does not fit the research findings.

Research shows that frustration is not necessarily a bad thing when it comes to learning. Moderate amounts of frustration or anxiety do not reliably inhibit learning but *stimulate* it under at least some circumstances.[17] Even more challenging to frustration level claims is the finding that some degree of frustration is *required* for learning to occur. Too much frustration and learners may lose motivation, but too little frustration and there is no learning. The ideal environment poses difficulty or challenge to students without overwhelming frustration.

Emmett Betts had some inkling of this. His concept of the instructional level was meant to result in book assignments that would provide some amount of difficulty so as to facilitate learning—there would be a degree of failure, but not frustration. He surmised that any psychological frustration would be ferreted out by observing students' tension signs during reading.[18] Nevertheless, there was never any real connection between his criteria and learning. Unlike the extensive body of frustration studies, his efforts were singularly ungrounded, circular, and unconvincing. Their only real connection to frustration theory was the use of the term. In the one small sample of students on whose performance he based his criteria, he documented the presence of tension signs that he thought signaled frustration (e.g., blushing, finger pointing, slow rates, pitch changes). But he provided no evidence linking these to any failure in learning. Betts's operationalization of instructional and frustration text levels was more logical than empirical, and its connection with frustration theory and the extensive body of research that it spawned was mainly by analogy.

Later studies of larger and more diverse samples of students reported striking differences in the degree of text challenge required to generate tension signs.[19] At some grade levels, tension did not materialize until oral reading accuracy dropped to about 80 percent. In the polygraph studies that sought to identify latent signs of frustration, none was apparent until students were reading texts more difficult than Betts's recommended.[20] None of these studies measured learning either.

Another inconsistency in the relationship between frustration theory and instructional level theory has to do with *mitigation*. In the reading theory, the notion is that frustration must be avoided. If a text might frustrate it should not be taught. However, in frustration theory, the idea is that frustration often cannot be avoided, and therefore needs to be mitigated, and the research has identified many ways that relaxation, cognitive restructuring, and counseling can be used to accomplish this. Instead of avoiding the instructional benefits of challenging texts, teachers can provide supports and guidance that will allow learning while mitigating potential frustration.

HIGH ACCURACY LEARNING THEORY

Behaviorism dominated American psychology through the middle decades of the twentieth century. It focused on human and animal behavior without any consideration of thoughts, feelings, or motivations.[21] According to behaviorism, learning is the result of conditioning. Conditioning refers to the process by which our behavioral responses become linked to environmental stimuli. To behaviorists, positive reinforcement is the glue that connects a stimulus and response. Thorndike's law of effect held that the likelihood that a stimulus will elicit a particular response depends on the consequences of the response.[22] Basically, behaviors that were reinforced with a reward would be repeated, and those that elicited punishment would not be. Thorndike developed this theory by placing hungry cats in puzzle boxes. Initially, the cats clawed at the box unsystematically, but eventually hit the release lever which allowed them to be rewarded with yummy fish. Thorndike timed these efforts and found that, with those rewards, the cats' behaviors became more systematic and facile; they learned to let themselves out of the box quickly. Thorndike and other behaviorists generalized this experiment to people.

In reading, for example, we may want students to say "was" when presented with the letter string, "w-a-s." The teacher might show this word to a student saying, "It says, 'was.'" The student then repeats the word. If his or her response is correct, then there should be some positive reinforcement (e.g., pat on the head, encouragement, piece of candy). Subsequent trials may be complicated by mixing this word in with several others, and correct responses are again reinforced. Over time, this S-R (stimulus-reward) link becomes certain. The word is learned.

The most specific applications of behaviorism to reading have been through programmed instruction and machine learning applications. Both emphasize three features that appear to dovetail—at least superficially—with the instructional level. Programmed instruction and machine learning both emphasize the teaching of tiny behavioral changes, with lots of repetition, and on the need for high accuracy in student responses.[23] That does not mean that these approaches ignored complex behaviors, only that these were seen as a concatenation of sequences of smaller behaviors. Behaviorists would break behaviors down into tiny parts and try to condition these sub-behaviors, eventually stringing them together.

Behaviorism was often referred to as "pigeon psychology," because one of its most famous demonstrations was B. F. Skinner's conditioning of pigeons to play table tennis.[24] He had them use their beaks to peck a ball back and forth across the table to each other. This was accomplished in small steps. If a pigeon came close to a ping pong ball, it was rewarded. If it pecked a ball, it was rewarded, and so on. None of these skills could be learned in a single trial, so each was repeated until mastered. By focusing on small steps, each of which led the pigeons closer and closer to the complex behavior, Skinner taught them to volley ping pong balls successfully (none, apparently, ever was able to compete in the World Table Tennis competitions).

Programmed learning for children is much the same.[25] The desired outcome is divided into a sequential series of frames or boxes, each containing one small question or task to which students respond. Each frame introduces a single skill or provides opportunity for review. The skills may be individual words, a phonic element, or a spelling pattern. As with conditioning the pigeons, frequent repetition is essential. Positive reinforcement matters, too. The pigeons received pieces of cereal to reward their actions. Thorndike's law of effect did not require external rewards, only positive consequences. As investigations shifted from animals to people, and from physical tasks to academic accomplishments, the reinforcing power of getting an answer correct came to be recognized. In programmed learning the reward to the students is immediate feedback on their responses.

What are the connections between instructional level theory and programmed learning? The instructional routines of both emphasize small amounts of learning. Programmed learning breaks tasks into tiny steps. Instructional level theory places students in texts that, by design, can foster only very limited amounts of learning—students may start out reading correctly as many as ninety-eight out of one hundred words. Not much to learn there, but the idea is that these tiny amounts of learning will eventually accumulate enabling students to read more challenging texts.

Most reading authorities in the 1940s believed that reading proficiency came from learning words. They pooh-poohed the idea of explicit decoding instruction, and championed high frequency word lists and memorization routines. Programmed learning and the instructional level both depended heavily on repetition as the key process in teaching. You may remember that textbook designers worked hard to build specific repetition schedules into their textbooks. Placing students in books with a few unknown words would facilitate learning by ensuring that those unknown words would be repeated so often that they would stick.

Finally, as with programmed instruction, the positive reinforcement came in the form of success rather than external rewards. As students learned to respond properly to a word, they not only could read the word, but would be able to enjoy and understand the story in which it was embedded. However, for this to work, "a low rate of error is necessary to ensure continued positive reinforcement of correct responses."[26]

High accuracy learning theory was used to defend instructional level theory since it seems to ensure that text assignments result in especially small learning steps, frequent repetition, and the natural reinforcement of learning through successful reading. That the guided reading situation is so different than the behaviorist conception was not recognized as a problem. Programmed instruction contexts were designed to ensure that students recognize what is to be learned and to minimize distraction from those items, so students would be aware of their success. However, when students are asked to read a text at their instructional level, it is not clear which reading skills must be mastered, nor is any learning success obvious. Students would be unlikely to recognize whether a correctly read word was previously known or unknown. Without clarity on such points, not much learning progress would be expected. This gets even knottier when the point of the learning goes beyond mastering certain words. Think of the various skills that must be implemented to comprehend a text (e.g., vocabulary, syntax, cohesion). The actual connections between behaviorism and instructional level theory are cursory at best.

VYGOTSKY'S ZONE OF PROXIMAL DEVELOPMENT

Recently, I was making a presentation on the importance of teaching reading with challenging texts. When I finished an unhappy audience member—a school principal—replied wryly, "Well I guess that means we can ignore Vygotsky from now on." His passive-aggressive response was based on his supposition that instructional level theory is supported by the influential Russian psychologist's "zone of proximal development." For that principal, my rejection of instructional level was seen as a contradiction of the august theories of a widely esteemed psychologist. He was dismissing what I was saying because, well, let's face it, I'm no Vygotsky. This principal believed that Vygotsky's zone of proximal development supports the instructional level—maybe even that it came from Vygotsky—and these misconceptions are widely held.[27]

Given how often the Vygotsky connections are posed these days, it seems pertinent to point out that American educators had widely adopted the instructional level idea decades before Vygotsky's work appeared in the US, and that he, in his lifetime, had never heard of our instructional level, nor did he write about placing students in books at students' instructional levels. Any superficial connections or similarities that seem to exist are more than outbalanced by the profound differences in the two perspectives.

Lev Vygotsky's social theory of how we learn, and his "zone of proximal development" were formulated during the years 1924 to 1934. This work was unknown in the US until one of his books was translated into English in 1962. Even then, his work was not widely recognized until late in the 1970s, long after the development and widespread adoption of the instructional level in reading. Unlike the previous three theories which may have, at least indirectly, influenced the instructional level idea, there is no way that Vygotsky's theories of teaching and learning could have played any role. Vygotsky did write about literacy learning, but his work never addressed the issues at hand.

Vygotsky was aware of American thinking about teaching and learning during his lifetime. He knew, for instance, of the view that development determined learning and of the heavy emphasis on readiness. He explicitly rejected both notions. In his view, learning influenced development every bit as much as the reverse. He also rejected the notion that instruction should wait for readiness. Vygotsky's theorizing focused heavily on the social dynamics of how adults mediated children's cognitive development. In his view, learning was not something to be waited for. Instead, he argued that instruction—or rather mediation—could be adjusted to meet the needs of the child.[28]

An important concept in Vygotsky's theory—and the one most relevant to this discussion—is the zone of proximal development (ZPD). According to Vygotsky, social mediation is the major determinant of cognitive development, and the zone of proximal development is the difference between what children can do independently and what they can accomplish with the assistance of a more able adult.[29] He believed that learning takes place in that ZPD space, and the mediation provided by the adult should provide sufficient support to allow for the successful implementation of a task or application of an ability. Basically, an adult helps a child to carry out a task successfully while providing useful and supportive explanation. As the child becomes more proficient, the ZPD shrinks—that is, the distance between what the child can do on his or her own and what can be accomplished with the help of an adult lessens. Here is a useful description of the process:

> The two work together, in a manner controlled by the adult, to reach a meeting of the minds. The adult intends to affect the child's understanding, the child is aware of this intention, and the child works to create a new understanding of the task, one based on the adult's intentions. In true instructed learning the child leaves the interaction with an internalized dialogue that represents a coordination of the participants' mental representations during the instructional process.[30]

Perhaps a homely example would help. A young child is unable to tie his shoes by himself (and Velcro is not an option). Learning to do this will entail a series of social interactions about this with his mother. Initially, Mom might do all the actual tying, while directing the child to observe as she describes the steps. This talk is the source of the "internalized dialogue" that the child absorbs.

Later, Mom asks the child, "When I tie your shoes, what do I do first?" If the child remembers that the laces must be crossed, she has him do that step himself, and then completes the remaining steps while he watches. Of course, all of this is accomplished with social interaction—Junior explains the step he can do, or Mom fills in the explanation; she praises his cleverness in crossing the laces properly and describes the steps the child still cannot do. If the child is unable to remember that first step, then the guided observation and explanation starts there again. Also, each time, no matter how little of the task the child can implement independently, the adult makes certain the task is completed successfully.

All the steps in this process take place in the child's ZPD—initially, he knew none of the steps, but the shoes always ended up getting tied. Over this series of episodes, the ZPD shrank as the child mastered more and more of the shoe tying routine himself—right up to the point that it could be said that he knew how to tie his shoes. The process was accompanied by lots of talk, both on the part of the adult and the child—describing or explaining what they were doing and internalizing that talk (remembering it) is an important part of social learning.

What was not part of this process? There was no formal assessment or consideration of readiness—except in the most general and commonsense way. No parent would likely try to teach their toddlers to tie their shoes themselves before they could put their shoes on. Also, there was no attempt to determine the child's instructional level, at least not in the sense that it is used in reading education. The mother did not delay teaching shoelace tying until the child showed that he was able to make a loop with a string, for instance. No, according to Vygotsky, delay is not the road to learning, but adjusted social mediation is. Mom made sure the task was completed successfully and provided sufficient support to ensure this success each time. The less the child knew, the more the adult contributed. As the child accomplished more and more, adult support was withdrawn (no wonder that later educators knowing Vygotsky's model described this support as "scaffolding," referring to how scaffolds are used in building).

The instructional level idea runs counter to this description. The instructional level, if implemented to specification, minimizes the amount of adult support, and ideally keeps this in a steady state from task to task—since the ideal would be to have all students always working with instructional level text. In the shoe tying example, the goal line is clear—by the end of the process the child will be able to tie his shoes. In the reading example, the goal line is constantly moving. There is never any sense of accomplishment, since the amount of help the adult provides should always be the same, since the difficulty level stays constant. Vygotsky would not tell third-grade teachers to delay introducing third-grade text but would advocate immersing their students in such texts while providing them with social support.

What of those students who are reading at a "second-grade level"? Vygtosky would want the teacher to adjust the amount and type of social interaction and support, not the task—being able to read that third-grade text would still be a legitimate social goal. Remember, the idea is to make sure the task is completed successfully—in this case, the text is read with comprehension—with the students doing as much of the work as possible, and with the adult providing necessary support and explanation to allow for this success. A child reading a year behind his or her peers would receive more support and explanation than the child who is already able to do much of the work independently. An apt example of this is provided by a small experimental study that showed that with adult mediation students were able to make solid reading gains when placed in texts two grades above their instructional levels.[31]

Some educators—that principal for example—confound the two concepts, considering the instructional level and the ZPD as identical. Others, seem to see both points of similarity and difference. After pointing out that the two concepts are "remarkably similar," Robert T. Ackland, Professor of Literacy and Teacher Education at SUNY Plattsburg, then suggests recasting the instructional level to bring it into alignment with the ZPD: "Instead of attempting to specify an instructional 'level' let's consider a zone or 'range' similar to the ZPD. The instructional range can be envisioned as the space on a column above a mark for the level of independent performance and below a mark for the level of frustration. . . . There are probably several ranges for each student, especially when we consider the importance of a learner's interest and prior knowledge."[32] Other educators have argued for a similar broadening of the concept, viewing student-text matches not as single-point decisions, but as a determination of wide ranges of performance, each requiring a different degree of instructional support from the teacher.[33] These reconceptualizations of the instructional level idea radically alter it into something much more akin to the Vygotsky theory. That the instructional level must be so substantially altered to accomplish this, reveals how superficial the oft-recognized correlation of ZPD and instructional level is.

The instructional level assumes children are not ready to learn from a text until they can read a certain percentage of words. Vygotsky's theory does not encourage such delay. The instructional level tries to limit the amount of social mediation teachers provide by severely shrinking the ZPD—the easier a task for a child, the less teacher mediation required. The instructional level promotes differentiation of instruction by varying what is taught to students, while ZPD supports differentiation through variation in the mediation. The instructional level emphasizes the selection of texts for pedagogical reasons alone (to match student ability and text demands), instead of selecting texts for their curricular or social value. The instructional level minimizes useful social interactions among the students by segregating them based on what they can and cannot yet do, reducing the possibility of valuable peer exchanges.

CONCLUSIONS

One reason the instructional level idea has been so persuasive to generations of educators has been the ease with which it has been connected to the major intellectual movements of the times. Each generation has relied on superficial similarities with whatever theory was then most persuasive. It may seem like the instructional level idea dined on psychological theories at Golden Corral and loaded up on generous helpings from the readiness, frustration, behaviorism, and ZPD steam tables, but that was not the case. For the most part, the instructional level idea neither emanated from those theories, nor is it consistent with their deepest tenets.

If instructional level is at sixes and sevens with those theories and their most basic principles and premises, then it must stand on its own. One cannot convincingly depend upon these theories to provide evidence by analogy in support of the instructional level. Instructional level only makes sense if it leads to greater learning success for children. The instructional level must live or die based on its own effectiveness.

CHAPTER 3

Does It Help Children Learn to Read?

Students are taught with below-grade-level texts because teachers have been led to believe that such books hold the greatest promise for learning success. Educational traditions and scholarly theories have encouraged this practice—without much consideration of viable alternatives. What if teaching with such books does not improve learning? What if it offers no advantages while encumbering teachers with lots of testing duties and students with pejorative labels—segregating them and limiting their exposure to grade level language or content? Even worse, what if the instructional level holds kids back, suppressing learning and leading to other unfortunate consequences? The issue has to do with the validity of the instructional level concept itself. If students do not learn more when taught at their instructional level, then it has no purpose. If they learn less, then it is malpractice.

The purpose of this chapter is to examine research studies that have attempted to *directly* evaluate the validity of the instructional level in text reading instruction. Over the past eighty years, there have been several empirical attempts to evaluate the instructional level. First, there are studies that measure the relationships between oral reading accuracy and reading comprehension. These studies were first used to justify the design of the instructional level. I find this kind of validation dubious since it does not consider the impact of instructional level text assignments on learning. However, proponents of the instructional level believe that progress in learning will depend on how well the students comprehend the instructional texts. Accordingly, they seek criteria that will identify texts that students will be sure to comprehend no matter the instruction.

A second set of studies has measured the correlations between text placement and learning. These studies include investigations in which text assignments were not manipulated as well as instructional experiments that lacked a control group. At best, such studies may imply that instructional level teaching leads to greater learning, but they cannot prove it. This evidence, too, will be considered.

Finally, a third set of studies, investigations of the experimental impact of placing students at the instructional level, will be explored. These studies allow for clear comparisons between what happens when students are taught with instructional or frustration level texts. As such they offer the strongest research evidence on which to determine the value of the instructional level theory in reading.

Before plunging into the research, it is worth noting the evidence that is often marshalled to support the instructional level. Proponents of the theory have often depended upon research that is far afield, such as studies focused on math computations, seatwork activities aimed at memorization, or the content learning of college students.[1]

For example, it is often noted in support of the instructional level that a meta-analysis of 180 studies of instructional interventions for students with learning disabilities reported that, "Interventions that included instructional components related to controlling task difficulty . . . were significant predictors of effect size."[2] However, that study focused on a wide variety of instructional variations, including the provision of teacher assistance, sequencing of tasks from easy to difficult, and scaffolding—and these supports were not necessarily aimed at supporting learning to read.

Such evidence is used to "prove" that some tasks may be too hard to foster learning. That may or may not be the case, but the purpose of the instructional level is to determine the books that students should read under the guidance of a teacher. The relationship of challenge levels in other domains or the provisions of other kinds of instructional scaffolding can only provide weak support for the instructional level, proof by analogy. The reasoning behind such arguments is something like: "This study proves that some math problems may be too challenging to stimulate math learning or that students learn better when teachers control task difficulty. Therefore, there must be an instructional reading level, too, and the level that I support must be the right one." Not especially persuasive. I think this is the kind of thing Gen Z'ers dismiss as "delusionship."

It is also worth noting that even when this kind of distant evidence is the basis of the instructional level argument, its advocates are often selective in its use—cherry picking supportive studies while ignoring large amounts of contrary data. They fail to point out that research has overwhelmingly rejected the potency of easy tasks or unambitious lessons in other verbal learning domains—the "too easy" side of the ledger that they tend to neglect in their defence of the instructional level. As Richard A. Schmidt and Robert A. Bjork, professors of psychology at the University of California, Los Angeles, summarize an extensive body of such research: "Manipulations that maximize performance during training can be detrimental in the long term; conversely, manipulations that degrade the speed of acquisition can support the long-term goals of training."[3] Admittedly, such studies are not easily generalized to a directed reading instructional situation, but if studies from other domains is the evidentiary basis for supporting the instructional level, then we should not ignore this burgeoning body of contrary evidence on "desirable difficulty" as instructional level proponents always do. Nor should an important lesson from that paragdigm be blithely ignored: Schmidt and Bjork go on to conclude that instruction and practice delivered at an easy level tends to stimulate immediate learning, which then fades quickly. In other words, short term evidence showing quick learning from relatively easy tasks is misleading; one should depend on such support with great caution.

Another example of neglected evidence can be drawn from an intriguing body of literature that paradoxically shows better comprehension or greater learning from more demanding texts at least for some readers.[4] More learning is likely when students must think more deeply and, perhaps, longer about a text—reading and rereading to gain the ideas. More demanding texts require such engagement. Easier texts do not. To gain advantage of the benefits of more challenging text, readers must have sufficient knowledge.[5] Many of these studies, however, have involved proficient readers usually at a college level, and their focus has been on comprehension or content knowledge, not reading improvement. Again, tantalizing information, and yet, not immediately applicable to what is being discussed here.

Given the purpose of this chapter—to evaluate the validity of the instructional level—only direct evidence will be considered. Only studies that evaluated the role text difficulty plays in learning to read will be analyzed. I concede that under some circumstances—such as when students are working independently—that there may be levels of difficulty that could interfere with learning. That, however, tells us nothing about what texts teachers should use to teach reading.

CONNECTIONS OF ORAL READING AND COMPREHENSION

As we recall from chapter 1 Betts claimed that all students have independent, instructional, and frustration reading levels, and proposed a way for teachers to determine those.[6] His informal reading inventory (IRI) required that students read, orally and silently, a series of passages drawn from the different grade levels of the reading textbooks used in their schools. Teachers were to evaluate oral reading fluency and comprehension to place students in the books deemed most appropriate. His criteria were:

	Oral reading fluency	**Reading comprehension**
Independent level	99–100%	90–100%
Instructional level	95–98%	75–89%
Frustration level	0–92%	0–50%

He credited these to a doctoral dissertation of one of his students.[7] Despite Betts's claim of learning benefits, the Killgallon study did not measure learning.

This thesis was never published so few scholars had access to his data. I did not read it until the 1980s. I was writing a chapter about the instructional level—I was a big fan of the idea since I had used it in my classrooms—and needed to summarize that study.[8] Fortunately, Pennsylvania State University, where the work was completed, lent me a copy. As I began reading it I was puzzled. I remember going back to the title page multiple times, reassuring myself that I had the right book. I could not understand the reasoning that led from these data to Betts's criteria.

In the 1940s, there had been considerable speculation about how best to match students to text. Bolenius, Thorndike, and Durrell—major reading scholars at that time—all provided armchair conjectures about how many words students must be able to read for a text to be a good candidate for instruction.[9] Betts himself had speculated informally on the matter in the form of mimeographed procedures used in his reading clinic. Killgallon's dissertation considered those sources, but he was the first to turn to student data.

Given Betts's claims, I assumed students were placed in reading books using those criteria and that they had learned more than students assigned to books by some rival scheme. I assumed, mistakenly, that the study proved the instructional level stimulated learning. That, however, was not the case. Actually, forty-one students were tested, and their oral reading was scored for accuracy and comprehension. The accuracy results were compared with tension signs that had been observed during testing (e.g., squinting, grimacing, flaring nostrils, blushing, sighing, frowning, gritting teeth, gripping chair, rubbing chair, scratching). Those behaviors appeared when word reading accuracy fell to 93.5 percent. Without explanation the researcher rounded that to 95 percent to set a lower bound for the instructional level.

From the dissertation itself, it is not clear from whence came the 75 percent comprehension criterion. In Betts's mimeoed guidelines, the criterion for comprehension had been 50 percent. H. O. Beldin, a professor at Western Washington State College, reanalyzed Killgallon's data decades later, and concluded that the criterion from the dissertation was arrived at by identifying the average comprehension for students who had read with 95 to 98 percent accuracy.[10]

Killgallon and Betts had correlated oral reading accuracy, comprehension, and tension signs, without any consideration of learning. Their aim was not to determine if the instructional level worked, a woefully inadequate validation. That, however, is not a universally held view.[11] Many authorities may disagree with Betts over the specifics of his criteria, but unlike me they accept his reasoning that it is enough that instructional text assignments ensure comprehension.

For example, William Powell, a professor at the University of Illinois, Urbana-Champaign, tried to put Betts's criteria on firmer footing. He employed the same research design as the one used by Killgallon but improved on it by expanding and diversifying the subject sample and altering how errors were counted.[12] Powell's data were drawn from a larger sample of students ($n = 178$) in grades 1 through 6.[13] He counted only oral reading errors that correlated with reading comprehension. Killgallon had counted word repetitions as errors—the largest category of mistakes—but later research reported that repetitions improve comprehension rather than detracting from it, so Powell chose not to count them. He also allowed the passages to be read silently first, while the original subjects had performed "cold reads"—reading aloud texts not seen before.

Powell's study reported very different results. Because the students in his study were drawn from multiple grades, he could see that the correlations of accuracy and comprehension varied by grade. For Powell, there was not one instructional level, but several. For grades 1 and 2, he reported that students accomplished sufficient levels of comprehension even when reading texts with only 85 percent accuracy. With the older students, the necessary levels of accuracy ranged from 91 to 94 percent. Based on this data, Powell recommended the use of more challenging texts to teach reading, especially for younger readers.

Later, he expanded this data pool by supplementing it with secondary analyses of several extant studies of children in grades 1 through 8.[14] Again, he found differences between lower grade and upper grade students and concluded that the Betts criteria were placing students in texts too easy to facilitate learning.

More recent studies have continued to pursue this line of inquiry. For instance, Homan and Klesius, in a study of 150 students in grades 1 through 5, found that the word accuracy scores that ensured 70 percent comprehension ranged from 93.75 percent to 96.42 percent, with no significant grade differences.[15] "The initial results of this study confirm previous research findings . . . strongly indicating that the word recognition criterion for instructional reading level should be set at about 95% for students reading at grade levels 1 through 6."[16] These estimates are averages across many students. There was considerable variation, meaning the 95 percent accuracy criterion would place some children in books they could already comprehend well and many others in books they could not. A similar study examined eighty-three students in grades 1 through 6 and concluded:

> The traditional Betts criterion of 95% for word recognition was generally not supported. Students in grades four through six achieved word-recognition scores of 93% or 94% when miscues such as omissions, substitutions, repetitions, insertions, and deletions were counted. Students in the primary grades achieved average word-recognition scores about 4 percent below Betts's criterion. When only significant miscues were considered (those that affected meaning), students in the primary grades achieved word-recognition scores one or two percent above 95%. Students in the intermediate grades achieved an average of 98% word recognition.[17]

These kinds of studies have usually recommended the use of at least slightly harder texts than Betts's criteria would lead to. This is even true of the original Killgallon dissertation, since he had rounded up the word accuracy statistics by about two points to set that 95 percent accuracy criterion.[18]

What that means is that all the studies aimed at establishing instructional level criteria through the correlation of word reading accuracy with comprehension ended up with criteria that would lead to significantly different book assignments for many children than would be obtained with Betts's 95 percent. This is especially true of Powell's criteria which required only about 85 percent word accuracy. One may assume these results were earth shaking in the reading world given the degree to which they contradicted

Betts. In fact, Powell's findings barely registered—when they were noted they were dismissed. Beldin, for example, points out that the Betts's levels had been "validated through use," meaning, I guess, that they had been around for a generation and children were learning to read.[19]

Despite these contradictory data, Betts's theory continues to be espoused by leading reading educators,[20] and his approach is built into most commercial instructional programs used in today's classrooms—reaching the vast majority of America's children (e.g., *Accelerated Reader*, *Achieve3000*, *Guided Reading*, *Read 180*, *Success for All*, *Units of Study*). Several informal reading inventories are commercially available for placing students at their instructional levels and these are widely used in teacher preparation and reading specialist courses.[21] Many of these employ Betts's criteria or slight adjustments of them. Most primary-grade teachers, and many upper-grade elementary teachers strive to teach students at their instructional levels—as do middle school and high school teachers.[22]

CORRELATIONAL EVIDENCE

Instructional level theory posits that placing students in texts in a particular way leads to more learning. Placements above or below the instructional level are thought to depress learning. The earliest empirical effort to measure the impact of instructional level on reading achievement was J. Louis Cooper's ambitious doctoral dissertation at Boston University in 1952.[23] This study pre- and posttested more than eight hundred students in grades 2 through 6 from eight different schools with two different reading achievement tests. It also administered intelligence tests to each student.

The difficulty of the instructional texts was determined by having students read aloud the books they were being taught from and tabulating the errors per hundred words. These data were then grouped into five categories: 0–1, 2–3, 4–6, 7–9, and 10 or more errors per hundred words. Cooper did not assign students to treatment groups or anything like that. This was a correlational study. He accepted the teachers' book placements and determined the degree of challenge these posed for students. He then examined how much learning the students in each category accomplished over a school year.

Unfortunately, student ability was totally confounded with book placement. All stuents who had scored high on the intelligence test had been placed in books that were relatively easy for them, and all the kids with lower IQ scores were taught from books that generated many errors. As a result, book assignment provided no additional explanation of learning beyond that due to IQ differences. Smarter kids learned more. That was it. Ironically, the biggest learning gains accrued to students who worked in books they could already read perfectly—100 percent accuracy, 100 percent comprehension. Students learned most when taught from texts from which there was nothing to be learned; a possibility Cooper himself rejected: "One must challenge whether or not the group with the fewest errors made the greatest gain in reading achievement because of its superior intelligence to the other groups or because it was working with easier materials than the others. . . . The gains of the other groups might be questioned on the same basis."[24]

Other correlational studies have reported similar results: more learning when there was nothing to be learned.[25] First graders who made the fewest errors tended to be promoted to harder books more quickly. But did they make the fastest gains due to propitious book matches, or were placements confounded with initial ability? The answer seems obvious. Cooper wisely suggested caution in interpreting his results. Without controls on initial reading levels, aptitude, language ability and the like, one cannot determine whether the learning advantages came from the easy books or the readers' superior learning ability.

Another such study was conducted by David Berliner, a psychology professor at Stanford University. His oft-cited data are not of the instructional level per se, but of a scheme that accounted for task difficulty more generally. He labeled classroom activities as "high success," "medium success," and "low success" based on whether the students had made observable errors and seemed to understand the tasks. Low success tasks were not understood at all. He reported that classrooms in which students were engaged in high success tasks more than half the time made the greatest learning gains: "The average student . . . spent about half the time working on tasks that provided high success. Students who spent more time than the average in high success activities had higher achievement scores in the spring, better retention of learning over the summer, and more positive attitudes toward school."[26]

But, again, was it the ease of the activities or that the best and most advantaged students tend to find school relatively easy? The analysis neither sorted out the impact of existing student performance levels nor of other covariates like amount of instruction.

These caveats aside, several correlational studies with older students have failed to replicate these patterns. Notably, these studies, by considering the instructional level match specifically, overcome to some extent the neglect of student background variables. As such, their results are more reliable. For example, in a study that tracked forty-one boys in grades 3 through 6 over a school year,[27] there was no relationship between learning and how well the book assignments matched the students' initial reading levels. Students learned as well when they were in frustration level books as when working at their supposed instructional levels. In another study, this one of text assignment effects with 304 sixth graders, there was no difference in learning between students placed at their instructional levels and those assigned to books one-half to one grade level above the instructional levels.[28] Again, frustration level placements did not appear to attenuate learning.

In a more informative study with a similar design, the effects of the student-text matches made by the teachers in their grade 2 through 6 classrooms were evaluated.[29] A variety of book assignments led to learning and these advantages varied by grade level. The greatest amount of learning went to those grade 2 students assigned to texts that they could read with 85 to 95 percent accuracy, third graders who were taught from texts they could read with 89 to 97 percent accuracy, and students in grades 4 through 6 who worked in the texts that they could read with 60 to 90 percent accuracy.

This study raises provocative possibilities. It points out that the instructional level calls for especially narrow placement decisions—95 to 98 percent accuracy. But this correlational study, like the two reported previously, found success for a much wider performance range. This was particularly so with the older students. In all cases, a wider range of performance levels was related to maximum learning. It also should be noted that the expansion of the ranges placed students in relatively more difficult texts—texts that Betts would have judged frustrating. Students could tolerate and benefit from books that presented wide ranges of difficulty, including texts that instructional level theory would shun.

It also should be evident from this that the instructional level notion—that book placement is the major determinant of learning—is too simplistic. It ignores too many other student and contextual variables that play a role in learning. One wonders about the differences in student abilities and classroom instructional supports that allowed maximum learning for students placed at either 60 percent or 90 percent accuracy levels. The difference maker(s) in these cases could not have been the texts. It will take further study to determine if these results are due to the resilience of learners, supportive instructional moves made by the teachers, or their combination.

In still another study—this one a no-control-group intervention conducted in 2005—first and second graders were taught using Fluency Oriented Reading Instruction (FORI).[30] FORI reformulated basal reader lessons to place a greater emphasis on fluency development, with daily teacher modeling, echo reading, and repeated reading opportunities. Students worked in grade level texts, rather than being matched to reading level texts. The students made nearly two years growth each year. Given the complexity of this intervention, one could not conclude that grade level text placement was the "active ingredient" that made this teaching so effective, but it is evident that these more challenging text placements did not prevent students from making markedly greater than average learning gains.

Often proponents of the instructional level idea will cite evidence that they claim supports the approach.[31] For instance, in one oft-cited large experiment on peer mediation and tutoring, it appears that the first-grade students who made the best gains were in books they could read particularly well.[32] This study, conducted by Linnea Ehri, a professor at City University of New York, and her colleagues provided tutoring to groups of struggling first graders. Those who made the greatest gains read books with 98 to 100 percent accuracy, while those who made the least progress worked in books at the 90 to 97 percent range.

This result has been misinterpreted, however. In this study, text level was confounded with instructional procedures. As the authors indicated, "the high accuracy levels that proved important occurred on text that was read independently *after* [italics added] prior coaching."[33] Although this was an experiment, text difficulty was a correlational variable, not an experimental one. The students' oral reading performances were not used to determine which books to assign but were computed after students had already been tutored in those books. Students were able to read these books at instructional or independent levels *because* of the teaching—not as the antecedent to its success. The most successful learners ended up able to read the instructional texts better than the less successful learners. Kids who made the greatest gains with each book used for instruction ended with the highest overall gains in reading.

This pattern is fascinating, not because it suggests the value of the instructional level, but because it presents the possibility that the instructional level criteria may be a better learning target than a starting point. Perhaps it would be best if teachers placed students in frustration level books, and then worked with those until students could demonstrate an ability to read them as if they were at the instructional level—an approach more in line with the instructional implementation in the Ehri study. Teachers are often uncertain of when to discontinue working with a text. The instructional level may provide such an end point.

In any event, this collection of studies shows two patterns. Studies that reported more learning for students who found the instructional texts to be easy, and studies that found no learning differences due to text assignment (instructional or frustration). The former studies could not unequivocally attribute learning benefits to text assignment, since it seems likely that the greater learning and the easy text placements were both due to initial learning advantages that these students possessed.

The latter studies may have attenuated those initial ability effects to some extent by classifying the students by reading level. Those studies found no learning differences due to text assignment. Kids matched to frustration level texts learned as much as those matched to instructional level ones. Even levels of reading that were far below any version of the instructional level, such as accuracy rates of 85 percent and comprehension rates of 60 percent, fostered learning success. Unfortunately, those studies provided neither sufficient information about the students to know if some may have possessed greater persistence or other advantages that allowed their triumph over frustration, or if teachers provided mediating support. These studies serve as demonstrations that learning is possible from a wide range of text difficulties, but little more.

EXPERIMENTAL EVIDENCE

Beyond these ambiguous correlational findings, there have been a handful of experimental studies of book placement. These studies are preferred because they allow an evaluation of the causal impact that teaching with instructional level books has on learning. However, it is not just type of study that matters but also quality. Initially, the experimental investigations into this matter were not especially sophisticated, ambitious, or informative. One study, for example, examined seven boys ages eight to eleven who were thought to be reading one to three text levels below their grade levels.[34] Students were placed in texts for instruction at various levels of proficiency (no one was placed in a text they could read with less than 80 percent accuracy, but initial comprehension levels ranged from 55 to 95 percent). Despite the varied text assignments, all students made learning progress across a school year. The text assignment variation had no effect, though the study included few students, and the text variations were not systematic (i.e., equivalent differences across groups).

Another such study examined forty-nine fifth graders who were taught for ten days from instructional level texts and ten days from texts that were two to six levels above the instructional level.[35] No learning differences were evident in oral reading or silent reading comprehension, which is not surprising given the short treatment duration. However, even in a somewhat longer study (fifty days) of sixteen students with learning problems in grades 1 through 4, no differences were found in oral reading fluency gains.[36] The students placed in frustration level texts did as well as those placed at instructional levels. Also, in a study of sixty-seven randomly assigned intermediate grade special education students it was found that there was as much learning for those who worked in texts they could read with 90 to 95 percent accuracy as for those in easier texts (98 to 100 percent accuracy).[37] In other words, text level—independent or frustration placement—made no difference in eliciting learning over ten weeks of instruction. Other studies that have intentionally taught second graders with frustration level texts (e.g., two to three levels above instructional level, 85 percent oral reading accuracy), reported successful learning.[38]

Not all such studies have reported no benefits to instructional level placements. One study examined twelve students' oral reading fluency improvements with instructional level and frustration passages (passages one grade above the students' instructional levels).[39] This study had students practicing their oral reading with instructional or frustration level passages and found faster gains in accuracy and speed with the instructional level texts—though this was only true with first grade texts. No such differences in learning were apparent with second grade texts. It should be noted that the teachers provided no instructional assistance to the students during the reading in this study.

Although these experiments consistently have shown that teaching reading with frustration level texts was supportive of learning, they suffer from various limitations and flaws. Most included few students, so their ability to determine significant differences is restricted. They also have measurement problems (e.g., tests of unknown reliability) or design flaws (e.g., short training durations, lack of appropriate comparison groups, lack of random assignment). As such, their evidence in either direction is wobbly and not particularly convincing.

More recent reports appear a bit contradictory—some supporting the instructional level and others challenging it. For example, a recent practice guide on reading interventions for students in grades 4 through 9 issued by the Institute of Education Sciences, the research arm of the US Department of Education, included the following advice: "Provide students with opportunities to practice making sense of stretch text (i.e., challenging text) that will expose them to complex ideas and information."[40] Stretch text is above students' reading levels—at grade level or slightly below the grade level mark. This recommendation was designated as having moderate evidence, meaning there was support but that it was ambiguous. The studies found the interventions that included substantial doses of stretch text either outperformed business as usual interventions (instruction presumably at instructional levels)[41] or led to substantial learning but not any more than resulted from the comparison interventions.[42]

However, these were complex programs of instruction. They included several instructional components, making it impossible to attribute success to any single part. It is impossible to conclude that grade level text instruction was the reason for success, though its inclusion obviously did not prevent learning improvement.

Classroom instructional studies aimed at a wider range of students have provided similar results. The Bookmark program emphasizes teaching students with grade level texts, but also includes several other innovative features including heavy emphasis on vocabulary development. This program has fostered higher reading achievement than business as usual teaching.[43] Similar studies with older students working with grade level texts in complex instructional regimes also report positive results.[44] It is reassuring that complex programs of instruction that focus on grade level text can have a powerful positive impact on learning, but one cannot unequivocally attribute success to the more difficult texts.

A recent meta-analysis reported that students make greater gains from oral reading fluency interventions when they work with texts at the instructional levels—using several operationalizations of the instructional level—than when the texts are above the students' instructional levels.[45] It also reported that, of these operationalizations, the one that did best was 93 to 97 percent words correct per minute, a measure that captures both accuracy and automaticity but ignores comprehension. That analysis suffers from so many serious substantive and technical flaws that it is impossible to credit those findings. This analysis failed to include several studies that met its selection criteria, included at least two studies that did not, combined experimental and correlational effects, and used dubious statistics for combining single subject or multi-baseline studies with group comparisons.[46] The researcher treated as equivalent studies of several months of classroom instruction delivered by classroom teachers and evaluated on commercial reading assessments with reports of short-term learning trials that offered twelve to twenty minutes of teaching on single passages with outcomes measured in terms of the amount of immediate carryover to other passages with the same words.[47]

There were even studies in which it was impossible to reliably determine the text levels at which the students were taught. Although the results of this meta-analysis are questionable, any of the studies included in that analysis that had evaluated the instructional level as an experimental variable will be discussed thoroughly here.

No definitive conclusions can be drawn from any of the studies discussed so far. However, over the past two decades, there have been some true experiments aimed specifically at validating instructional level theory. The first of these validation studies was published in 2000, a full fifty-four years after Betts first proposed the instructional level. In that study, fifty-one second graders who were struggling with reading were randomly assigned to one of three treatment groups. One group worked in texts at their instructional levels (preprimer through grade 1), and the others worked with texts two and four grade levels above their instructional levels. This study employed Betts's criteria, but the higher-level placements would be classified as frustration by anyone's criteria. Students, no matter their placements, were paired with better-reading second graders, and these pairs worked on fluency for fifteen minutes per day across ninety-five days. If instructional level text assignment was superior, then the students who worked in instructional level texts would be expected to make the greatest learning gains during this semester long intervention. Nevertheless, the study reported, "We found that dyad reading with materials two grade levels above the instructional reading level was superior to dyad reading at the instructional reading level."[48] Text placements two full grade levels above the instructional level led to substantially greater learning as measured by the Burns and Roe informal reading inventory. The group that was placed four grade levels above did better too, though their advantage was smaller and was not statistically significant.

These unsettling results were later replicated with third graders.[49] Of course, these findings were disappointing to many reading educators and scientists. Not only had the instructional level failed to confer a learning advantage, but frustration placements had resoundingly done better. It appears, from these two studies, that instead of avoiding frustration level texts teachers should embrace them.

These studies were not without limitations. All the students continued to be taught during the remainder of the reading period in the traditional way. That means children in the control group—the instructional level group—worked only with instructional level texts while the kids in the experimental groups experienced a mix of texts: instructional level during regular reading instruction and frustration level during the experimental intervention.

Perhaps what was really being evaluated here were the relative benefits of a steady diet of instructional level instruction versus a more varied daily reading routine that included more challenging materials.

Another possible explanation for the greater learning that accrued for students placed two or four grades above their instructional levels could be attributed to an interaction between text placement and instructional method. Activities like repeated reading in which students read text selections aloud two or more times may be particularly supportive of learning when the texts are relatively difficult, and not so beneficial when students can already read most of the words.[50] Although this explanation seems apt, it contends that students can make greater learning gains when matched to challenging texts as long as they receive appropriate instructional support—an idea not well aligned with instructional level theory.

If that is the case, then this replicated research finding would not be a demonstration of the superiority of teaching with more difficult text. It would suggest that such placements could *possibly* be superior, but only when matched with the correct amount and type of teaching. Some authorities who suspect that to be the case bemoan it since, according to them, such teaching would be beyond the skills of average classroom teachers.[51] This argument seems specious given that the frustration-text instruction in both these studies was delivered, not by classroom teachers, but by better reading second- and third-grade students, a degree of teaching quality that should be easy to duplicate.

In another experimental study, second-grade classrooms were assigned to one of three conditions.[52] In two of the conditions, the students read and reread aloud grade level texts, while in the third, teachers taught guided reading with texts at the students' reading levels. The two groups taught from grade level texts made significantly greater gains than those taught from instructional level texts. "This suggests a different approach than the commonly used notion (e.g., Fountas & Pinnell, 1996) that instruction should be matched to children's skill level."[53]

Unfortunately, the guided reading instruction was not closely monitored in this study, so it is impossible to be certain as to the accuracy of the instructional level placements. Also, the group differences here were not limited to text levels. Unlike in the previously discussed experiments, students who worked with frustration level texts received a different instructional regime than that provided to the instructional level groups. The harder texts were accompanied by more emphasis on oral reading fluency. It makes sense that instruction with challenging text would require some adjustment. But those adjustments make it impossible to attribute the superiority in learning to text difficulty alone. Perhaps if the guided reading classes had received more fluency teaching, they, too, would have excelled. The best we can say from this study is that frustration text instruction, when adjusted to address the difficulties those texts present, can be more beneficial than traditional instructional level teaching.

Rollanda O'Connor and her colleagues have reported two experimental evaluations of the instructional level that seem to complicate this picture a bit.[54] In the first of these studies, low performing students—students who had received Individualized Education Programs (IEPs)—in grades 3 through 5 were randomly assigned to one of three groups. Two of the groups received one-to-one tutoring, and the third served as a control. The tutored groups were taught with either reading level or grade level texts, and the instruction focused on phonemic awareness, phonics, vocabulary, text reading fluency, and reading comprehension. The study was designed to evaluate whether this extra tutoring provided a learning advantage, and if it did, whether instructional level or grade level texts were best.

This study was well-designed. Unfortunately, the clarity of the design was undercut by serious implementation flaws. During the study, the researchers altered the group placements. Bizarrely, students who were not doing well after sixteen weeks of instruction in either condition were shifted to the opposite treatment condition for eight weeks. That adjustment severely weakens the text level comparisons and makes it impossible to truly evaluate them since many students received both treatments. Nevertheless, because this study is so often cited in support of the instructional level, it is worth considering its findings.

The study reported that both tutored groups outperformed the untutored group and that there were advantages to being tutored with texts matched to students' reading levels. Students who ended up in the reading level group made significantly greater gains than those who ended with grade level texts, an advantage evident for the word identification and decoding measures (word attack), but not reading comprehension.

The researchers further examined individual performance. They reported that the reading level match conferred benefits only to the lowest performing students in the study—those who began the study with the lowest reading levels. The overall superiority for the instructional level was entirely due to gains made by the students who were reading at the first-grade level or lower (the best readers in this study started out at a beginning second grade reading accuracy level).

A later study reported by these researchers—in the same journal—noted a concern with the earlier study.[55] Each participant had been instructed one-on-one by a tutor, and the tutors varied in how they had responded to miscues during oral reading. The researchers wondered if those variations biased the results. Accordingly, in the later study, they standardized the tutors' responses to miscues, doing away with this variance altogether. They also avoided the crossover design in which students shifted groups. Without these confounds, one can draw firmer conclusions as to the benefits of instructional level text placement for students with learning disabilities.

This follow-up study randomly assigned 123 low readers in grades 2 and 4 to the tutoring conditions. In this case, students were taught with reading materials that they could read with 92 to 98 percent accuracy or 80 to 90 percent accuracy. Students read aloud with adults for fifteen minutes per session, three days per week for twenty weeks. The intervention led to improvements in reading rate and reading comprehension, but not word identification or vocabulary knowledge. However, even though the differences in text placements were starker in this study than in the original, this time there were no learning differences attributable to text placement. Even when students were taught with frustration level texts by anyone's criteria, there was no detriment to learning with presumably the most vulnerable learners.

It is interesting that the seriously flawed study that had concluded that instructional level texts were beneficial to students with learning disabilities is highly cited despite its serious confounds and implementation problems, while the more rigorous study is not. According to ProQuest, a collection of databases of scholarly journals, books, and dissertations, the study that supported the instructional level has been cited 123 times while the non-supportive study appears only sixty-three times. This could be due to the differences in publication dates, as the older study has had more years to rack up mentions. However, even if one limits the pool to citations that have appeared over the past five years, the pro-instructional level study was cited seven times, while the study that reported no benefit to the practice has not been cited at all. This uneven—biased—use of the research data is illustrative of how the instructional level has been promoted.

In a more complicated experiment, thirty-seven classrooms in grades 3 through 5 with 869 students were randomly assigned to one of two treatment groups.[56] One group received reading instruction delivered to whole classes and the other focused on homogeneous small group instruction in which the teachers attempted to match the students' reading levels or to reduce the distance between their reading levels and the text demands. The whole class instruction group was further divided, with some classes taught with on-grade level texts and the others with texts one level above grade. The researchers provided the following explanation of this approach:

> In the present study, the difficulty variable was manipulated by assuming that materials that were too easy would produce less learning than materials that were more difficult. Since there is an ethical problem in asking students to spend a year in materials that might not produce learning, below grade level materials were deemed inappropriate. Consequently, it was decided to manipulate this variable by using materials that were on or above assigned grade level. Although this solution does not allow for all possible comparisons, it produces a range of discrepancies across ability groups, since high group students are using materials that are relatively much "easier" than the materials that low group students are using.[57]

This study does not provide a direct and complete evaluation of the instructional level, since it does not consider the impact that discrepancies between reading level texts and grade level texts have on learning. Nevertheless, if the instructional level is beneficial, then we should see more learning for the small ability groups (since more students in those groups would be placed at an "appropriate" level), though any result will then necessarily be confounded by differences due to the whole class/small group variation. Likewise, one should expect the above level placements to lead to a greater proportion of frustration level teaching, so the on-grade level group should make the greatest learning gains.

Surprising to advocates of the instructional level, neither of those results was obtained. Whole group instruction did as well as the presumably more powerful small group teaching, even though a smaller percentage of students in the whole class condition were taught with instructional level texts. As for the comparison of on level and above grade level teaching, the researchers reported: "Difficult materials seem to have produced higher scores. The instructional implication is that when choices are to be made for instruction, more difficult materials should be selected rather than less difficult materials."[58]

Finally, in a study of ninth graders, the instructional level again fell short of providing any kind of learning benefit for most students.[59] This study assigned 293 students to groups that worked with either challenging texts or easier versions of texts designed to increase student comprehension. The groups were supported by instruction that emphasized either K-W-L (Know-Want to Know-What I Learned), a strategy that engages students in reviewing their background knowledge, setting purposes for learning, and reviewing/summarizing what was learned) or Listen-Read-Discuss (instruction in which the teacher more formally builds appropriate background knowledge and guides students through text discussion). Most students—except for the lowest performing English language learners—learned equally well from the easy and challenging texts over a twelve-week period both in terms of comprehending the texts and improving their ability to comprehend. The authors' conclusion: "This study provides preliminary evidence that many students who read below grade level can learn from both easy and challenging versions of texts *when receiving supportive instruction* [italics added]. It may be time to think of text difficulty as a characteristic of the support offered around a text rather than the text itself."[60]

What can we make of this review of experimental evidence? These experimental studies, with one exception, either concluded that the instructional level provided no learning benefits or that it attenuates learning. In some cases, students learned from the harder texts as well as they did from the easier ones, while in others, the instructional level placements suppressed student learning. The one exception to this pattern was the first O'Connor study, the one in which students were shifted from one experimental group to the other, the findings of which were not replicated in more rigorous later study.

These studies not only reject the idea that easier text leads to more learning, but provide other valuable insights for reading instruction. It should be noted, for example, that all these studies took place with students in grades 2 through 9. There were no studies that considered the benefits of teaching with instructional level texts in grades K through 1.[61] This gap in the evidentiary record alone should be enough to recommend restraint in applying these findings to younger readers. If the reading level text exerted any advantage in the first O'Connor study it was with learning disabled students who were reading at a first-grade level or lower. Also, the high school study reported learning benefits from easy text placements, but only for students whose English was severely limited; and it should be noted, in that regard, that the instructional scaffolds in that study offered these students no linguistic supports.[62] There are theories that explain why younger students might benefit from working with relatively easy text.[63] That issue and related considerations will be explored more directly and completely in chapter 6.

Another important idea that arises from this body of research has to do with the instructional support and guidance provided to students working with more challenging texts. In none of these studies was frustration text reading done without instructional support. This was especially apparent in the studies that reported greater learning gains from harder texts, studies in which fluency supports were provided.[64]

The conclusions of the high school study concerning the benefits of combining text challenge *along with* appropriately supportive instruction are pertinent. It echoes the Vygotskian principles discussed earlier. Instead of protecting students from potential frustration by matching them with texts that they can already read reasonably well, students should be exposed to more demanding texts *while* being provided with stronger and more extensive scaffolding and support aimed at mitigating any potential negative effects of the difficulty. Vygotsky's idea was that social support for learning needed to increase when the distance between student performance and the desired level of proficiency was greater.

THE INSTRUCTIONAL LEVEL AND LEARNING TO READ

This chapter examined a variety of studies aimed at validating the instructional level. The earliest studies tried to establish criteria for identifying the right texts, procedures that neglected the most important issue—whether being taught at the instructional level made any difference in learning. Accordingly, the correlational and experimental evidence that addresses the instructional level construct were examined. This review of evidence revealed no consistent benefit to being taught in instructional level texts. Students who were placed in that way either did no better than students taught from more difficult texts or learned less. Depending on the teaching, students from second grade on, repeatedly made progress in learning from texts at a wide range of difficulty—including from texts that every version of instructional level theory deem to be far too hard to foster learning.

Many of these studies show that it is possible for students to learn from instructional level texts. However, in none of these studies did the instructional level *outperform* frustration placements. This is likely because placing students in instructional texts will always have two outcomes: it makes the texts easier for students to read, but reduces the opportunity to learn by exposing them to fewer of the text elements that must be mastered to become proficient readers. As suggested by the Ehri study, it may be wise to start with texts that students cannot read well and then work with those texts to the point at which they can. Chapters 6 through 9 will explore how that may be best accomplished.

Why Instructional Level Teaching Doesn't Work

Teaching students with texts at their "reading levels" provides little or no learning advantage. Frustration level texts may increase learning. Those conclusions may be surprising but there are good reasons why instructional level teaching fails to deliver the desired benefits. This chapter explains those reasons. To implement this approach successfully students' instructional levels must be identified accurately, text levels must be ascertained reliably, and then the small group arrangements that students are assigned to must intensify instruction sufficiently. If teaching students at an instructional level can boost achievement, it only can do so if all three of those steps are successful—something research shows to be dubious.

MEASUREMENT PROBLEM ONE: IDENTIFYING STUDENTS' READING LEVELS

Various tests have been recommended for determining students' instructional levels. Betts recommended the Informal Reading Inventory (IRI).[1] IRIs are individually administered oral reading tests that evaluate word reading accuracy and comprehension. Originally, IRIs were to be constructed from the instructional texts themselves. Word reading errors included mispronunciations, substitutions, insertions, omissions, repetitions, reversals, hesitations, and refusals. Betts indicated that students were at the instructional level if they could read a text with 95 to 98 percent accuracy and answer 75 to 89 percent of the questions about it. Over the decades, there have been dozens of refinements, revisions, and alternative approaches, but none have been adopted universally.

In the 1970s, Edward Gickling adopted Betts's theory and procedures, though he adjusted them in important ways, and his curriculum-based assessment (CBA) version has continued to evolve.[2] Gickling proposed that instead of reading a single passage that represented a text level, students should be evaluated by the median score of three one-minute reads of such passages, something that should enhance reliability.[3] Gickling settled on 93 to 97 percent as the appropriate accuracy criterion and he validated this by showing that students comprehended texts at that level better than they did more difficult texts, and students were more likely to stay on task during seatwork when assigned to work with such texts on their own.[4] Other versions of CBA have operationalized the instructional level as any text that students can read at 70 to 119 words correct per minute.[5]

Marie Clay created "Reading Recovery," a first-grade reading intervention program. The assessment she developed for this program, the running record, has been expanded up the grades by Irene Fountas and Gay Su Pinnell.[6] Running records add some controversial analytic steps for interpreting oral reading errors and divide grade levels into multiple discrete sublevels. The test administration steps are the same as those for an IRI, though with different placement criteria (90 percent accuracy and 80 percent comprehension).

In a survey of more than 1,500 primary grade teachers, 75 percent reported using IRIs and running records[7] and many special education teachers did as well.[8] More recent surveys have reported wide use of the IRI.[9] There seem to be no similar surveys concerning the use of CBAs for establishing student reading levels. Curriculum based assessments such as *DIBELS* (Dynamic Indicators of Basic Early Literacy Skills) and *aimsWeb* are ubiquitous, but they are mainly used for monitoring student progress with oral reading automaticity—not to place students in books.[10]

Research shows that these oral reading measures are not sufficiently reliable to provide highly accurate individual placements. Reliability refers to a test's consistency or stability of measurement. An assessment would not be useful if each time it was administered, students were placed at different levels. If text placement matters so much in learning, then the accuracy and consistency of the measures is paramount. Admittedly, these are not "high stakes tests." Teachers can change placements whenever they choose, though there is an extensive body of research showing that few such changes occur in actual practice.[11] "Once a bluebird, always a bluebird." The instructional level—despite how scientific and precise those placement criteria may appear—is at best an approximate concept. It is not likely, with such tests, that students will be placed accurately at a level that will sustain maximum reading growth.

There are several ways to determine reliability. Test-retest reliability estimates how likely students will obtain the same result across multiple administrations. Alternate form reliability compares the consistency of results across different versions of a test, such as comparing performance on different text passages deemed to be equivalent. Inter-rater reliability gets at whether different people administering the same test will reach the same conclusions.

Usually, reliability is reported by a decimal number ranging from .00 to 1.00, but with most reliabilities in the .50 to .99 range. IRIs are reliable in conventional testing terms. Most interrater, test-retest, and alternate form reliability coefficients range from .70 to the high .90s,[12] though the design of some of these studies (e.g., aggregation of scores across grade levels) may inflate estimates.[13] It should be noted that CBA analyses report comparable levels of reliability, sometimes higher.[14] These better results may be due to the exclusion of comprehension, which is notoriously more difficult to evaluate, and because of the use of timing and multiple passages. However, there is also clear evidence showing that environmental factors such as who administers the CBA or where it is administered have a significant impact on CBA scores.[15] Running records have more mixed results, sometimes with acceptably high reliabilities.[16] However, Fawson and his colleagues reported that for running records, acceptable levels of reliability could only be obtained when students read aloud four different texts at a level, while D'Agostino reported the need for a burdensome eight to ten such reads.[17]

Nevertheless, the value of these general estimates of reliability are questionable. Consider the scores for ten students participating in an alternate form reliability check (table 4.1). Each student was tested on two different third grade passages. The test appears to have perfect reliability. However, those are not the reliability estimates that we are interested in. Our concerns need to be, not with test scores, but with placement decisions. As table 4.1 shows, despite high reliability, one test version would place 60 percent of the students in a third-grade text, and the other only 30 percent!

The best way to sort this out is to examine standard errors of measurement (SE_M). If someone is evaluated repeatedly with the same measure, no one expects the scores to be identical. There is always some variation, and statisticians devised the SE_M to identify how confident we can be about the range of scores that a test will elicit. For instance, we can estimate with 95 percent accuracy how often a student's score will range between two points.

For example, in analyses of a popular IRI, the standard errors ranged from ten to fifteen words in one study and eleven to twenty words in another.[18]

TABLE 4.1 Differences in instructional placement with a measure with perfect alternate form reliability

Students	*Form 1 accuracy*	*Form 2 accuracy*
A	98	96
B	97	95
C	97	95
D	96	94
E	95	93
F	95	93
G	93	91
H	92	90
I	91	89
J	90	88

Note: Shaded scores are at Betts's instructional level.

The smaller the SE_M the better, so let's use that ten-point estimate—the one based on the highest reliability—to build a 95 percent confidence interval. If a student read ninety out of one hundred words correctly, we can assume that 95 percent of the time that students' scores with that level of text will range between seventy and one hundred! We can say with a high degree of certainty that texts at that level will be at that student's independent, instructional or frustration level. Big yikes! That is neither a precise nor worthwhile result.

In analysis of another widely used IRI, fifth and sixth grade students were organized into four separate cohorts (high or low in print processing skills and vocabulary knowledge).[19] The IRI used in this study does not report reliability statistics, so let's say it is .90. The SE_Ms for these eight groups of students ranged from 1.76 to 7.30. The confidence intervals would not allow teachers to distinguish instructional and frustration level placements for three of these eight cohorts.

In still another study that considered standard errors, this one focused on the *Ekwall IRI*, the results were the same.[20] With that test, the average fourth grader would be expected to be placed in texts between the second and fourth grade levels 95 percent of the time. The fifth-grade placements would range from grade 2 to grade 5, and the sixth grade from grade 4 to grade 5. Remember, the difference here has nothing to do with what the students know or can do. This is just the expected variation in a students' placements based on such tests, given their lack of precision.

These studies all focused on word reading accuracy. What about comprehension? In an analysis of the Qualitative Reading Inventory (QRI), it was found that:

> Overall, the authors note that SE_Ms for comprehension scores at all reading levels were relatively large, a finding that indicates low reliability. They illustrate the implications of this finding using the example of a student who responds correctly to 75% of the comprehension questions for the passage Sequoyah, which has a SE_M of.18 (or 18%). With this SE_M, the student's estimated true score is anywhere from 39% to 100% correct. . . . This is problematic because the QRI-3's cut-off for the instructional level is 70% comprehension.[21]

This result should not be surprising given an earlier study in which teachers wrote questions for an IRI passage (two factual questions, two inferential and one vocabulary).[22] Researchers randomly selected three sets of questions from this pool and administered them to fifty-seven students in grades 2 through 5.

> The highest level of agreement was between set one questions and set two questions, where, for approximately 65 percent of the subjects, there was exact agreement. Further analysis revealed that approximately 65 percent of the subjects were being assessed as being at different instructional levels by at least one of the three sets of questions. Indeed, 14 percent of the subjects were assessed as being at three different instructional levels by the three sets of questions.[23]

For the most part, reliability studies of oral reading CBAs focus on words read correctly per minute (wcpm), and not on percentage of accuracy—the statistic usually used for instructional level placements. We can estimate the reliabilities and standard errors of measurement for CBAs, but it is not possible to translate these into meaningful estimates in terms of Gickling's instructional level. CBA studies show these tests to have reasonable levels of reliability, but with large standard errors of measurement.[24] For example, in a study of 8,200 students in grades 1 through 5, Christ and Silberglitt reported an SE_M of ten words correct per minute (wcpm). This would mean that if students read 100 wcpm, their true scores would be expected to range between 80 to 120 wcpm 95 percent of the time. Some studies report much larger standard errors.

These estimates are likely more reliable than what we could expect from teacher administered tests in regular classrooms. Early IRI studies identified serious problems with inter-rater reliability.[25] Teachers varied greatly in how accurately or consistently they recorded errors. By contrast, more recent evidence suggests high inter- and intra-rater reliabilities.[26] Several testing adjustments have supported this improvement: use of specially trained test administrators, testing students outside the classroom, using audiotapes to allow repeated accuracy checks, and so on—procedures not practically available to teachers. Even with those supports, there still may be significant variations due to how non-standard dialects are considered. If students pronounce "car" as *kah*, "cold" as *coal*, "here" as *he-ya*, or "out" as *oot*, are those reading errors?[27]

As Gickling himself noted, "When you stop to realize that the SE_M of these procedures actually exceed the range of skill of most poorly performing students then you get some idea of the variability within the 'match'. . . . There is no such thing as an accurate 'level of difficulty' or 'level of frustration' as typically used by educators to facilitate the match for most poorly performing students."[28] Trying to identify especially narrow ranges of performance (93 to 97%) with a measure that has a SE_M greater than that is going to be wrong a lot of the time.

Gickling was writing only about the criteria he developed, but his insight is as apt for any of the others. For example, Betts was similarly cautious: "Since so many factors must be taken into consideration for determining the instructional level, perhaps *Probable Instructional Level* would be a better description of the term."[29] Of course, one could arbitrarily widen the IRI or CBA criteria to enable the more consistent placement of students. But making such adjustments without proof that these would better characterize an instructional level would just be cutting the man to fit the coat.

Wider criteria would also exacerbate another problem with these assessments. The idea has been both to match students to the right books but also to differentiate instruction to better meet diverse learning needs. Reading levels accomplish neither. As Matthew Burns and his colleagues concluded, "Research also found that students performed differently on similar levels of text because of the text structure, prior knowledge, the nature of the assigned reading task or how the reading level was defined."[30] The within group variation in these kinds of skills is likely to be as large or nearly as large as it is across groups.[31]

TABLE 4.2 An example of results from an informal reading inventory administered to a third grader

Passages	*Accuracy*	*Comprehension*
1st grade	100%	90%
2nd grade	92%	80%
3rd grade	87%	80%

It is possible to improve the psychometrics of these instruments. Interrater reliability has been a source of error but the use of specially trained testers, removing testing from the classroom, and recording the readings improved that.[32] Solutions to some of the other many problems—increasing passage lengths or numbers of minutes of reading,[33] or selecting passages psychometrically rather than based on readability formulas[34]—are possible, though each makes these tests less manageable for teachers.

In any event, it is important to recognize that oral reading performance is often ambiguous. Consider the scores of a third grader in table 4.2. This student read the first-grade passage at an independent level, but no clear instructional level is evident. The second and third grade accuracy scores were below level, though comprehension was better. A teacher could decide to teach with a second-grade book, since those scores are closest to an instructional level. Another teacher might argue for a higher placement given those comprehension scores, while a third might contend that the testing ended too soon.[35] This latter phenomenon occurs because "higher level passages are assumed to be more difficult for students to read."[36] That assumption is usually correct—harder texts tend to elicit less accuracy and lower comprehension.[37] However, as Fuchs and company note, with the test performance of an individual on a small set of passages, things are not always so consistent. A student who struggles with a third-grade passage may do well with a fourth-grade one. It does happen.

Betts originally required that students read the passages silently prior to evaluating their oral reading of those passages.[38] This approach survives with running records, but not with CBAs or most IRIs which judge accuracy on "cold reads." In a comparison of these procedures 80 percent of the students were placed in texts at least one full semester higher when allowed to reread the passages.[39] In a case study of an eleven-year-old with learning problems, the student made twenty-two errors on a cold read, but only eleven on a reread.[40] Another study reported that "only 20% of the errors incurred in the first reading of passages at both functional levels [instructional, frustration] were repeated upon rereading."[41] The interesting thing here is how much students' oral reading improves without instruction. Rereading significantly changes our judgments as to whether students can learn from a text or not, and these substantial improvements on a second reading are evident even when the first reading would have clearly been at a frustration level, although one study with four students reported that the rate of such improvement is better with instructional level than frustration level texts.[42] Studies show the possibility of raising performance levels simply by teaching students some of a text's words.[43] Such quick improvements should warn against depending too rigidly on cold reads to make long-lasting placement decisions.

There are also concerns about oral reading assessment and comprehension. Timed readings have reasonably strong reliability, but students may read differently when asked to read for speed rather than comprehension.[44] Similar concerns have been raised about the use of multiple brief reads; there are stronger connections between word reading and comprehension when longer and more complete texts are used. Matthew Burns, Fein Professor of Special Education at the University of Florida, focuses heavily on the degree to which instructional level placements determined by CBAs facilitate word memorization, but the purpose of directed reading lessons is to guide students to orchestrate all their reading skills towards successful comprehension, not just to make gains in one or another isolated skill.

The point of all this is not to denigrate the overall value of oral reading testing, only to reveal the serious lack of precision that such tests have when it comes to text placements. Given their consistent inability to distinguish reading performance across text levels, it should be evident that at best these tests will indicate that a student is at one of several equally likely reading levels. That these tests result in a specific text placement may seem helpful to the dutiful teacher. Test results that indicate a fourth grader will learn best if placed in a third-grade book is solid information that can enable practical action. However, that such tests, if readministered, may place this same student in texts ranging from grades 2 through 6, should give one pause as to the value of this "practical" information.

MEASUREMENT PROBLEM TWO: READABILITY AND TEXT LEVELING

Now we turn attention to the second part of that equation, book leveling. How are text levels determined and how precise are they? There are four basic problems with readability measures and text leveling systems. First, there are many ways to set text levels, and these often disagree. The adage—a man with a watch knows what time it is, while a man with two watches can never be sure—holds here. That different measures of readability result in different text designations means teachers cannot trust the accuracy of text levels.

Second, many estimates of readability tend to have large standard errors of measurement. Modern text measures have done much to reduce this unreliability. But these improvements mask the great amounts of within-text variation that exists in any text. Placing students at the average level of difficulty of a text means that they will spend considerable time reading text not at their level.

Third, texts assigned the same levels will vary greatly in their conceptual, linguistic, and textual features. Leveling systems predict a sequential gradient—level G is easier than level K, a 500L is harder than a 400L. Those levels are mute when it comes to identifying *why* those texts are at those levels. Some readability measures can now provide clues to at least some of the factors that contribute to text difficulty—a real advance—but they are cumbersome, and the information they provide does not match well with student assessments. Difficulty is always a product of text and reader.

Finally, and most importantly, readability measures have never been validated for enabling optimum learning. They do a fine job of predicting comprehension, not learnability—and those are not the same. Ensuring easy comprehension of a science or social studies book makes sense, and readability predicts the likelihood of content retention.[45] But knowing the level of a text divulges nothing about how much learning progress young readers would likely accomplish with that text.

The ancient Greeks recognized that texts varied in difficulty.[46] It was not until the twentieth century that psychologists developed objective means for measuring this and for placing texts on a difficulty continuum.[47] Over the past century, text difficulty estimation has evolved into a more sophisticated and technically reliable enterprise. These days we have both highly reliable quantitative readability measures as well as alternative qualitative or subjective leveling procedures.

Scientific explorations of readability depend upon the same methods bookies use to set betting lines for football games. Their purposes, fundamental conceptions, and algebra are identical. Sports betting establishments identify correlates of outcomes of interest—which team will win, how many points they will score. They use those correlates as predictors, things like average points per game, passing yards, and turnovers; variables that can easily be counted or computed.

Bookies use statistics to weight and combine these predictors into algebraic formulas or algorithms that allow them to predict the likely scores of an upcoming match. Some variables turn out to be better predictors. Others may be valuable but do not matter much because they capture the same information provided by other variables. Eventually, bookies end up with algorithms that predict outcomes well enough that they can make money. Different bookies will end up with different algorithms depending on which data sets they used and the variables they included. No matter how rigorous their formulas may be, there is always error—teams beat the point spread or win despite the prediction.

Why the focus on gambling here? Because everyone recognizes that sports betting is guesswork. The games have not yet been played and no one "knows" what the scores will be yet. A fallible prediction is the best we can do. When a sportscaster announces the home team is favored to win by three points everyone gets that it may not turn out that way.

Educators are not as cognizant of the predictive nature of readability or the error inherent in this kind of estimation. Our language reveals how we think about it. We speak, for instance, about *readability measures* or *tests of readability* or a *text's level*, when what we are really talking about are predictions, estimates, or guesses. The gambling analogy reminds us of the fallibility of these predictions. We tend to treat text-level designations as properties inherent in texts, rather than guesses about who is likely to comprehend them. We treat text levels as if the game has already been played, since a text already exists. But we are not guessing about the properties of the book, we are using those properties to guess who may struggle to read it—something that cannot be known until the game is played.

The surest way to determine how well students can read a text is to have them read it. That was Betts's original plan. Students would read passages from the books that would be used for instruction. It turns out that even this straightforward plan is fraught. The variations in difficulty within any book ensures that at least some of the time the reader may be a bit overmatched. That may be one of the reasons why student reading ability seems to decline when the amount of reading required in the assessment increases—longer texts may increase the possibility of greater variability in reading demands.

Testing each student with a series of texts from their classroom would be an expensive proposition it terms of teacher and student time. It would be more practical to have an algorithm based on easy to count text features that would result in sound predictions: "my seventh graders are likely to beat this book by six points," or something like that.

Researchers who conducted the earliest readability studies posited long lists of potential predictors. They identified word frequencies, sentence lengths, numbers or proportions of different parts of speech, types of sentences, inclusion of adverbial or prepositional phrases, and so on. Over decades, hundreds of such variables were examined. Many turned out to be duds.

Eventually, the statistical formulas were able to do a reasonably good job of arraying books on a difficulty continuum. For instance, they could put books in the same order as publisher's grade level designations. However, they eventually figured out those grade levels were arbitrary, so they had been trying to predict sequences that had never been validated and that "lack[ed] reliability and comparability."[48] Over time, they shifted to predicting comprehension.

The most ambitious of those early studies selected 48 one hundred-word passages and counted their features.[49] They evaluated each passage on more than two hundred different content, style, format, and organization characteristics. Some of those variables were countable, while others proved unmanageable. The researchers had eight hundred adults read those passages and tested their comprehension on each. With that data, they could arrange the passages from easy to hard. Their final algorithm included five variables that together could predict the relative difficulty of the texts with about 40 percent accuracy.

Different schemes could be woefully different in their accuracy.[50] This was because the different readability schemes included different predictors or because they measured or weighed those predictors differently. Even when formulas were aimed at the same outcome—reading comprehension—they might measure it differently; some formulas used children's comprehension, others adults. Criteria for comprehension success differed, too. Some formulas predicted 50 percent comprehension while others aimed for 75 percent.

Readability estimates also suffered from large standard errors of measurement.[51] "Depending on the formula, the standard error can be one-half to one year. When formulas are compared . . . they are usually, but not always, within one grade level. Occasionally, formulas vary up to two grade levels."[52] Think about what that means. A formula with the smallest of these standard errors—one-half year—could say that with 95 percent certainty a text's level ranged over three grade levels, say second to fourth grade, a huge difference for the teacher trying to place students in just the right books.

These large SE_Ms were a result of the onerous counting of text features. All this work was done by hand. Try counting the number of words in each sentence in a book or determining how many of the words appeared in a list of ten thousand high frequency words. For longer texts, like school textbooks, books could only be sampled—evaluating a handful of passages from each book. Because the passages within any text will vary in difficulty, the use of different samples may lead to different readability estimations.

In the 1960s, attention shifted to efficiency and usability. It turned out that most of the heavy lifting was done by two predictor variables—vocabulary sophistication and sentence complexity. Other variables did little to improve the predictions. Accordingly, formulas were stripped down to those two variables.

Perhaps it was not obvious when scientists were sifting through hundreds of variables for the keys to estimating difficulty, but with only two easily countable variables it became crystal clear that readability is an index and not a measure. These formulas do not identify what it is that makes texts hard to comprehend, only what correlates with the real sources of difficulty. No one believes the average number of letters per word is what makes a book hard. Those kinds of counts may seem silly, but they do provide sound prediction.

Vegetarians are less likely to miss their airline flights. That may be true, but only fools would eat more broccoli to increase their chances of catching their planes. We can expect a wide range of reading performance from students assigned to texts of a given level.[53] Even when a readability estimate is correct—a group of fourth-grade level readers are reading a fourth-grade text with approximately 75 percent comprehension—it is impossible to know what these students would need to be taught to enable them to progress to a higher level. "Findings of within-grade variability in passage complexity can contribute to uncertainty about students' instructional reading levels when different passages are used to compare performances across readers or the same reader over time."[54]

Another problem with the simplicity and indirectness of readability schemes is how easily they can be gamed.[55] Let's say a publishing company wants to market a book that would be interesting for eleven-year-olds but readable by third graders. The editors identify a terrific book on ultimate sports. Their readability index puts it at a fourth-grade level. They could search for an alternative, but they want this one. So, they make this book fit the bill by shortening some sentences or swapping out some multi-syllable words. Presto change-o, problem solved! Readability now predicts third graders will comprehend this book well. However, nothing that made that text difficult changed—we're eating vegetables and still missing our planes. These adjustments did not make the book more comprehensible; they just ruined the prediction. Research shows that such mechanical adjustments can alter readability estimates, while increasing a text's difficulty.[56] This kind of gaming takes place. No one knows to what degree because it is undetectable. Texts can be revised to improve comprehensibility, but not with those kinds of trivial alterations.[57] Sometimes successful revisions improve comprehensibility while making the readability estimates appear harder.[58] Revisions that increase the measured difficulty of the texts have been found to benefit both good and poor readers.[59]

Lexiles have, perhaps, pushed the boundaries of efficient readability prediction about as far as they can go. This index is based on those same two predictor variables, but because of the digital revolution, instead of sampling texts—extracting a handful of passages and predicting book levels from those—they measure entire books. This does away with standard error as a measurement problem, though it continues to be an irksome pedagogical one. The Lexile algorithm predicts reading comprehension and its equation is based on an unusually large sample of readers. By any estimation, Lexile does a good job of predicting comprehension, certainly as good or better than any rival readability scheme—including some of the newer more sophisticated methods. However, it is important to note that MetaMetrics, the publisher of Lexiles, makes no claims that matching texts to students using their levels facilitates learning to read—they are honest that they predict comprehension, not learning.

As for standard error of measurement, because Lexiles are based on analyses of entire texts, there can be no sampling error. That is true in traditional measurement terms, but it disguises important variations that matter instructionally. Bradley and Ames divided a fourth-grade textbook into 110 228-word segments and reported that the segments differed in readability levels from first grade through twelfth grade![60] Students differed in how well they could read these different passages drawn from the same book. Lest anyone conclude that such textual variation is peculiar to basal readers or to the period when this study was conducted, consider more recent evidence.[61] Lexiles are not calculated based on a single analysis of an entire book but instead, a book is sliced into a series of 125-word segments. The Lexile for such a text is an averaging of this collection of segment scores. They have implemented this procedure, analyzing all these shorter segments in literally tens of thousands of texts, and concur that such variation is commonplace.[62]

The reliability of the overall estimate obscures variations that matter pedagogically. These "texts are judged to be relatively the same in comprehensibility. However, the variability across individual parts of texts can be extensive. Within a single chapter of *Pride and Prejudice,* for example, 125-word excerpts of text had Lexiles that ranged from 670 (beginning grade 3) to 1310 (college)."[63] This amount of variation requires a major alteration to instructional level theory and all the authoritative pronouncements about the importance of placing students at just the right level to avoid frustration. Given these measurement problems, according to instructional level theory, students will be placed at their reading levels only a fraction of the time.

Validity is "the degree to which evidence and theory support the interpretations of test scores for proposed uses of tests."[64] As such, we cannot say that a test or measure is valid. Its validity is dependent on purpose. According to James Cunningham, professor emeritus of literacy studies at the University of North Carolina and Heidi Anne Mesmer, a professor of literacy at Virginia Tech, "It may seem obvious to say that the reading comprehension performance of real students should be the criterion variable used to develop a tool for predicting the difficulty of texts."[65] However, these authors go on to rightly point out that, "Just because a tool was developed using a criterion measure of student performance does not mean the tool will produce estimates of text difficulty that are valid for every use to which those estimates can be put."[66]

These authors go on to criticize the Common Core State Standards (CCSS) for establishing text levels that students should be able to read by certain points in their education, because of the lack of precision inherent in such readability estimates.[67] They fear that these standards may encourage teachers to teach with texts that students will not already easily comprehend. In other publications these same authors champion the idea of teaching reading with instructional level texts. According to these experts, readability can be used to make highly precise text assignments for instruction, but they lack sufficient precision to set educational goals—even though these outcomes are expressed in multi-year ranges aimed at accommodating the reliability issues.[68]

CCSS's use of readability should be enlightening.[69] Many states have moved away from CCSS standards but have continued with their grade level text goals. Those text standards are expressed as ranges—rather wide ranges—for each grade level, and the levels are stated as multigrade spans of two or three years. Each multigrade span is assigned text levels that vary in ranges of 200L to 400L. There is also considerable overlap across grade spans. Students in grades 4 through 8 would be meeting their grade level standards if they could read texts with 925 Lexiles. These ranges and overlaps reveal the lack of precision and specificity of readability estimates and the need for accommodations to make them useful. This also should reveal the unlikelihood that one could accurately assign students just the right books based on these tools.

It is also important to consider the widely used qualitative leveling approaches. These days, when teachers speak of "text leveling" or "leveled books," they are most likely referring to the Fountas and Pinnell levels, though there are other qualitative systems.[70] P. David Pearson, former Dean of the School of Education at Berkeley, and Elfrieda Hiebert, president and CEO of TextProject, provide a useful history of the development of this qualitative leveling plan.[71] An early version of the approach was developed for use in first grade with Reading Recovery,[72] and Fountas and Pinnell refined and expanded it to texts from beginning books to eighth-grade. Quantitative readability measures are not especially accurate with beginning reading materials. The amount of word repetition and other approaches aimed at easing students into books (e.g., decodability, rhyming, illustrations, sentence patterning) can undermine the accuracy of readability predictions. Qualitative gradients were created to offer a more accurate appraisal of such texts.

According to Glasswell and Ford, the Fountas and Pinnell scheme requires that texts be evaluated by judges who place them on a multi-point continuum (from A to Z) based on ten separate text characteristics: genre/forms, text structure, content, themes and ideas, language and literary features, sentence complexity, vocabulary, words, illustrations, and book and print features.[73] Complicating matters further, there are extensive lists of criteria within each category. "Across those 10 characteristics, 66 specific criteria are further identified. . . . a K-level text is analyzed using the same ten characteristics with 71 specific criteria."[74] There is no guidance in how to weight these variables, and which ones matter most seems to be in the eye of the beholder, which may be why books can vary so greatly—what Pitcher and Fang refer to as "gross inconsistency among books within the same level—in particular dimensions."[75]

No studies have evaluated the reliability of these judgments, but one investigation suggests that this gradient correlates reasonably well with the better-validated quantitative readability measures.[76] Another study confirmed that these levels were related to how fluently or accurately students could read texts,[77] but none of this work has explored the relationship between these levels and learning to read.[78]

Publishers have leveled tens of thousands of books using this scheme. But given its complexity—the simultaneous qualitative evaluations of ten factors and dozens of features with no explicit prioritization rules and no validation studies—it is unclear how accurate any of these levels may be, something Fountas and Pinnell themselves admit.[79] This approach lacks the scientific rigor of the quantitative approaches and may result in varied book placements depending on who is making the judgments. There is no reason to expect these approaches to be more reliable or valid than quantitative estimates. In an analysis of the text features of leveled books, researchers concluded: "It is ill-advised to rely on such a measure to determine text difficulty and hence reader-text match. In fact, concentrated attention to text levels may be detrimental."[80]

Another complaint about this system has to do with its use of length of text as a determiner of difficulty. Students tend to score lower when presented with longer texts so taking account of this in a determination of difficulty seems reasonable. However, as some observers point out, when text difficulty determines book assignment, the readers who are most in need of practice are provided the least reading experience.[81] Indeed!

These days, there is greater interest in readability estimates that go beyond correlates to determine why a text is challenging.[82] This is possible now because of the existence of sophisticated theories of language and cognition that can guide these efforts, and the ubiquity of computers and other digital resources that allows for the efficient and reliable analysis of subtle and complex language features.[83] These newer measures—Coh-Metrix,[84] Reading Maturity Metric,[85] and TextEvaluator[86]—can determine vocabulary sophistication, syntactic complexity, degree of cohesiveness, narrativity, and other variables that matter in reading comprehension, but they do no better than existing measures when it comes to predicting comprehensibility.

Nevertheless, as these newer tools become increasingly available, they should be a valuable contributor to the kinds of teaching proposed here.[87] Instead of trying to predict which levels of text students might learn from, they should be able to tell us what challenges a text poses. In other words, they can reveal text features that students could be taught to negotiate. Rather than avoiding the difficulty, these tools should allow difficulty to be confronted in a more pedagogically powerful way.

What was true for student reading levels is true for book level estimation. These tools have value, but they lack the precision that would either allow students' reading levels to be accurately determined or for placing them in books that accurately match those levels. The joint use of two systems of approximation reduces the likelihood of proper text placement.

ABILITY GROUP TEACHING WITHIN THE CLASSROOM

It is widely believed that small group teaching is more powerful than whole class instruction. This small group teaching is supposed to be better, at least in part, because it allows for differentiation—which is also thought to be a key to improved learning. The third leg of the instructional level stool is the teaching of students in small ability-based groups. This approach is meant to supercharge learning. But does it really work that way?

Often when providing professional development to school districts, a curriculum director may say: "We'll know if today was a success if our teachers teach small groups more often." The first time I heard that I was taken aback. That is not how I would determine success in school improvement.

Then there was the day I observed a second-grade teacher in Chicago. When I entered the room most kids were doing seatwork, and the teacher was at her horseshoe-shaped desk with three children. It was some kind of guided reading activity with a *Weekly Reader*. The reading was done, and the teacher was quizzing them about the text. She soon dismissed them and summoned three more students. They read the same short article, and she asked the same questions, with the same responses. Believe it or not, the third group did the same. It was *déja vu* all over again. I fled before she could beckon more groups.

What a horrible waste of time. It is nonsensical because grouping does not exert a "main effect" on reading improvement. Main effects are those direct impacts that independent variables exercise on outcomes. Research shows "there are no significant main effects or significant interaction effects being in high or low ability groups. Apparently there is no particular advantage or disadvantage of being in a high or a low ability group."[88]

As Hiebert explains: "Contextual variables such as a grouping scheme are secondary or even tertiary variables that affect learning indirectly. A particular grouping scheme does not require any particular set of instructional or learning behaviors. Even . . . accommodations in materials or pace, can vary depending on the teacher."[89]

The purpose of placing students into small within-class reading ability groups is to "manage heterogeneity."[90] The idea is to cluster the children together based on similarity of skills and capacity to learn. With grouping, the teacher can vary the difficulty level of the lessons and pacing to better meet the needs of all students. The best students need not be slowed by the strugglers, and those most in need can be taught what they do not yet know.[91] At least that is the way it is supposed to work. In the classroom, things are considerably more complicated, for a few reasons:[92]

- Teachers differ in their purposes for grouping, how much they use it, the size of the groups, and in mobility among groups.[93]
- How students are assigned to groups varies too. Groups may differ in homogeneity, who ends up in the low groups, or how well students are matched to the texts.[94] Teachers may group based on behavior as much as on academic criteria.[95] As one scholar put it, "Differentiated instruction is neither good nor bad because it is differentiated."[96]
- Grouping implies no specific instructional practices. Even sound instruction may not be equally distributed across groups, so grouping may carry benefits and disadvantages.[97] Research shows overlaps in books for different groups—meaning that children with supposedly different abilities may be working with the same books.[98] Grouping provides no consistency of learning experience, so it exerts no consistent impact on learning.

Grouping should be thought of as a tool, akin to what a wrench is to a plumber. Wrenches are great for some tasks, but no journeyman plumber sets out to use a particular wrench more often or for a specified amount of time each day. Tool use depends on the job. That is rarely how grouping is viewed. Educators often see it as a positive approach to be employed often.[99]

The idea that small group pedagogy is superior to whole class pedagogy has long been held. A. H. Turney was already able to review sixty-six studies on its effectiveness ninety years ago.[100] Grouping became a mainstay when class enrollments included fifty or sixty children. Instead of fading away as class sizes shrank, it became even more widespread, morphing into more groups with fewer kids in each.[101] What once was a ubiquitous three groups per class, now has some teachers juggling four to six groups despite working with lower enrollments.[102]

The success of instructional level theory depends on the potency of small group instruction. These groups tend to be assembled within each classroom, though there are schemes (e.g., Joplin plan, circling, walking reading) for shifting kids from class to class to perfect the text matching. Matching text levels to students' abilities supposedly ensures differentiation, and there is great faith that it delivers learning success.

Kids are not always assigned to groups to match them to books. This distinction matters. Grouping in kindergarten is common, even though most kindergartners cannot read. These groups may focus on letters and sounds, for instance, varying the content. There are clear benefits to providing teacher-directed phonics instruction to students low in decoding skills, while other students engage in independent language-oriented activities.[103] Such studies reveal that small ability group instruction can be beneficial since it allows teachers to teach students what they need to learn. Grouping may also support more intensive teaching. It is easier to engage each child in a lesson or to monitor learning with a small group than a whole class. Some kids may be shy in the classroom but more participatory in a group, especially students who are less familiar with English.[104]

But as good a tool as it may be, on the job it may fall short. One wrench might have too short a handle to provide the necessary torque, while another might be too long to work in the available space. When it comes to grouping, there are many such shortcomings.

One obvious problem is the necessary tradeoff between increased differentiation and decreased instruction. The assumption is that getting exposure to just the right text for relatively brief amounts of time will outweigh any reductions in the amount of teaching. If a teacher has ninety minutes to teach reading and divides her class into small groups for sixty minutes, the amount of instruction provided to each student drops considerably. Three groups would lead to a forty-minute reduction: a whopping 120-hour diminution in reading instruction over a school year. What is taught to a small group may be learned better, but the reductions in what can be taught offsets this benefit.[105] Independent seatwork is usually not very effective in fostering learning.

There are other problems with small group teaching as well, in terms of whether kids are placed in the right groups or whether they are working with the right content. Many teachers admit that they consider classroom behavior or the children's work habits when making group placements.[106] They also may equalize group sizes or allow the numbers of low achievers to determine the numbers of groups,[107] adjustments not likely to support text matching. Race and language differences sometimes get into the mix as well.[108]

Researchers, too, make the common mistake of assuming small group teaching necessarily leads to more learning. Studies often treat grouping literally as a main effect, as if grouping caused the learning, an approach that ignores or lumps together all the benefits and disadvantages of grouping.[109] For the most part this research is correlational. Experimental studies comparing whole class teaching with small group teaching are rare; those that do exist find whole class teaching to be superior.[110] The correlational results are mixed: sometimes grouping offers no learning benefits,[111] and other times small gains may be attributed to it.[112] Some grades or groups seem to benefit, while others do not.[113] According to Steve Amendum, director of the School of Education at the University of Delaware, and his colleagues: "One implication is that it is not possible to say that a particular instructional characteristic is 'better' or 'worse' for children's reading achievement. Such an implication may work against the grain of 'common wisdom' or results of at least a few prior studies . . . that implies, for instance, that small group settings . . . are generally 'best' for beginning readers."[114]

Studies often report positive benefits only for the kids at the top.[115] The best readers learn more when grouped, while the lowest languish, falling further behind. Even that is not universal. Different groups within a classroom often receive unequal treatment and have different learning experiences.[116] Low groups may experience more time off task,[117] less silent reading,[118] less engagement,[119] and so on, though sometimes they receive enriched learning experiences.[120]

Sadly, within-class ability grouping has tended to resegregate classrooms, since African American and Latino children so often are relegated to low reading groups,[121] especially by white teachers.[122] It also turns out that children of single parents end up more often in low groups.[123] The consequences of this can be catastrophic in terms of social justice given the potentially long-term negative effects of within class ability grouping.[124]

> Grouping is not neutral with respect to inequality of educational opportunity. There appear to be stronger race differences in how much is learned of what is taught in grouped classes. Since less material is also taught in grouped classes, and since black students in this sample tend to be in grouped classes more often than whites, race differences are increased by grouping according to ability. Finally, grouping appears to increase inequality of educational outcomes. Students assigned to high groups are taught more than students in low groups. These better opportunities for learning in high groups appeared to be statistically reliable. . . . grouping appears to increase inequality of achievement.[125]

I remember when I first read that paragraph. I was not disturbed by it, not as I am today. I had bought into instructional level theory, so I dismissed these data as unfortunate. Then, I did not recognize low group placement as a problem, but as a solution. If children were to become literate, they had to be taught to read with books at their levels. I assumed those low group placements would facilitate the delivery of the most appropriate and beneficial teaching.

Now I recognize that matching kids to text is not the boon I thought, so I am horrified by this research. It is only reasonable to place students in below grade texts if that enhances learning. If it does not—and research shows that it does not—then resegregating classrooms and stifling the learning of the children with the greatest needs is wrongheaded.

There are several examples in the literature of teachers forgoing ability grouping without apparent loss. In a case study of first-grade reading, the guided reading of texts was accomplished successfully with the whole class.[126] In an experiment that compared ability groups and mixed ability groups—small group instruction, but not based on instructional level considerations—fourth and fifth graders did best in mixed ability groups who worked with grade level texts.[127] These studies cannot "prove" that ability groups are ineffective, but they do show that success is possible without that ubiquitous and potentially discriminatory approach.

CONCLUSIONS

Chapter 3 showed that instructional level placement does not raise reading achievement. To make the instructional level approach work, teachers would need to correctly identify students' reading levels, publishers must correctly identify text levels, and then students must be taught in grouping arrangements so powerful as to outbalance the reductions in instruction that grouping usually requires.

Research shows that none of these requirements is likely to be satisfied. Tests used to identify student reading levels have neither been validated for that purpose, nor are they sufficiently reliable to allow the precise ability estimations required. Text level estimations suffer from the same problems. With student and text measures that may be off by one or two years in either direction, it is likely that many children will be placed in the wrong texts.

Some may claim that instructional level theory does not require such precision, that IRIs and book leveling systems are only meant as approximations. I do not believe that to be the case, but if it were, then the wisest conclusion would surely be that most children should be taught at grade level rather than at supposed reading levels, since the confidence intervals for these measures will almost always include a students' grade level. Only students far below level—perhaps three or four levels below their grade—would gain any benefit from being relegated to easier texts.

This is a good place to acknowledge that one of the studies that reported learning from frustration level texts[128] has been criticized. Mesmer and Hiebert indicate that they evaluated the levels of the texts used in the Morgan et al. study and that their readability estimations differed.[129] According to them, the texts were not as difficult as claimed. That sounds like a serious blow to my argument, but I believe it is just the opposite. That different readability measures assign books different levels illustrates why instructional level theory makes so little sense. If matching students to just the right text is so haphazard and the resulting small group instruction so weak, no wonder evidence does not support the instructional level. Placing students in just the right text can only promote greater learning if it is really just the right text. Mesmer and Hiebert's demonstration reveals why this is so implausible.

It is time to set aside the notion that we need to teach students at their reading levels. As Alfred Tatum, provost and vice president for academic affairs at the Metropolitan State University of Denver (and a former student of mine) has said, "leveled texts lead to leveled lives."[130]

Teaching Reading with Challenging Text

This chapter provides an alternative to instructional level theory. As we recall, instructional theory holds that if students are to be successful learners they must work with texts that they can already read with few errors (90, 93, 95 percent accuracy) and with at least 75 percent comprehension. Certain student-text matches are supposed to be propitious for learning, students are thought to learn best when grouped with others at the same reading level, and limiting difficulty is claimed to be motivating. This approach constrains the amount of teaching by severely limiting the gap between what students can already do and what instructional texts necessitate. Instructional differentiation is achieved by assigning students to books of different levels, which is why so many students now are taught with below-grade texts. The use of such books ensures that students will not be asked to deal with language complexity much beyond what they can already negotiate proficiently and constrains the depth and complexity of content to which they will be exposed. Teaching with instructional level books focuses on guided reading practice, supplemented with a spoonful of vocabulary teaching, some practice answering questions thought to elicit certain cognitive responses, and instruction in cognitive strategies that are virtually useless with easy text. Student progress is gauged by the students' steady march through the levels. Students are expected, for example, to work with Level G text until they can perform at the instructional level with Level H books.

In any event, that is what is recommended. Implementation is not so pristine, and research and practice have exposed a plethora of problems. Chapter 3 showed that this approach provides no learning advantage to students and chapter 4 detailed the improbability of accurately and reliably estimating student reading levels and text readability levels, and the unlikelihood that the product of these two rough approximations would be optimal student-text matches. Instructional level proponents are correct about the potency of small group instruction, but they ignore the countervailing forces that reduced amounts of teaching have on learning, and the unfortunate tendency to relegate racial, ethnic, economic, and linguistic minorities to the lowest groups, segregating them from their classmates.[1] These denizens of low reading groups are fed a steady diet of below-grade books, while their more advantaged classmates are nurtured on challenging texts, rich language, and grade level content. This is a soft version of retention (flunking), without the usual requirements for informing parents or other protections of student rights.

Other evils inherent in this "easy books all the time" regime include pejorative public labeling of students by reading levels.[2] Student reading levels are to be monitored closely to facilitate rapid advancement, so that students can switch groups as needed—though, in truth, such group shifting occurs rarely.[3] It is hard to catch up with those reading the more challenging books without exposure to the more advanced content, vocabulary, grammar, and the discourse and structure that the more advantaged kids are experiencing. Even when text leveling seems to match a student to an apt text, knowing the students' reading level reveals nothing about needed instruction. When the main goal is to *avoid* incomprehension and miscomprehension, there is no point in trying to figure out what text features are blocking student understanding.

It is time to place reading instruction—text placement, curriculum design, differentiation, classroom organization—on a different footing; one more in line with the assessment limitations, advances in text theory, empirical research findings concerning what works, and the social demands of a pluralistic society. This chapter sets out to redefine reading, and offers a new model of instruction, and an explanation of the major tenets of this approach. Basically, it is recommended that most children should be taught with grade level texts even when that would mean teaching many at their supposed frustration levels. Doing this will require serious reforms of classroom practice—including adjustments to the curriculum to increase attention to teaching students how to make sense of text, approaching differentiation in a new way, and establishing more specific and attainable goals for reading lessons.

Over the past century, educators have promoted a plethora of definitions of reading and reading comprehension. These have tended to describe reading in ways that favor certain approaches to teaching. Wiener and Cromer classified definitions of reading into three categories: those emphasizing identification of letters and words, those with a focus on reading comprehension, and those that link the two.[4] When identification/decoding is heavily emphasized, "the defining attribute of reading is the correct 'saying' of the word."[5] There are also important distinctions to be made among definitions that emphasize reading comprehension. Some definitions emphasize the extraction of an author's intended meaning, while others stress the idea that readers construct their own meanings—and, again, some definitions, such as that promoted by the RAND Reading Study Group, include both.[6]

These days definitions seem to be less popular than models of reading. The "simple view of reading"—a model that indicates reading comprehension is the product of decoding ability and oral language comprehension ability—for instance, has been widely embraced because of the clarity of its combination of only two constituent elements.[7] Other scholars have expanded upon that model by unpacking its elements, revealing the separable parts of decoding and comprehension and their nature.[8] Newer attempts, such as the Active Model of Reading, provide even more complex perspectives, detailing additional components, and exposing more intricate relations among the parts.[9]

All these definitions and models have value. None, however, emphasizes the central role that text plays in reading. Readers' actions predominate, while the role of text is assumed. The point here is not to minimize the importance of readers' knowledge or readers' actions, just to acknowledge that reading is a kind of dance between a reader and a text; a dance that cannot take place if either is missing. The idea of "dancing" with a book may seem awkward. Afterall—despite Gene Kelly and puddles, umbrellas, and lampposts—we do not usually dance with inanimate objects. But books are not inanimate in that way. Books are written by authors to communicate with readers. As such, they include a surfeit of textual affordances meant to accomplish that communication, and barriers—intended or not—which may interfere with or complicate that communication. Nascent readers must learn both to take advantage of those affordances and to negotiate those barriers—making that interaction between the reader and the author's text into a dance. The better the reader gets at anticipating the affordances and responding to the barriers, the better the reader and the reading.

This neglect of text is evident in the language components of any of these models. They all include language processes without any explicit recognition of distinctions between oral and written language—some even seem to claim that readers simply read oral language that has been translated into print. The permanency of text greatly complicates the role that memory and language play in comprehension.

What is reading? For our purposes, reading is the ability to make sense of the ideas expressed in text by negotiating the textual, linguistic, and conceptual affordances and barriers of a text. Reading is best characterized by this interaction of reader and text, and learning to read means gaining insights and abilities that would allow one to carry on those negotiations successfully.

Let's break this definition down a bit. First, reading is about comprehending, it is about making sense of ideas expressed in text. The RAND definition cited in note 6 above holds that what is referred to here as "sense making" includes both recognizing ideas expressed explicitly in text as well as those ideas that readers must construct—via inferring and reasoning—taking care to respect the ideas the author meant, rather than overriding the text with their own ideas, beliefs, and prejudices.[10] As such, reading entails cognitive processes but also ethical ones. Our job as readers is to make sense of what the author tried to say, not to replace his or her ideas with our own. This is harder to accomplish in reading than in most listening situations, given the absence of the author. Readers must read critically, judging the information expressed in the text, and creatively, using texts as a jumping-off point for their own idea formation, while respecting the author. Those are all part of reading comprehension.

Text includes both linguistic and conceptual information. In the models of reading noted earlier, decoding is usually separated from language comprehension. Here, print is thought to include a great deal of information, and it does this through its dependence on its phonological, semantic, syntactic, and pragmatic features. The linguistic features of text require decoding—they also require other interpretive efforts—making sense of word meanings, sentence structure, cohesive relations, and discourse structure, all of which are communicated through print, and textual apparatuses and conventions.

Likewise, there are the ideas themselves—that's the conceptual part of comprehending. When it comes to concepts like *bunny rabbit*, *esophagus*, *compassion*, *infield fly rule*, *Socrates*, and *war*, there is more to understanding and appreciating these ideas than just the definition. Each of these ideas may carry with them visual, auditory, haptic, tactile, and olfactory information, as well as a rich network of related ideas, memories, and experiences. Some ideas are more complex than others—amoebas are less complicated life forms than human beings and require much less detail to explain. Shallowness or depth of information—sparseness or extensiveness—play significant roles in promoting and preventing comprehension.

Another important idea is that the information the author has coded into text includes affordances. Examples of affordances are things like precise diction, plain syntax, unambiguous cohesive links, explicit revelations of structure, repetition, graphics, and so on. Affordances are less about text itself and more about the relationship between the reader and the text. Authors code the information in ways that they believe will afford a reader the greatest possibility of comprehending the text or, at least, in comprehending it in the way the author wants.

For example, an author of a short story might describe a meal as "sumptuous," wanting to give the impression that it appeared to be something special and probably quite expensive. As such it would reveal something about the character who ordered it—that he was monied and likely had good taste or an understanding of good taste, and that he provided this meal to a young woman he had just met suggests an interest in further relations with her. An adjective like *sumptuous* can convey a lot of information about the meal, the character, and his motivation, and it accomplishes all of this quite efficiently. That is a powerful affordance to write into a text, but it only works as an affordance if the reader knows the meaning of the word and recognizes its implications. Some readers may get part of it; they might recognize that *sumptuous* is positive and that this must be a grand meal. Maybe they will even draw conclusions about the character's motives, but maybe not. Affordances are possibilities, not guarantees.

Or consider this famous sentence from Abraham Lincoln's Gettysburg Address: "It is rather for us to be here dedicated to the great task remaining before us, that from these honored dead we take increased devotion to that cause for which they gave the last full measure of devotion, that we here highly resolve that these dead shall not have died in vain, that this nation, under God, shall have a new birth of freedom, and that government of the people, by the people, for the people, shall not perish from the earth."[11]

Until this final sentence, the speech is super simple—lots of declarative sentences and common vocabulary. Why such complicated syntax for the climax? Here is where Lincoln communicates the major point that he is trying to make, and it is here that he forces us to slow down and reread to try to make sense of this exquisite complication. These ideas are what Lincoln wanted his listeners and readers to pay the greatest attention too, and he used complicated syntax not to make a complicated idea easy, but to get his most thoughtful readers to pause and think hard about the point he wanted to make.[12] Again, some readers will just plow through that, noticing the "of the people, by the people, for the people" cadence, without grasping the relationship between the reader and the men who fell at Gettysburg. In this case, the affordance is the selective complication of sentence grammar.

By this example, I do not intend to suggest that affordances are grand and subtle features built into texts for the most sophisticated readers. Of course, there are such features, and they are potentially powerful affordances, but so are simple word and structural choices like "See Dick run," or "STOP" imposed in large white letters on a red octagonal background. That means that there are simple affordances that readers need to learn early on—such as that letters represent phonemes and spelling patterns represent pronunciations, or that periods reveal breaks between ideas. There are also those more sophisticated affordances, like symbolism in a literary novel or the relations between words and graphics in a science text.

Authors build affordances into text to communicate with readers. But, of course, for some readers, these constructions may pose barriers to understanding instead of working as affordances. Becoming a reader means that you are learning how to recognize and use the affordances the author has relied upon to express the ideas, and how to surmount them when they turn out to be barriers to understanding. An author's diction may be perfect—using just the right word to communicate the exact intended idea—but it can only convey the intended idea if the reader is able to ken its meaning.

Providing students with instructional level texts—texts they can already read with a reasonably high degree of accuracy and comprehension—limits their exposure to text affordances that they cannot already utilize. This lowers the possibility of teaching students how to negotiate them. Instructional level teaching aims to minimize the possibility that words or sentence structures will interfere with immediate understanding—all other potential barriers are ignored, and the accompanying instructional question-answering and comprehension strategy routines do nothing to help teachers identify these hurdles and to respond to them pedagogically.

The theory of instruction inherent in the instructional level idea is that students can raise their reading levels by practicing reading with relatively easy texts. As students work with each text, they are to master the small number of unknown words that are the hallmark of instructional level texts, accumulating vocabulary knowledge as they progress. They also are to benefit from their consistently high levels of comprehension, as if comprehending an easy text will somehow automatically enable comprehension of other texts. This high comprehension experience is usually monitored and bolstered by quizzing the students about the selections using questions aimed at providing practice with essential reasoning skills. That's why teachers are told to ask literal recall, inferential, drawing conclusions, comparison, application, and analysis questions. Despite the allure of this approach, the instructional value of this kind of questioning is specious.[13]

Recent textbooks retain these questioning routines, bolstering them with instruction in the use of cognitive strategies—getting students to take an active and intentional role in comprehending. These strategies usually do not deal with recognizing and dealing with text barriers as much as providing self-control over one's own attentional or mnemonic limitations. There is substantial research supporting the value of comprehension strategies,[14] and yet, there is good reason to believe that too much time is devoted to them; students can master many strategies with much less teaching than is often allocated.[15] Strategy teaching has great value but there is a serious flaw in any strategy teaching in the instructional level classroom. The only time good readers consciously use a comprehension strategy is when they are having difficulty making sense of a text. Teaching strategies with texts that students can already read well engages them in a fantasy game. "Let's pretend you are having trouble, and I will show you how to make believe you are solving the problem." (Programs like Reading Recovery[16] or Guided Reading[17] also focus attention on alternative ways to read words in text—encouraging students to use "multiple cueing systems"—another approach of dubious value).[18]

Placing a greater emphasis on the role of text—and on the reader's operations on text and negotiations with text—unveils several important learning goals too often ignored or minimized. The instructional level often distracts us from those curricular goals by making their relevance so subtle as to merit no explicit attention at all. The use of complex text for the teaching of reading brings those text affordances and barriers to the forefront—making the need for explicit guidance in dealing with them a central part of reading instruction.

Unlike the books used in reading instruction, social studies and science texts are often difficult for students—presenting unfamiliar content using language and expository discourse features with which many students lack experience. These content-focused textbooks are often beyond students' reading levels. Experiences with those should serve the needs noted here, but they rarely do. I have spent considerable time in classrooms over the past fifty-five years, and my observations suggest the reason for this failure is not in our textbooks but in ourselves. Often teachers read these books to the students, intimating they are too hard for kids to even attempt. These days they may use *Audible* or some other recorded books service to do the reading. Many teachers still rely on "round-robin reading" or "popcorn," with the best readers presenting the text, just another version of "listen-don't-read." Teachers usually comment on the snippets of text as they are read, telling students what they meant but with no guidance in how to make sense of the cryptic parts.

The idea here is not to set a high standard and then lose all who fail to meet it, but to set such standards and then to provide the teaching necessary for their accomplishment. Students need to learn to read and comprehend texts—even complicated and difficult texts that they cannot easily grasp on a first attempt. To accomplish that, instruction must engage students in dealing with such text demands without telling them what the text says or reading it to them!

Placing students in challenging text and then not teaching them how to deal with the demands of those texts is foolish. Those who prepare teachers rarely provide training in how to effectively teach reading with demanding texts. I suspect this omission is due to instructional level theory. Its adherents do not prepare young teachers to teach with complex text, since that would be, according to that ideology, bad teaching.

The levels of the texts that students need to learn to read have—at least for the time being—been established by the Common Core State Standards (CCSS).[19] Many states have diverged from those standards but have maintained the text levels that they established. These standards are a worthy target since students who graduate from high school able to comprehend texts as difficult as specified should be able to read well enough to meet the demands of beginning level jobs, freshman year of college, or military service.

These levels have not been without controversy. One complaint has been their unevenness. CCSS established those graduation requirements and worked backward down the grades to set goals for each lower grade. Larger text level increases are evident for some grades than for others, and some of the biggest jumps are in the early grades.[20] Some critics are concerned that since many students are not already reaching these outcome levels they will be left behind. They fear that teachers will take these standards literally and try to teach students to read with more challenging texts—criticism aimed at maintaining the instructional level approach.[21] Again, their emphasis is more on preventing students from engaging with texts they cannot already read successfully rather than on teaching them how to do it.

BASIC PREMISES OF A TEXT COMPLEXITY APPROACH TO TEACHING

The remainder of this chapter is devoted to explaining the basic premises of a Text Complexity approach to reading instruction and to text teaching in the content subjects. These tenets provide the basic principles of a theory of text teaching that will be further fleshed out in the ensuing chapters.

Instruction Can Be Too Difficult or Too Demanding to Foster Success and Text Can Be a Source of That Difficulty

It would be wrong not to concede the very real possibility of learners being overwhelmed by too many demands or for demands at too high a level to allow for success. The argument is not about whether instruction can ever be too demanding but about what the proper response is to such situations. Any theory that calls for the teaching of challenging text must account for the possibility that text difficulty is potentially off-putting for some students. Ignoring the problem is not an option. Rather than avoiding the difficulty needed for learning, instruction must provide the scaffolding students need to confidently take it on effectively. It is always worthwhile to monitor students' responses to instruction and to try to increase their engagement when it is flagging. Text is neither the only element of a lesson that can pose difficulty for students, nor—given its curricular role—should changing it be the solution to maintaining students' motivation. Teachers can make a lesson sustainable by lowering difficulty, but this also can be done through adjustments in the amounts and types of scaffolding the teacher provides or by easing the task demands.

Monitoring Success Is Critical

Not only should teachers be sensitive to students' responses to the difficulty of text, but they also need to be vigilant concerning incomprehension and miscomprehension. Comprehension questions should not be aimed at providing students certain kinds of thinking practice—such as asking an inference question so the students can rehearse their inference skills—but to find out if they made key inferences, and then, if they failed to, to try to determine and address what caused the failure. Instead of preteaching words the text defines or explains contextually, those items should become comprehension questions. It is important to know if the students made sense of the definition or were able to determine the word meaning some other way. Questions should be used to reveal failures to comprehend, and each comprehension failure should elicit instruction, taking students back into the text to see if, through rereading, the problem can be solved and providing explanations for how to use context, or make a connection, or generate a reasonable inference.

Read Instructional Texts Ahead of Time

Too many teachers over rely on textbook lessons. That does not mean that they should give up using textbooks, nor that the lessons in the textbooks are without value. Nothing could be further from the truth. However, unless the teacher has already read the text the students are being asked to take on, it is nearly impossible to anticipate the problems students might have or what advice or direction should be provided to support learning. When teaching students to read a text that they are likely to read well, comprehension will rarely go far afield. But this can happen when students are struggling with a text and the teacher must be able to head off these problems before they capsize an entire lesson. Catching a misinterpretation early can make all the difference. I remember a fifth-grade social studies lesson focused on the US Civil War. The text used the word "bigotry." Unfortunately, a student confused it with "bigamy," a word he knew, so he ignored the affordance of an explicit definition. If the teacher had not noticed the problem quickly, a good deal of miscomprehension would have resulted, since it was a key and frequently repeated word in the chapter. A teacher who had not read the text could have easily missed the problem until the student was hopelessly confused.

Text Learning Depends on Three Variables, Not Two

Instructional level theory posits that teaching reading is a two-variable process. To be effective, teachers must attend to students' reading levels and the levels of text difficulty. Successful teaching, according to that view, is largely accomplished by making certain that the texts do not outstrip the readers' current abilities. With such a match, learning is assured. But comprehension is a product of student, text, and task—the latter including activities and instructional conditions that may be set by teachers. Tasks, as such, are malleable, and can be used by a teacher to make a text more accessible for the reader.[22] The following chapters will describe many tasks that can be used to guide students to surmount specific comprehension barriers. Study after study has demonstrated that teaching can successfully facilitate students' interactions with challenging texts. A directed reading lesson is not a two-variable problem, but a three-variable one. The scaffolding a teacher provides can transform potential failure into pedagogical success. Students can overcome text difficulty with teacher guidance.

Increasingly, research is demonstrating this possibility. Explicit teaching of sight vocabulary can transform frustration texts into instructional level ones.[23] That simple teaching routines can advantage learning undermines the central tenet of instructional level theory. That teachers can so easily convert frustration text into instructional level text by teaching sight vocabulary, meaning vocabulary,[24] text reading fluency,[25] or through various comprehension scaffolds[26] means that there is no need for a specific level of text to facilitate learning. It may make sense to protect against too much difficulty when it comes to seatwork, homework, or independent learning tasks. In those cases, students are on their own with the books and their affordances and barriers. But in the guided or directed reading situation, teacher support and guidance can mitigate any difficulty a text presents. Instead of avoiding difficulty, alleviate it.

Differentiate Teaching Not Curriculum

When I speak about this topic, I often get the response, "So you don't believe in differentiation?" I strongly support differentiation, but not the notion that it means placing kids in different levels of books. We need to differentiate teaching—not the curriculum. Curriculum differentiation means teaching different things to different kids. Different levels of books provide different language experiences. Easier books use more prosaic vocabulary and simpler syntax. They also provide different content exposure since more complex language allows for a greater depth and sophistication of coverage. Basically, teaching students with different text levels means teaching them different things. But our goals for students should be the same.

The instructional level starts from the premise that some students should learn different things and that we must accept that many students won't reach the same outcomes as the others. Instructional differentiation is something else altogether. It teaches everyone the same thing but alters how that thing is delivered to ensure success. A teacher, for instance, might seat some students nearer where she can reach them, because of concerns about attention. Or she might engage some students in writing the new words because of memory concerns—the other kids seem to remember words with greater ease and facility. Another example is the whole class lesson that gets through to some kids and not others. In that instance, the teacher might pull some students aside for another run through—maybe simplifying the explanations or adding new examples—to make sure they all reach the intended outcome. Research shows that the harder the text, the more scaffolding that will be needed to ensure learning success.[27] The greater the disparity between reader and text, the more assistance and support that will be necessary.

Comprehension Is Essential

A big part of the instructional level idea is that students must comprehend a text to benefit from it. This comprehension is accomplished by placing students in books that they should be able to read with a high degree of accuracy. Ensuring comprehension success makes sense. However, when ensuring such success is the main goal, then current "read-it-to-them" or "tell-them-what-it-says" approaches are reasonable instructional choices. They are not. The scaffolds teachers provide must be instructive; their purpose is to help students comprehend the text at hand, but also to provide them with generalizable insights and actions that can be applied to other texts in the future.

Think of learning as emerging from the transformation of incomprehension to comprehension. Students benefit from taking on texts that they cannot initially read well but that they transform into ones they can comprehend *through their own efforts*. This transformation is a more certain route to learning than constant practice with texts one comprehends easily. This approach accepts the idea that it is important for students to comprehend what they are reading,[28] but rejects the notions that such comprehension need be immediate or easy. Nor does it ignore the important role of teachers and instruction. When students confuse who or what is being talked about in a text because of a failure to make the right pronoun links, it is not enough to correct them but to show them how to keep that from happening in future reading.

Rereading Should Play a Key Role in Directed Reading

When a text is easy, readers can plumb its depths with a single read. However, when a text is difficult, it may be necessary to read it and reread it, or to reread key portions. The importance and value of rereading tends to be lost in instructional level theory. The late Donald Graves, the writing expert, once told me that, "too many people these days are caught up in first draft living." What I think he was complaining about was the careless human tendency to stay on the surface, our willingness to accept our ignorance—not even recognizing our lack of understanding or the imperfection of what we produce. Directed reading lessons need to foster a sense of revision: "When I read it the first time I thought this, but now that I have gone back and examined it more carefully, now I think. . . ."

Lessons need to include both returns to the text to address key affordances that students need be conscious of as well as barriers that tripped them up. It can also make sense—after all the discussion—to go back and read the whole text again. There can be real satisfaction in that when students see how well they can understand such a text. (Don't worry too much about the boredom that students may claim this causes. Many of them have seen *Frozen* fourteen times.)

Not All Instructional Texts Need To Be at the Same Level

Students can benefit from exposure to texts of varied levels of difficulty. Reading educators do not seem to think much about the advantages of this kind of variation. The instructional level idea so persuaded teachers to focus on student-text differences—getting everyone to just the right level—that the value of varied difficulty in practice has gone unnoticed. The idea of gradually inching students up a text gradient has encouraged a linear view in which students move only in one direction: up.

Other fields of study—near and far—have a more complicated view of what it means to nurture learning and development. Special Educators, for instance, have focused on the interleaving effect. Studies show that when engaged in memorization tasks like learning spelling words, rehearsal focused on a mix of both known and unknown items leads to more learning.[29] Similarly, kinesiology, the study of muscles and joints, has developed training schedules for strengthening athletes and preparing them for participation in sporting events.[30] There are training schedules for marathon runners, for instance. These schedules do not prescribe that runners run three miles a day for a week, and then four and five each of the following weeks, continuing until the runner can go for twenty-six miles. No, the runners start out with three miles on one day, and a couple of days later they run four, which is followed by another three-miler. This kind of up-and-down variation is evident throughout. Even after a runner has done an eight-mile run, the follow up is only three miles.

Learning and development are best supported by a mix of easy and more challenging tasks. Progress is best thought of as a *jagged* progression; that is, it goes up and down repeatedly, though always tending towards higher levels of performance overall. In that marathon schedule, while the runners keep dropping back day to day, the number of miles accumulated each week keeps rising.

Students should learn to read grade level text. That means that many students will need to read texts that are challenging for them. It should not mean that they read only such texts. The point here is not that students should be taught with hard books and allowed to read easier books on their own. Nor is it a call for teachers to read hard books to kids, exposing them to that language and content, while keeping the students' own reading to instructional levels. No, students should deal with a continuum of difficulty both in their instruction and in their independent reading. Learners need opportunities to consolidate their learning gains, and switching among demanding texts that require a great deal of teacher scaffolding and simpler ones—including markedly easier ones—allows for such consolidation. This variation in text difficulty also likely plays an important role in motivation, in keeping kids' heads in the game.

The instructional level proponents are correct that a steady diet of frustration could be discouraging. Students, however, do not need a continuous dose of such texts, just enough to provide them with opportunities to learn. One way to accommodate this kind of variation is to simultaneously vary the lengths and the difficulties of the selections. When dealing with very demanding texts, the focus might be on only a few pages, while with relatively easy texts, students should read much longer and with less interruption and teacher support.

Short-Term Learning Benchmarks Are Valuable

Directed reading lessons guide students through a text, whether in a reading lesson or a content class. The lesson is usually finished once the text has been read, though there might be some additional skills work added on. Perhaps the students write something about the text or complete some kind of worksheet. Learning may be monitored by a meaningless chapter or unit test focused on the skills or strategies that were presented—tests with little pedagogical or psychometric value.

The intentional use of texts the students cannot read well without the support of a teacher suggests a better conclusion to these communal reading activities. Research shows that students learn best when there are clear learning goals of which both teachers and students are aware.[31] In a well-done intervention study conducted with struggling first-graders, the students who made the greatest progress were able—by the end of the lessons—to read the lesson's text at an instructional level.[32] It seems sensible to have students work with a text until they can read it fluently (90 percent, 93 percent, or 95 percent accuracy with 70 or 75 percent comprehension). Aiming at such short-term benchmarks should provide students with a clear sense of accomplishment—"I couldn't read that book before, but now I can." A benefit of this approach is that students can see their own progress. With instructional level lessons, students read a text. That is the outcome. There is no sense of success. There is no sense of improvement. One wonders if this is part of the dissatisfaction many students express about reading lessons.[33] Teachers are likewise afforded a sharper understanding of what it is they are trying to achieve, a focus on learning rather than on the smooth delivery of lessons.

Beginners Do Not Need Harder Texts

Too often sound educational theories are overgeneralized. What might be a good idea under one set of circumstances might be a bad one in another. When it comes to teaching students with challenging texts, there is little research with children earlier than second grade. That means there is no clear evidence that this is a good idea with beginning readers. Furthermore, there are strong theoretical reasons to suspect that young students may not be well served by especially hard text.[34]

The reason for this has to do with the role of decoding in reading. What makes texts difficult for beginners are not the linguistic or conceptual demands but the words and the students' ability to translate those from print to pronunciation. Several of the studies that showed students could be successful with more challenging texts were conducted with second graders. That means students need not accomplish total proficiency with decoding, only that a firm grasp of these fundamentals may be needed. Making text harder at the beginning means making the decoding requirements more opaque and reducing word repetition, steps likely to diminish learning. Once students have mastered these basics, then more challenging texts can be beneficial. Perhaps the problem with the instructional level is that it applies something that is beneficial for a brief initial period to all students at all levels!

Beginning Reading, Decoding, and Fluency

The purpose of this chapter is twofold. First, I will explain why it would be imprudent to try to teach beginning readers with more challenging texts, and will explore the types of text that will advantage learners in kindergarten and grade 1. The reason beginning readers are an exception to the major pedagogical thrust of this book has to do with the importance of developing the foundations of decoding. It will also explain how best to meet the needs of older students who still struggle with decoding. Research suggests that once the foundations of decoding are in place—say those of a typical beginning second-grade reader—students can benefit from working with more challenging texts. But students who reach that point of reading development may still struggle with the words in harder books. Teachers may need to scaffold this aspect of reading when placing older students in grade level texts and advice is provided on how that can be accomplished successfully.

THE BEGINNING READER EXCEPTION

English is an alphabetic language. That means that the written form of English refers to the sounds and pronunciations of the letters and words rather than to the meanings. English spelling is complicated. There are many reasons for this. English has forty-four phonemes (discrete units of sound that distinguish one word from another) and only twenty-six letters to represent them. That mismatch leads to the use of double letters to represent single sounds and to multiple sounds assigned to the same letters and letter combinations. Also, English is a melting-pot language. Loanwords like *ballet*, *opera*, *coyote*, *freight*, and *ski* become common in English despite their deviation from its spelling patterns. There is considerable dialect variation among English speakers as well—oral and written language may correspond differently depending upon racial, ethnic, economic, and regional differences.

Nevertheless, English spelling is much more systematic than is commonly recognized.[1] Studies of tens of thousands of English words show a great deal of consistency when factors like letter position and morphology are considered.[2] That is why explicit phonics instruction has repeatedly been found to provide beginning readers with learning advantages. Kids who are taught phonics tend to make faster and more certain early reading progress. Because of the systematic nature of English spelling, it is possible for students to learn to read without phonics instruction. But this can only occur if they manage to infer or figure out how decoding works.[3] Phonics instruction neither guarantees reading success, nor does the lack of it ensure failure. Phonics eases the way for most beginning readers, and for those with dyslexia it can be an essential lifeline.

It is often assumed phonics is about sounding out words. A child laboriously sounding letter after letter may come to mind. That is not how proficient readers read. Initially that kind of sounding plays a role. But phonics instruction is more about helping students to think about how words are structured. It is about teaching them to remember words. Linnea Ehri, a professor at City University of New York, has probably done more than any other scientist to identify how readers come to almost instantly recognize words.

At one time, it was assumed that it was necessary to memorize large numbers of words to become readers. Those memorized words are usually referred to as *sight words* because they were words that the reader appeared to recognize immediately on sight without any obvious mediation or sounding. That makes sense for the words that students studied, but what about other words?

When I taught first grade, I noticed that early in the year, memorizing words was brutal. The children needed extensive amounts of drill-and-practice to remember the simplest of words. But something funny happened. Later in the year, something had changed. It was not just that the kids knew more words. They were now learning new words amazingly fast, often from a single exposure. Somehow their memories had been transformed into something quite different than what they started out as.

Dr. Ehri has shown how those letter-sound connections bond pronunciations, spelling, and meanings of words in memory.[4] Instead of learning how to sound out words, students are developing a system that allows them to remember and recognize words efficiently, to be able to recognize words with automaticity (that is, without conscious attention and with a minimum of cognitive resources). She has described a series of four stages—prealphabetic, early alphabetic, later alphabetic, consolidated alphabetic—that young readers go through from initially trying to remember words with any visually salient cues they can discover (like remembering the word *monkey* because it has a tail at the end) to the point where they are able to recognize letter patterns and combinations automatically (e.g., morphemes, syllables).

However, there is more to beginning reading instruction than explicit phonics teaching. One of those other things is the texts that students are exposed to. Text plays an important role in fostering beginning decoding development. Accordingly, curriculum designers and researchers have puzzled over how to optimize beginning reading texts for more than a century. "On one hand, we want to teach first graders how to read print on their own. To this end, the earliest texts need both to be easy enough to be penetrable by true beginners and to progress by some design that will continually work to strengthen and expand beginning readers' independence with print."[5]

In that pursuit, two fundamental ideas of how best to construct beginning reading texts have been proposed: controlled vocabulary texts and decodable texts. If you remember from chapter 1, an important part of textbook development was the idea of controlling vocabulary—introducing new words slowly and then repeating those words frequently over a certain number of pages. This approach also focused on the frequency of usage of words. Words like *to*, *is*, *was*, *the*, and *of* were treated as having greater value than less frequently appearing words, even if their spelling patterns might be unusual. These high frequency words were introduced early and repeated often. Memorization of words was thought to be the mechanism for propelling beginning reading success, and the systematic introduction of new words and their repetition were the scaffolds those texts were designed to provide. Controlled vocabulary texts may differ in how quickly they introduce new words, the numbers of repetitions, or over what stretch of text these repetitions take place, but the basic approach is consistent.

Decodable texts, on the other hand, are designed to provide students with practice applying their decoding skills. Some decodable books limit the words to those that follow the most consistent spelling patterns. Others are more specific. They try to focus on any words that can be decoded using the specific skills that have been taught up to then. The word *mad* follows a common spelling pattern, but if students have not yet learned the correspondence between the letter "a" and the /ă/ phoneme ('short a"), then for them, the word is not yet decodable. In either case, the idea is to help students to recognize and use those most consistent and useful spelling patterns when they read. Given the complexities of English—and the exceptional nature of some of the highest frequency words (e.g., *the*, *of*, *where*)—it is impossible to use only decodable words in such texts. That means that decodable texts will vary in the percentage of words that are truly decodable.

Both these approaches to beginning reading texts are based on the understanding that the thing that makes beginning reading texts hard is the *words*. That is the reason the instructional approach is different with beginning readers and why it would make no sense to try to increase text levels for them. If you want to make beginning reading texts more difficult, introduce more words and introduce them more quickly, introduce more uncommon words and words with exceptional spelling patterns, and repeat words less often.

Each of those actions will make the texts more challenging to read, but they also are sure to slow down and disrupt the construction of the memory systems on which future reading development depends. Think back to the studies summarized in chapter 3. Researchers taught students to read with texts designated as frustration level. None of those studies found learning advantages from the easier texts, but none of those studies considered beginning readers. Much of that research was carried out with second-graders, children who should already have developed at least a rudimentary understanding of the decoding system—possibly not all the way through Ehri's developmental sequence, but far enough along so that the use of harder text was not disruptive.

Unfortunately, despite the amount of scholarly consideration devoted to these issues, it is still not possible to say definitively what the best text choices are for beginners. Research provides some valuable hints, but it has not yet settled the question. Part of the problem is that beginning readers seem to be able to learn to read from many approaches—everything seems to work, though there are at least subtle differences in their degrees of success. Also, research has revealed that there are multiple ways that reading texts can be made simple and scrutable enough for beginners.

During the 1950s when controlled vocabulary was the major approach to the design of beginning reading texts, reading research was a rather limited enterprise. Government agencies and education advocates were not demanding adherence to empirical studies. The notion that controlling the vocabulary of beginning reading books smoothed the way for beginning readers was convincing on the face of it. If evidence was needed, one could see that large numbers and percentages of American children were learning to read.

Despite the lack of rigorous research into the specifics of that approach, there is research showing the importance of word repetition in reading programs. Elfrieda Hiebert has done more than anyone to point to the importance of word repetition in kindergarten and first-grade reading texts, and the problems that lack of repetition can pose for beginning readers. She and her colleagues have traced the historical record of repeated words over the past six decades and reported that as repetition declined—with many more words appearing only once, "singletons"—beginning reading has become more difficult.[6] The gradual introduction of high use words with a reasonable amount of repetition benefits readers. (Recently, she has speculated on the value of controlled vocabulary texts for older readers who continue to struggle with word reading, and has even designed some innovative prototypes of these kinds of texts.[7] Such texts would necessarily be easier than the grade level reading regime recommended here. Hiebert recommends these as supplements to grade level texts, not as a replacement.)

We live in a more research-oriented time and yet the situation is not much better when it comes to what we know about the effectiveness of decodable text. Some form of decodables has been available for more than sixty years. The idea was first broached by the American linguist Leonard Bloomfield.[8] The idea was to present children with texts that introduced spelling patterns and word families. Several publishers (e.g., Merrill, Lippincott, Harper & Row, Miami) issued "linguistic readers" during the 1960s. Their titles alone provides insights to their design: "*Nat the Rat*," "*Tug Duck and Buzz Bug*," and "*Biff and Tiff*."

In the 1960s, a massive comparison of the effectiveness of various approaches to beginning reading instruction was undertaken.[9] It considered a wide variety of ways of teaching reading: basal readers, phonics, linguistic readers, programmed readers, individualized reading, initial teaching alphabet, and so on. The researchers concluded that none of the methods was superior to the others, though programs that provided some kind of decoding support consistently outperformed the others (linguistic readers were in that category).

That is where matters stood until 1985. In that year, a study was published that tracked the progress of first graders taught with controlled vocabulary readers or decodable texts.[10] In the early parts of the study (November and February), the kids who worked with decodables outperformed the others in word reading, nonsense word reading, and the ability to read words they had not previously encountered. However, by the end of the year there were no differences in the groups when it came to decoding ability or overall reading achievement. Decodable text advocates have focused heavily on the early advantages those decodables provided while ignoring the lack of durability of those benefits.

Another widely cited study provided phonics instruction to two groups of first graders.[11] The phonics was supplemented with decodable text for one group but not the other. At the end of fourteen days of lessons, the students in the decodable group read highly decodable texts more accurately and they were more likely to apply their knowledge of sound-symbol relationships than the comparison group. Both groups were learning decoding, but the opportunity to practice applying those skills had a positive effect on the ability to apply them.

There have been several studies that have included decodable text in more complex interventions or along with explicit phonics instruction. The comparison groups did not read the decodable texts, but neither did they receive the rest of the instruction.[12] That makes it impossible to determine if decodable text exercised any impact on the learning outcomes, though they do show that quality interventions that include decodables can be effective.

The results of such studies are not always this positive. For example, in a study of at-risk first graders, students were assigned to a nontreatment control group, or to one of two experimental interventions, both of which received phonics instruction.[13] One of these experimental groups worked with texts with 85 percent decodability (that is, 85 percent of the words should have been decodable given the phonics skills taught up to then) and the other used texts that were only 11 percent decodable. Both intervention groups outperformed the comparison, but there were no differences in outcomes due to degree of decodability.

A recent meta-analysis correlated text conditions with learning using the data from ninety-seven intervention studies.[14] The researchers coded studies as including no text, decodable text, nondecodable text, or a combination of decodables and nondecodables. They found that the text conditions did not differ. Overall, working with decodable text was no better than working with no text when it came to learning. The only condition that even came close to a statistically significant advantage was the combined text group. Also, when it came to gains in decoding ability, the students who had the opportunity to work with both decodable and nondecodable texts outperformed those whose reading was limited to decodables alone.

There are now almost as many research reviews on decodable text as there are primary studies to include in those reviews.[15] These reviews all draw the same conclusions. Though they acknowledge that decodable texts help students to apply phonics skills, this transitory effect is only apparent during a brief period during the first several months of first grade. Mesmer speculates that the benefits accrue during a specific stretch of Ehri's stages of decoding development: "Beginners may benefit from decodable text when they have learned enough letter sound correspondences to begin to sound out words but not enough to handle the full range of English patterns presented in uncontrolled text. Decodable text may mediate readers' use of code information during connected reading as they transition from the partial alphabetic stage to the full alphabetic stage."[16]

These research reviews also concur that students are best served by working with a combination of texts that includes a range of decodability. This makes sense both because of the lack of strong evidence supporting any of the beginning text schemes, but there are also worrisome concerns that high decodability, if overdone, can be problematic. It is essential that young readers develop "mental sets for variability" rather than "for consistency."[17] The complexities of the English language require readers to be flexible in applying decoding skills. Many letters and spelling patterns correspond with more than one sound each. For example, the letter "e" matches to three different sound values in the word *extremely*. Also, in most words with a *CVCe* (consonant-vowel-consonant-silent e) spelling pattern the vowel makes a long sound (it "says its name"), hence *cone*, *bone*, *note*, and *robe*, but then there are also words like *done* and *come* that require a different pronunciation despite the use of that common spelling pattern. Students who too rigidly rely on pattern consistency are at a marked disadvantage over those who more flexibly choose among the alternatives.[18]

Statistical learning appears to play an important role in reading development.[19] Studies of language and concept development have shown that human beings summarize their cognitive experiences statistically, allowing for more optimal responses to future events. Similar abilities appear in reading. Readers tabulate their experiences with the *CVCe* pattern and weigh the likelihood of the alternative pronunciations. When beginning reading text differs too much and for too long from the statistical properties of English there can be long-term consequences that reduce accuracy and fluency, even for adults.[20] Likewise, decodables may represent English as being more consistent than variable, encouraging rigidity over suppleness in decoding.

Decodable texts simplify English reading by making it more consistent and less flexible than it is. The use of a range of texts that vary in decodability or that provide other forms of simplification—such as controlled vocabulary readers—are less likely to promote misunderstandings of how decoding works. Some experts argue persuasively for the use of texts that include a combination of vocabulary controls and high decodability.[21] The idea is to make sure that students do not just see the patterns that are being taught, but also the exceptions to these patterns.[22] One study intentionally combined these two approaches, exposing students to texts that depended both on the gradual introduction of high frequency words with much repetition along with high decodability. The learning results were positive.

TEXT RECOMMENDATIONS FOR BEGINNING READERS

Unlike what is being recommended for grades 2 and up, it is essential that the texts in kindergarten and grade 1 be simple and easily accessible. Text difficulty should be severely limited early on. Additionally, beginning reading instruction should include the following:

- Explicit phonics instruction that initially teaches letters and sounds, and then gradually introduces students to more complex spelling patterns and morphological structures (such as *ed*, *ing*, *es*, and so on), and these should be provided to any students who have not already mastered them.
- Early instruction should teach high frequency words that students are likely to know the meanings of or with which they have had much oral language practice. This emphasis should come both in the form of explicit teaching and through frequent inclusion in their texts. Some authorities would limit explicit word teaching to those with exceptional spellings. Although evidence is limited on this, that may be a mistake. Given the uncertainty about what it is exactly that students are coding into memory, it may be beneficial to learn words that may serve as exemplars of spelling patterns.
- When words are introduced for direct instruction, students' attention should be drawn to the spelling patterns and decoding relationships, even with words that have exceptional spellings. Some claim that it is harmful to teach students words they will eventually be able to decode. There is no evidence that this is true, though emphasizing the structure of words and their sequences of letters does seem the surest way to ensure that the full benefits of this teaching are accrued—memorization of the words, but also information about where that word fits in the memory system children must develop.

- It makes sense to provide students with decoding practice as the various phonic skills are taught. This practice should include both the reading (decoding) and spelling (encoding) of words that fit the instructed patterns. It also should include opportunities to deploy these skills in text reading, and decodable texts provide a potentially beneficial opportunity for highly concentrated practice of this kind. The benefit of this practice seems to be most pronounced from the beginning of first grade through about February (or for children whose skills development are comparable to those of an average reader over that time span).
- There is no period when it makes sense to use only decodable texts. Other simple texts that rely on the gradual introduction of new vocabulary with much repetition have value both in supporting students' word learning but also in counterbalancing the potential problems of decodables. No one should conclude from this that decodables are bad and controlled vocabulary is good. Any simplification—including both of these—entails altering the statistical properties of the language. The effectiveness of a mix of texts has the potential for preventing these simplifications from misleading learners about the nature of the language.

A final note on the texts to be used to teach beginning reading. The emphasis here has been on decoding alone. Reading instruction, however, requires more than that. All reading models emphasize the importance of both decoding and language development. Decoding has received so much attention here because it is the reason why the beginning reading period is an exception to teaching with harder text. It is essential that we not ramp up text difficulty on beginning readers because of their need to develop the fundamentals of decoding.

Shared reading—teachers reading books to children—is especially valuable during kindergarten and first grade because the simple texts that will best foster decoding development rarely provide much support for language development. Until students can decode well enough to read texts with sufficient depth of content and complexity of language, reading challenging texts to students has an important role to play in instruction. Children should be engaged in as much comprehension activity as decoding activity, and early on much of that will be done with the books that are read to the children, and the books used for this need not suffer the same language complexity limitations that are so common in beginning reading texts. In fact, the books to be read to the children should be selected on the basis of their rich language, valuable content, and potential enjoyability.

SCAFFOLDING WORD ACCURACY AND FLUENCY WITH CHALLENGING TEXT

Older students who lack fundamental decoding skills will need to receive the same instructional regimen recommended for K–1 classrooms—explicit phonics instruction supported by decodable and vocabulary-controlled texts. What of those students who have these basics—who can decode as well as an average end-of-year first grader—but who still struggle to read the words in their textbooks? In the past, we would have avoided that situation by immersing them in texts that they could already read with a high degree of accuracy, hoping that continual practice with readable texts would eventually lead to progress. Research has shown that by grade 2, protecting students from these supposedly frustrating books is not necessary. However, that is not to say that they should be cast into harder texts, sink-or-swim style. Teachers need to provide helpful teaching, guidance, scaffolding, and support to ensure maximum progress. Unlike with the instructional level approach, the assumption is not that students will make largely automatic gains from reading texts at a certain level, but that *with instruction* grade level texts will bc productive. The remainder of this chapter will describe the kinds of word reading/decoding supports found to be effective for these older students.

Word Reading Supports

All students should spend time studying words and parts of words. The kind of explicit word instruction that makes the best sense during the upper grades is an amalgam of morphology, spelling, and phonics.[23] That kind of teaching should help students to continue to develop an understanding of how words work. However, as valuable as such teaching can be, it is not likely to be sufficient or rapid enough to enable struggling students to read the grade level texts used in their daily lessons. Such teaching is appropriately aimed at improvement over the long run—it is not meant to pay off right away. More immediate support must be provided through the scaffolding of these students' interactions with texts.

Research has identified two approaches to scaffolding the word reading challenges that grade level texts may pose for many students. Both approaches have been found to be effective in multiple studies. These are approaches that have long been used more generally to teach reading. The difference is that instead of using these techniques only to contribute to general reading improvement, in this case, we want to focus them on the grade level texts that students need to read. Our priority is to reduce the distance between what students can do now and the immediate demands of text that they are about to read. As we do that and students are enabled to read more and more difficult texts successfully, overall reading achievement should rise.

Matthew Burns is a well-respected chaired professor of Special Education at the University of Florida. He and I strongly disagree on the value of the instructional level. He is, these days, the chief advocate of the Gickling version. Nevertheless, his research provides some of the most convincing evidence that it is possible to successfully teach students to read with the kinds of books he cautions teachers against. Dr. Burns argues that students learn best from texts they can read with 93 to 97 percent accuracy. But in a series of studies, he has demonstrated that teaching words from frustration level texts can efficiently transform these into instructional level texts.[24] Given the possibility that frustrating texts can be rendered productive through teaching means that it should *not* be necessary to send kids to reading purgatory—relegated to below-grade-level texts until they manage to do better.

Most reading programs encourage the preteaching of words with their main focus on explaining word meanings than supporting the students' ability to read those words. Admittedly, recognizing a word and remembering its meaning are closely interconnected, and the introduction of these words likely addresses both issues to some extent. However, what makes Burns's instruction different from typical guided reading lessons is the emphasis on adding these new words to the students' sight vocabularies prior to the text reading. The words are more than introduced or familiarized, they are taught.

Burns' studies focused on students—third, fourth, and eighth graders—with learning disabilities. In one study, teachers evaluated students' ability to read the words in texts used in regular classroom reading lessons. If students could not read a word within two seconds, it went into the pool of items to be taught. A pool of known words was also identified. Students then worked with these words for ten to fifteen minutes three times per week, for twelve weeks. The words were printed on index cards and were practiced in sets of ten; nine known words along with one unknown word. The teacher showed the unknown word to a student and said the word. The student was to repeat the word and use it in a sentence. If the student could not do this, the teacher defined the word and used it in a model sentence, and the student tried again. Finally, there would be drill-and-practice with the ten cards until the student could easily read the word. At that point, a new unknown word replaced a known word in the deck and the process continued. In other studies, the teachers identified words key to comprehension that they presumed the youngsters did not know. In all the studies, these lessons resulted in significantly improved oral reading fluency with the target texts as well as in much improved reading comprehension. If unknown words are preventing students from reading a text well enough, then teaching some of those words should result in success.

The method described here was certainly effective, but it could easily be adjusted by adding some guided decoding support. That would mean not just telling the words to the students but demonstrating how to use the letters to arrive at a pronunciation. There are various ways such instruction could be provided. In some schools, special educators, Title I reading teachers, or teacher's aides might be deployed for this purpose. In others, volunteers and cross-age tutors might do it. These days there are even digital resources, such as sight word and spelling word programs that allow teachers to edit the word lists. Parents too could be helpful. If many students require such support, then classroom word lessons aimed at next week's texts would be a reasonable choice.

Oral Reading Fluency Training

As effective as preteaching words to the point that they become sight words has proven to be, this approach has obvious limitations. There is sure to be a point at which there are so many unknown words that instruction cannot efficiently bridge the gulf between student and text. If students can read a text with 80 to 85 percent accuracy, the anticipatory teaching of five to ten words should make a text accessible. If the texts are much harder than that, and they sometimes will be, then this kind of word work should be only a *supplement* to another scaffolding approach.

This other approach, oral reading fluency training, has become quite common in American classrooms, at least at some grade levels. Fluent readers must be able to read text accurately, with automaticity (without conscious attention to word reading), and with prosody (text reading should sound like language with proper pausing and intonation).

Guided oral reading practice with repetition and feedback can have a positive impact on reading fluency.[25] Reading gains are greatest when reading practice is with texts that students cannot already read fluently.[26] This improvement affects reading comprehension too. The National Reading Panel found that fluency instruction not only had a general impact on overall reading achievement, but that this improvement was mediated by changes in how well the students were able to read the texts that were used for practice.[27] My own classroom observations tell me that fluency practice is too often left to the end of a reading lesson. Quite often students will read a text for comprehension and discussion, and then once that is concluded, they may be required to read a page or two of the text aloud. If students are placed in grade level texts—and they struggle to read the words—then turning this approach on its head should be productive. Fluency work should come first, making sure the students can read the text reasonably well, and then shifting focus to comprehension. As with Burns's sight word studies, the fluency practice should improve students' ability to read the texts.

Those studies summarized in chapter 4, in which students learned more when working with frustration level texts, all accomplished this result through fluency instruction. In each of those studies, students engaged in some kind of fluency work with the frustration level texts.[28]

Perhaps, as in Burns's studies, the fluency work transforms frustration level text into instructional level text, enabling further learning gains. That seems particularly likely in the more than twenty studies that intentionally placed students in frustration level texts and found that oral reading practice improved performance with those texts.[29] Earlier, research was cited to the effect that reading a text aloud once without feedback resulted in accuracy improvements of about 50 percent. In many cases, that would be more than enough to tip a text from the frustration classification to the instructional one.

There are several ways that fluency training can be implemented. The key is to provide this support with the grade level texts from which students are to be instructed. In two of those studies in which frustration level texts paid off in more learning, students engaged in paired repeated reading, with the lower readers reading text portions to their better-reading classmates for about fifteen minutes per day. Many other studies provided both silent and oral repeated reading opportunities without feedback, and still others used choral reading or reading while listening to improve performance with the texts.

Again, there are many ways that this kind of instruction can be fit into a busy school day, utilizing whatever human and digital resources are available. Personally, I tend to favor paired repeated reading but with close teacher supervision. The teacher monitors both the reading and the partnering by moving from pair to pair for observation and guidance.

In conclusion, students need to read instructional texts with sufficient accuracy and fluency. Instructional level theory takes a rather static approach to this requirement, accomplishing it by limiting instruction to texts students can already read reasonably well. Reading is more malleable than that. Using instruction—changing what students know rather than avoiding the texts—can have a powerful impact on learning. Much can be gained from preparing students to read these demanding texts, and students and teachers can easily see the gains that are accomplished.

Scaffolding Reading Comprehension

The word reading scaffolds described in chapter 6 will be necessary for some students, and these should improve the comprehension of the instructional texts. However, there is more to supporting reading comprehension than making certain the students can recognize the words. Text includes conceptual and linguistic features that may serve as barriers to comprehension and that must be negotiated successfully for comprehension to be accomplished. This chapter explores those potential barriers and how students can be guided to overcome them effectively. Vocabulary, syntax, cohesion, text structure, cognitive strategies, and prior knowledge will each be addressed.

Many years ago, Keith Stanovich, a psychologist at the University of Toronto, proposed an interactive-compensatory model of reading.[1] This model explained how readers recognize words in text. He contended that readers could discern the right word by multiple paths. Young readers do whatever they can to figure out a word—sounding it out, guessing it based on semantic and syntactic context, using illustrations. But as they gain reading proficiency, their reliance on the orthographic-phonemic features of the words increases, with less reliance on those less certain cues.

The idea that reading involves compensatory processing is a useful way to think about comprehension too. Readers try to derive meaning from a text, and there is more than one way to accomplish this. Comprehension depends on both the information in the text and the readers' knowledge, and readers will differ in how they weigh these. Knowledge is important because it can be used to lessen the mnemonic and cognitive processing demands of reading, provide inferences, and diminish ambiguity. The most widely accepted theory of reading comprehension today holds that readers analyze a *text base* into a series of connected propositions or semantic units and then transform this information into a situation model.[2] A *situation model* results when readers combine information from the text with their own knowledge to form a coherent mental representation of the ideas. Individuals differ in how proficiently they process the text information, but they will also differ in how dependent on the text base they are, the background knowledge available and their reasoning abilities.

Scholars have long divided language into discrete components—phonology, morphology, syntax, semantics, pragmatics. Recently, empirical research has begun to suggest the importance of a more unitary theory of language. Statistical models fit the data better when gross indicators of language proficiency are used rather than separate measures of discrete components.[3] Language is a process. Under normal circumstances, we do not fire these components off in some predetermined order. We resort to them as needed. Readers can figure out text meaning in varied ways in part because text includes a great deal of redundancy. There are multiple ways readers may gain purchase on a text.

For example, consider this brief text: "The three soldiers were exhausted by the end of the grueling ride. They had served in the cavalry for only a brief time and had no idea how difficult crossing a desert might be."

The idea that there were multiple soldiers is signaled repeatedly: the adjective *three*, the plural marker at the end of the word *soldiers*, the plural verb *were*, and the pronoun *they* in the second sentence all conspire to convey plurality. These markers fit the semantic, morphological, and syntactic categories. The reader who misses one or another out of carelessness or a lack of proficiency may still grasp the idea that this was not a single man. Similarly, I might not know the meanings of *exhausted* or *grueling*, but I still might get the basic idea from the word *difficult* and that they were "crossing a desert" on horseback. That these were men is not stated in the text. In trying to develop a coherent mental representation of this text, I used my background knowledge: In the old cowboy movies, the cavalry was always a group of men riding horses.

Even this trivial example reveals the rich contextual redundancy of text and readers' ongoing or interactive dependence on various language components. Two readers reading the same text may appear to comprehend equally well. Nevertheless, their understanding and memory for the information may differ greatly. Even identical responses to a comprehension question can be reached by alternative routes. Readers may answer a query about *grueling* correctly but may have depended on background knowledge, while others got there through context. With a different text using that word, these students might not appear to know its meaning.

During a directed reading lesson, teachers can guide students to help them deal with the different language components. For this to be worthwhile, the texts should be sufficiently demanding to outstrip the students' language skills. They should not be able to comprehend these texts well using only the cognitive and linguistic tools they already possess. With teacher scaffolding and the students' own efforts, comprehension should improve markedly. Directed reading lessons are the appropriate locus for showing students how to bring the entire universe of their knowledge, language skills, and reasoning ability to bear on a text. Additionally, teachers may provide more specific "skills lessons" aimed at supporting more concentrated practice with any of those skills.[4] Nevertheless, the focus here will be mainly on what teachers can do to make frustration-level texts comprehendible for young readers. Because of the complexity of reading comprehension—and the many ways each of us comprehends any text—the scaffolding provided during directed reading lessons must be responsive and varied.

VOCABULARY

"It seems almost intuitive that developing a large and rich vocabulary is central to learning to read. Logically, children must know the words that make up written texts in order to understand them . . . Numerous studies have documented that the size of a person's vocabulary is strongly related to how well that person understands what he or she reads."[5] Indeed! An author's diction is a marvelous affordance. It allows for the communication of exact meanings. In a story, it matters if a character is "furious" or "angry," "happy" or "ecstatic," and a good author will make such distinctions. Those affordances quickly morph into barriers when words like "furious" or "ecstatic" are not in the readers' lexicons.

The importance of vocabulary can be inferred from the lesson plans of all major textbooks, and on sites like *Teachers Pay Teachers*. Everyone seems to recognize the value of preteaching unknown words, and research supports both the idea of teaching vocabulary to improve reading comprehension[6] and introducing challenging vocabulary prior to text reading to enhance the comprehension of that text.[7] At least one study showed this approach enabled students to comprehend texts that were significantly above grade level.[8] Another study showed that vocabulary preteaching boosted the comprehension of general education students and those with learning disabilities, though the latter did not reach the same comprehension levels as the former, likely because word meaning wasn't the only problem for these students.[9]

Nevertheless, I am often disappointed at how this scaffold is used. Instead of supporting reading development, it may hinder it. Science texts, for example, aim to teach students about concepts like *adaptation*, *ecosystems*, *force*, *motion*, *traits*, *absorbency*, *flexibility*, *weather*, and so on. Accordingly, explicit definitions or explanations are usually provided when such words are introduced in text. It is common practice to encourage teachers to familiarize students with these words *prior* to reading. Instead of teaching students to notice the introduction of new concepts and providing practice in figuring out scientific definitions, these preteaching practices seem aimed to discourage reading. Why bother to read a text if you already know what it is going to say? This approach encourages students to try to remember the teacher's explanations while ignoring the text. Maybe this is why so many students fail to recognize definitions in science texts?[10]

The same kind of problem is evident with many words the meanings of which could be determined through close reliance on context. Preteaching these words may improve the readability of the text for students who do not know them, but how to use context to resolve word meanings is both essential and undertaught. Context instruction can have a positive impact on reading comprehension and can be well taught through guided practice with text.[11] Words that can be figured out from context should not be pretaught. Proper guidance will not try to remove these barriers, but will guide students to surmount them. Comprehension questions should be posed to reveal whether the students understood these words. If they did not, then students should be returned to the text to help them determine the word meanings. Such scaffolding may take the form of a demonstration—showing students what to do when they meet such words. Other times, key information may be pointed out to help the students to grasp the meaning, and sometimes just encouraging rereading may be enough.

In such exchanges, I would encourage an emphasis on comprehension rather than vocabulary. Consider the following sentence: "When the prairie plants were uprooted, the animals that depended on them lost their food source." Students should be able to get the meaning of "uprooted" from context or morphology. Teachers could ask vocabulary questions: "What does "uprooted" mean?" or "What did the author mean by "uprooted"? It would be better to ask, "What caused the animals to lose their food source?" That is a comprehension question that can only be answered by interpreting the vocabulary. If a student responds, "Because the prairie plants were uprooted," then ask what "uprooted" meant. If they say, "Because the prairie plants died," then query how the author revealed that, what words conveyed that idea.

Preteaching the meanings of key words can significantly reduce the difficulty of a text. But if our goal is not to avoid challenge but to teach students to read, then preteaching can send us down the wrong road. It is a mistake to preteach words an author will define explicitly or contextually. Students should be held accountable—through teacher questioning—for understanding the meanings of the author's words. Students should be taught to recognize and comprehend explicit definitions, especially with science texts. Students should be taught to determine word meanings using context, morphology, and reference tools like dictionaries and they should be expected to do so. When they fail to, the teacher needs to scaffold those efforts to build these valuable habits of mind.

SYNTAX

There is more to reading comprehension than words. Readers have to make sense of sentences and their grammar or syntax. There is abundant evidence showing that miscomprehension is often due to readers' inability to fathom sentence complexity. Teacher guidance during reading can help students to deal with these syntactic barriers. Unfortunately, sentence intepretation guidance is all too rare; perhaps because it would not be useful with instructional level texts.

Over the past two decades, research on syntax and reading comprehension has gradually accumulated. What had been a desert is now an oasis. There is a slew of rigorous studies revealing the importance of syntactic awareness in reading comprehension.[12] In many studies this relationship was significant even controlling for differences in decoding ability, vocabulary knowledge, memory, and other relevant skills.[13] If all students were equal in those other abilities, there would still be variations in comprehension due to syntax. Kids who understand syntax comprehend better than those who do not. It matters in grades K–12, with regular classroom kids and those with dyslexia, and with both native English speakers and English language learners.

It is worth noting that syntax is particularly relevant to the idea of teaching reading with grade level texts because of the role syntax plays in measures of readability.[14] Texts with more complicated sentence structures are measurably harder to understand, something long acknowledged in readability measures. However, even relatively simple sentence structures may be a problem for elementary school students, which argues for greater attention to sentence comprehension.[15] Many intervention studies have included syntax.[16] Unfortunately, these studies were not designed to separate out the syntax effects from those of other language components.

As with vocabulary, teachers sometimes provide explicit syntax lessons. There is little research evidence supporting their benefits. But more applied approaches do appear to work. An example of this is sentence combining instruction.[17] In this approach, students are presented with two or more short sentences, and they try to combine them into a single grammatical sentence:

Simple sentences:	She did her homework. She watched a movie. Her brother watched the movie.
Combined sentence:	She did her homework, and then she and her brother watched a movie.

But there are also approaches that make sense for teaching students to succeed with challenging text. For instance, teachers can teach paraphrasing—teaching students to put the sentences into their own words.[18] It is a good idea for the teacher to model paraphrasing initially, showing students how to do it and explaining how it works. For instance:

Original sentence:	Ted took a cab to the zoo because he wanted to see the lions.
Paraphrase:	Ted rode a taxi to the zoo to see lions.

"I put the sentence in my own words, so I changed 'cab' to 'taxi,' and I thought I could use fewer words to say the same thing. Instead of 'because he wanted to see the lions,' I shortened that 'to see lions.'"

In a study of paraphrasing, Cheryl Scott and Catherine Balthazar report a syntactic error made by a ten-year-old with a language disability.[19] The student read the following sentence: "Rachel Carson, who was a scientist, writer, and ecologist, grew up in the rural river town of Springdale, Pennsylvania." He thought the noun closest to the verb was the subject of the sentence, and misinterpreted it to mean that a scientist, a writer, and an ecologist [they] grew up in Pennsylvania. Paraphrasing uncovers such misinterpretation and can help to prevent it.

As with vocabulary, it can be a good idea to anticipate problems, examining a text before a lesson to identify complicated sentences that may be barriers to comprehension. Then come up with questions about those sentences that would reveal incomprehension or miscomprehension. With the Rachel Carson sentence, the student was asked what he had learned about

Carson, and he responded that "they grew up together in the same place," revealing his bafflement. If students answer correctly—they recognize who Rachel Carson was and where she lived—then proceed. But if a sentence turns out to be disruptive, it should result in interpretation guidance. Take students back to the text to help them figure it out. A particularly powerful approach is to parse the sentence, breaking it into smaller chunks. For instance, the Rachel Carson sentence may be divided as follows:

Rachel Carson,
who was a scientist,
writer,
and ecologist,
grew up
in the rural river town
of Springdale, Pennsylvania.

This division attends to the internal punctuation in the sentence, and separates noun, verb, and prepositional phrases. It should lead to discussion and perhaps some paraphrasing or combining. In this case, a teacher might show the students how to turn the dependent clauses into independent ones: "Rachel Carson was a scientist. Rachel Carson was a writer. Rachel Carson was an ecologist. Rachel Carson grew up in Springdale, Pennsylvania. Springdale, Pennsylvania is a rural river town." This could lead to prosody practice, with students trying to read the sentence aloud so that it makes sense, or to a discussion of the need to identify the verb and its subject. Over time, students should be learning how to parse complicated sentences themselves to better understand them. The point is to scaffold comprehension, showing students how to translate frustrating sentences into comprehensible ones. Without this, complex sentences tend to be an on-off switch: students get the meaning or not, but if not, they have no way to surmount the barrier.

An alternative to sentence breaking is intensive questioning with the students reading and rereading the sentence multiple times. Who was the sentence about? Who was she? What did she do? Where did she do it? What kind of town was it? And so on.

Research shows the value of sentence breaking both for supporting fluency and comprehension. A fascinating study administered a traditional comprehension test to secondary students.[20] One group read the usual test passages, while the other read those same passages parsed with slashing lines (e.g., Rachel Carson,// who was a scientist, //writer, //and ecologist// grew up// in the rural river town// of Springdale, Pennsylvania). The students who read the parsed text earned significantly higher test scores. The idea here is to teach students to do that themselves.

Recently, I came across an intriguing study conducted with ninth and twelfth graders.[21] The students spent fifteen minutes a day reading and analyzing difficult texts sentence-by-sentence with their teacher—discussing main ideas, author's purpose, inferences, and literary styles as expressed in those sentences. They were taught how to divide and simplify difficult sentences, and to determine the primary functions of the various phrases and clauses. This regimen not only allowed the students to comprehend the texts they were working with, but it significantly improved general reading comprehension abilities as measured by standardized tests.

COHESION

Coherence refers to the meaningful connections among words, sentences, and ideas in a text. It establishes continuity and clarity and makes a text meaningful. Cohesion may be thought of as being analogous to the warp and woof of fabric, weaving the ideas together into a coherent unity. Linguists have identified and categorized cohesive links that create this kind of coherence,[22] psychologists have developed innovative techniques for measuring the degree of unity or cohesiveness in texts,[23] and there are scads of studies showing that cohesive tie interpretation is implicated in reading comprehension.[24] Such studies have found these relations with a variety of text types and with students across a wide range of ages and abilities.

The most widely acknowledged cohesion taxonomy was proposed by Michael Halliday and Ruqaiya Hasan. They described the purposes of these devices as specifying "the way in which what is to follow is systematically connected to what has gone before."[25] If readers are to understand a text, they must use the connections the author has included or infer the implied connections. The Halliday and Hasan taxonomy describes five types of cohesive links that convey repetition or express the relationships among ideas. Some cohesive links that can trip readers up include substitution ("Do we have any *books*? Only old *ones*."), ellipses ("I have two *oranges*. My brother has four *more*"), lexical (George Washington = president, general, father of our country), and conjunctions (in addition, to, consequently, unless, and so on). Miscomprehension occurs if readers miss or misinterpret these links—misattributing the action of one character to another, for example, or failing to grasp the implications of a causation signal. Failure to make such connections undermines the creation of a sound situation model, resulting in a failure to comprehend.

The explicitness of cohesive links in text impacts readability[26] and comprehension.[27] Reading comprehension often turns on the readers' abilities to identify or infer referential and semantic,[28] and causal and temporal connections,[29] as well as awareness of character motives[30] or the conventions of story structure.[31] Several factors determine whether appropriate and necessary connections are made, including readers' knowledge and awareness of linguistic connectives,[32] amount of repetition,[33] distance between references and antecedents,[34] and the extent to which readers are trying to comprehend the text and not just reading the words.[35] Texts are easier to comprehend the more explicit or straightforward the connections, the lower the potential for ambiguity (connecting a male character to associated pronouns is easier when there is only one such character), and the shorter the distance between the antecedents and referents.

As with syntax, cohesion is a text feature better dealt with during and after reading, rather than beforehand. Consider this passage from Peter Pan:

> "Surely," said John, like one who had lost faith in his memory, "he used not to sleep in the kennel?"
>
> "John," Wendy said falteringly, "perhaps we don't remember the old life as well as we thought we did."[36]

The teacher might ask, "What did Wendy mean when she said, 'as well as we thought we did?' As well as we thought we did what?" When asking such a question it can be a good idea to return to the passage so students can read and reread to determine the antecedent ("remember the old life") referred to by "did." This might seem like only a linguistic exercise. It is, of course, when separated from an effort to comprehend. This connection emphasizes a poignant element of this narrative—the children have been gone from home for a long time, their childhoods are slipping away. This repetition will only nourish readers' comprehension if the meaning of the referent is recognized. This kind of exchange can both ensure that the students end up with a coherent situation model and should provide them with insights about how to deal with such puzzling elements in the future.

It is reasonable to engage students both in explicit exercises aimed at building these skills as well as encouraging awareness of this aspect of comprehension during directed readings.[37] Consider the following paragraph. It includes a remarkable amount of co-referencing across five sentences, including some that may be ambiguous. In any event, if the connections are not made, it is unlikely that students will grasp the paragraph meaning—which provides an explanation of the origin of planets:

> Meanwhile, the nebula continued to orbit the new Sun until it formed a large flat ring around it. Scientists call this ring a "protoplanetary disk." The disk, or ring, was hottest where it was closest to the Sun, and coolest at its outer edge. As the disk swirled around the Sun, the Sun's gravity went to work. It pulled and tugged at the bits of rock, dust, ice, and gas until they came together in clumps of material we now call the planets.[38]

With such a rich paragraph, I recommend providing a copy students can mark up. Have students reread it to identify the first concept ("the nebula"). Have them mark those words with a color and then read on to see if it is referred to again (nebula arises twice more in the first sentence—referred to by the pronoun "it," but do not be surprised if some students think those "its" refer to the sun). Then have them read these sentences again, looking for the second concept (the sun), and mark it and its repetitions in the same color—a different color than was used for nebula. Then they need to take on "ring/disk," gravity, and my favorite: "the bits of rock, dust, ice and gas"="they"="clumps of material"="the planets." This string both reveals a synonymous relationship, but also a temporal transformation. This time sequence is signaled directly only once by the word "until," so it is easy to miss.

Once these connections have been identified and sorted out, it can be helpful to reread the passage aloud, replacing some of the references with repetitions and adding explanatory language where needed, such as expanding on what "until" is referring to.

> Meanwhile the nebula continued to orbit the new Sun until the *nebula* formed a large flat ring *around the nebula*. Scientists call this ring a "protoplanetary disk." The *protoplanetary disk/ring* was hottest where the *protoplanetary disk/ring* was closest to the Sun, and coolest at the *protoplanetary disk/ring's* outer edge. As the *protoplanetary disk/ring* swirled around the Sun, the Sun's gravity pulled and tugged. *The Sun's gravity* pulled and tugged at the bits of dust, ice, and gas and it kept doing this until *the dust, ice, and gas* came together in *clumps of material* that we now call the *planets*.

The purpose of this rereading is less to paraphrase than to make certain that all the ideas are properly understood and arranged in a way that accurately conveys the intended ideas.

Research shows that it is possible to revise texts so that these kinds of links are understood easily by elementary and middle school students. Such revision—increasing repetitions, signaling causation explicitly, and so on—results in higher comprehension and recall even when the resulting texts have readabilities above grade level.[39] But research also shows that, without altering the texts, students can learn to identify these textual connections and to draw appropriate inferences, improving their reading comprehension.[40] This instruction is beneficial to both average readers and those who struggle. Even when such interventions failed to generalize to overall reading achievement, they were successful at improving students' immediate comprehension of the challenging text.[41]

TEXT STRUCTURE

Cohesion describes how ideas in a text fit together at a microtextual level, connecting words and sentences and closely related elements. Text structure refers to the macrotext, a system of organization or "top-level" text, which holds together the elements of the microstructure. If cohesion is thought of as the warp and woof of a fabric, the structure is what determines whether the fabric will be a shirt, scarf, or towel. These woven items depend on the threads being woven together coherently, but a good deal of their functional power comes from whether they have sleeves or legs or certain dimensions. Regarding text, it is the top-level text structures that define what it is—a story, scientific experiment, or news article.

Occasionally an author will explain how an aspect of cohesion will be dealt with, such as revealing that "she" refers to teachers and "he" to students. That happens, but not often. By contrast, authors often provide explicit explanation of the top-level structure of their texts. An introduction to a biology chapter may explain that the text will be divided into three parts, one on certain organisms, both individually (part one) and how they interact within communities (part two), as well as how these communities contribute to an ecosystem (part three).

Narration (fictional stories and retellings of true events), exposition (informational texts that describe, analyze, or explain something), and arguments (assertions of opinion or attempts to persuade) differ structurally. Here we will only deal with narration and exposition both because of their strong research base and the limited role of argument in elementary school.[42]

Stories possess plot structure, organized around the purposes or intentions of characters. As such, stories include settings, characters, problems, goals, attempts to solve the problems, outcomes of those efforts, and psychological reactions. That stories have a common structure may sound reductionist and a bit boring, but authors do amazing things with those elements. Stories usually string together multiple episodes, with characters making multiple attempts to solve a problem, or—as in many novels—dealing with one problem after another. Perhaps more than one character has a goal, and those may conflict (think Hansel and Gretel who want to go home and the witch preparing Hansel for her dinner). Authors often alter the sequence of how these elements are presented, requiring listeners, readers, and viewers to reorder them. Few television dramas these days tell a single story sequentially—there are usually three or four plot lines that interact, and flashbacks and flashforwards are common fare. Despite all that complexity, knowledge of those core elements gives readers a valuable leg up on comprehension.[43]

Some scholars claim that informational text is more challenging than stories. Part of this added difficulty is due to text structure. Exposition is usually structured around five rhetorical purposes, and any combination of these may appear in a single text. These five rhetorical structures include: enumeration and description of facts about some concept or process, time sequences, cause and effect relationships, comparisons and contrasts, and problems and their solutions.[44] Readers identify these structures from explicit information authors provide, from headings and subheadings, and by signal or cue words.

Another way to think of structure is in terms of the content that may drive an organizational plan. Texts that depend on content organization will still employ those common rhetorical structures, but their content plan may be even more conspicuous and useful. A fourth-grade social studies textbook, for instance, may describe world cultures (e.g., Egypt, Greece, Rome, China). It would be beneficial if students recognized that each chapter included sections devoted to economics, religion, government, arts and culture, and history. This recognition of the analogous nature of the content in each chapter should help students to anticipate, compare, and remember the information, as well as providing them an appreciation of the structure of social studies itself. The rhetorical structures would still be useful since these chapters would employ several of them. The arts and culture sections may be enumerative and descriptive—presenting the cultural accomplishments of each civilization. The history sections may be organized sequentially, perhaps with a problem-solution approach. The government and economic sections might be comparative—categorizing these cultures into monarchies, democracies, and dictatorships. Guiding students to recognize and use these informational and rhetorical macrostructures can provide valuable scaffolds that make challenging texts comprehensible and memorable.

The recognition of top-level organizational text structure plays an important role in comprehension and memory. The National Reading Panel concluded, on the basis of seventeen studies, that poor readers have difficulty identifying story structure, and that teaching students how to use story maps has "a firm scientific basis for concluding that they improve comprehension in normal readers."[45] More recently, a synthesis of thirteen single-subject design experiments reported that "the story-mapping strategy was an evidence-based and very effective strategy in developing text comprehension" for students with disabilities.[46]

Even stronger evidence supports the teaching of expository text structure. In a synthesis of forty-four studies focused on grades 4 through 6, researchers at the Utrecht Institute of Linguistics reported: "In sum, our meta-analysis shows that text structure instruction has a positive effect on students' reading comprehension skills over and above regular reading programs. It improves their performance on comprehension questions, recall, and summarization tasks."[47] Another meta-analysis, this one with forty-five studies from grades 2 through 12, concluded: "We recommend that text structure instruction be included as one component of a comprehension approach to expository reading instruction."[48] Still another meta-analysis, this one based on nineteen studies, K–12, decided that: "It is evident that expository text structure instruction is an effective research-based reading comprehension strategy for a range of student abilities and grade levels. It is likely that text structure instruction is effective because it presents students with an organizational framework for approaching expository text that is often complex and dense with academic vocabulary."[49]

These expository text studies are particularly interesting because most of them took place in social studies or science classes, rather than reading.[50] That means that most of this evidence was obtained from studies in which the students would have been reading grade level content texts rather than the instructional level texts so ubiquitous in reading instruction. There are several ways this kind of scaffolding can be provided. One approach would be to prepare students for reading a text by explaining what the structure of the text is, how it can be recognized, and why it matters. This might be accompanied by a demonstration of how to read such a text. Another possibility is to provide students with a story map or graphic organizer that guides the identification of key structural information. With a story, students would note the characters, problems, goals, and attempts, while with a comparison, the comparable features of the concepts or processes would be charted. Students do best with this scaffolding when they receive elaborated feedback, providing them with not just the right answer, but showing them how to recognize and use the information to overcome barriers to comprehension.

COMPREHENSION STRATEGIES

Comprehension strategies are cognitive actions readers may implement when trying to understand or remember the information from challenging texts. Historically, reading comprehension has been viewed as a somewhat passive receptive process. Comprehension was thought to result automatically from reading the words. Consequently, reading instruction was viewed as little more than the teaching of words or decoding, along with some reading practice and, perhaps, a smidgeon of vocabulary. Such "instruction" tended to focus on having students read texts they could comprehend, rather than on improving comprehension or enabling them to take on more challenging texts.

> An important development in theories about reading comprehension occurred in the 1970s. Reading comprehension was seen . . . as an active [process] that engaged the reader. Reading came to be seen as intentional thinking during which meaning is constructed through interactions between text and reader. . . . According to this view, meaning resides in the intentional, problem-solving, thinking processes of the reader that occur during an interchange with a text.[51]

The idea that readers are vigorously and consciously taking deliberate actions to make sense of text may seem contradictory to the experience of proficient readers. This is because so much of our reading—especially pleasure reading—is carried out with texts in our wheelhouse, using language we already know, to explore information we are familiar with. In that context, drawing inferences or remembering key facts are automatic processes, actions accomplished without conscious effort. The situation changes, however, when reading demands increase. Enroll in a graduate program or get a promotion or transfer at work and reading may suddenly seem more demanding—harder to negotiate because of unfamiliar content (making it difficult to bring prior knowledge to bear) and what may seem like newly erected barriers to understanding (e.g., unfamiliar vocabulary, complicated sentences, unclear referents, impenetrable organization).

Perhaps an example will help. Summarization is a powerful comprehension strategy. It can help readers to remember—and possibly understand—a text. A reader reads a text portion, and instead of just launching into the next section, stops and summarizes. This does not need to be recorded or even stated aloud, though initially that can help. This summarization is ongoing, with each summary addressing both the new and the previously summarized information. Summarizing slows readers down, gets them to think about the content more than if they only read, creates opportunities to correct confusions and vagaries, and may encourage attention to the connections among the text sections.

Admittedly, I rarely use this strategy myself. Unless I need it. A while back, I was teaching myself to read French and took on a full-length, unabridged, literary novel, Alexis Jenni's *L'art français de la guerre*. This is a challenging book with many historical referents, shifts in time frame, and symbolic or metaphorical relations. It requires the reader to recognize parallels among Homer's *Iliad,* the French resistance in World War II, and the Algerian debacle of the 1950s. I looked up a lot of words in my French dictionary and sometimes resorted to those syntax and cohesion scaffolds. Those tools helped most of the time, and yet, their use interrupted my thinking, making it hard for me to keep track of the story and to make the connections needed to grasp and appreciate the subtle plot.

With a little experimentation I found that if I summarized each paragraph in the margin, often with just a few words—"they went to lunch," "he meets an artist," "his encounter with the resistance"—I could quickly regain the thread. This strategy was powerful. It helped me to understand and, importantly in this case, to remember what I was reading. Such strategies work—I came to adore that book—but strategies only make sense if readers appreciate their possibilities, recognize text barriers, and have a desire to conquer them.

The National Reading Panel (NRP) identified strategies that had received the greatest positive research attention, considering more than two hundred such studies.[52] Other research syntheses have added to that list.[53] Table 7.1 provides a description of those strategies. This list is not comprehensive; it only includes strategies that have been studied. There are many potential barriers to comprehension—and the strategies in this list could not possibly address them all. For instance, what do you do if you come to language, language that seems perfectly understandable, and yet is so opaque as to appear nonsensical? That is why there is a need for a strategy on how to recognize and deal with idiomatic expressions: it's a piece of cake, let the cat

TABLE 7.1 Comprehension strategies

Strategies	*Purpose*	*Actions*
Previewing	• Comprehension is improved if readers, before reading, can identify the genre and/or topic of the text and the direction it may take	• Read title and examine pictures • Skim introduction and/or conclusion • Read the subheadings
Prior knowledge/ purpose	• Comprehension is improved when students have easy access to their own knowledge on a topic. Reviewing that briefly before reading accomplishes this • Having specific reading purposes can increase the chances that students will identify relevant information. • Connecting information in text with prior knowledge during reading can increase understanding and recall.	• Brainstorming what is already known about text topic prior to reading • Predicting what the text may present—before and throughout the reading • Readers decide what they want to find out from the text • Readers think about the connection between ideas in text and what they already know as they read • Make inference using prior knowledge
Rehearsal	• It is not enough that readers understand what they are reading, later recall matters too. • Understanding of later presented information in a text often depends upon the readers' memory of earlier presented information.	• Self-questioning during and after reading • Summarization during and after reading • Graphic summaries during and after reading • Visualizing the text content • Review of text information after reading
Comprehension monitoring	• Readers must notice when they are not understanding a text or when their minds have wandered. • They must take actions to remedy those problems if they are to gain full understanding of the text.	• Reread • Look up word in dictionary • Compare information with graphics • Ask for help

out of the bag, call it a day, hit the sack, it's not rocket science, it's raining cats and dogs. Or what of the chemist who explained that when reading an important study, he previewed the text to identify any abbreviations or symbols and memorized them before reading. That comprehension strategy can pay off and handsomely, and yet it is too specific and unstudied to end up in a strategies list.

The point is that strategies need to be used purposefully and in contexts in which their use will help a reader to comprehend. A list begs to be taught, and that is fine, if the teaching does not mislead students into thinking that reading is about applying strategies, rather than about understanding text that will not necessarily surrender its meaning without a fight. One does not need to use strategies, but text barriers must be surmounted and having some tools available for surmounting some of the common ones makes sense. In some classrooms teaching students to use strategies has become too much the point, elbowing aside more significant concerns. Strategies should never divert student attention from the texts they are trying to comprehend. A teacher once told me that her students still "were not comprehending very well, but their predictions were improving"—missing the point of prediction instruction altogether.[54]

Unfortunately, textbooks devoted to educating teachers about comprehension strategies usually say little about the role played by text. Even when degree of text challenge is mentioned, it is usually as a warning that new strategies should be introduced with especially easy texts.[55] That sounds good—moving students along a gradient of difficulty sounds like good pedagogy—and yet, it belies what strategies are and why we teach them. Applying strategies to relatively easy texts, texts that one can presumably already comprehend well, is not an exercise in *problem solving* but in *pretending*. If the texts are not difficult—that is, if students can already comprehend them well—there is no point to implementing a strategy.

How should strategies be taught? First, teachers should introduce strategies as scaffolds. For instance, teachers may—when guiding students to read a challenging text—direct them to preview the text to see if they can figure out what it may be about or what genre it may be. They may have students brainstorm what they know about a particular topic, perhaps filling in the first parts of a K(Know)-W(Want to Know)-L(What I Learned) chart or making predictions. Then, when students can implement this guidance, an effort to put these actions under the control of the students themselves is appropriate. This means teaching them as strategies rather than just using them as teacher guided scaffolding. It is usually recommended that strategy teaching employ a "gradual release of responsibility" approach. Research has not proven this to be essential, though it has been used in many of the successful studies and seems logical.[56] Gradual release simply means that students initially implement a strategy under the direction of a teacher and that as the strategy becomes familiar they take on more and more of the responsibility for its use.

This is often described as the "I do it, we do it, you do it" model. Teachers are encouraged to demonstrate how to implement a strategy—explaining what they are doing, when they use the strategy, how they do it, and why they are doing it. Then, gradually, the students take over, first with direct teacher guidance, telling students what to do and why to do it, but then replacing these directions with queries. "If we want to be sure that we're going to remember this information, what could we do? What did we do with the text on Monday?," and so on, getting students to make the choices. If a teacher has already been scaffolding reading by having students apply these strategies during guided reading, then explicit modeling and guided practice may be less necessary. The teacher could jump right to the "explaining the purposes of the strategies" and "guiding student choices."

In any event, guiding students to preview text, to think about what they are reading, to connect what they are reading to what they already know, to notice when they are not understanding and to take action to remedy that, and to review the information they are reading all can have positive impacts on the comprehension of complex text. Scaffolding these actions and teaching students how to use them on their own when needed makes great sense and should help to transform supposedly frustration level texts into instructional level ones.

PRIOR KNOWLEDGE

Research has long shown the importance of readers' knowledge in comprehension.[57] Text cannot provide all the information necessary to allow readers to fully make sense of the ideas it expresses. Comprehension requires readers to fill gaps, make connections, resolve ambiguity, make judgments of credibility, and so on. Readers accomplish this by resorting to what they already know. The degree of text difficulty can be offset by the knowledge the reader brings to the text.[58]

There are many kinds of knowledge readers bring to texts.[59] The importance of linguistic knowledge (e.g., semantics, syntax, discourse knowledge) and procedural knowledge (e.g., strategies for processing those linguistic variables during reading) have already been explored. Readers also use their world or domain knowledge—what they know about a topic or content that a text addresses. This knowledge contributes to comprehension in myriad ways. If students are reading about electricity in their science class, what they know about electrons, currents, circuits, resistance, and the like will allow them to generate inferences (e.g., the text says copper is often used for wiring, leaving it to readers to deduce that is *because* it is a good conductor). Knowledge also reduces the load on working memory. Information already available in long-term memory reduces the need to hold the redundant text information in working memory.[60]

Personal, experiential, or general knowledge are part of this, too. This knowledge differs from academic knowledge. It includes what we learn from living our daily lives, interacting with our social and physical worlds: knowing that people do things for a reason, objects fall when dropped, the sun shines during the day, and we should help when someone is having trouble. This kind of information helps to contextualize text, such as supporting the visualization of a scene or the drawing of an inference as to a character's motivation. This also means that two good readers may end up with two very different interpretations of a text—readers may, for instance, differ as to which fictional character in a story they sympathize with, leading them to formulate very different themes.[61]

Knowledge—especially experiential knowledge—often has cultural significance. Because different cultural groups may have different experiences, their knowledge may differ. Students from low-income families or who are racial minorities may view the actions of police in a social studies book or short story differently—drawing very different inferences.[62] The meaning of actions like smiles, eye contact, or hand touching may be interpreted differently depending on the cultural background of the reader. Reading about unfamiliar social practices like *Bar Mitzvahs* (Jewish), *quinceañeras* (Latino), or *Rumspringa* (Amish) may be more of a challenge to some students than others because of their degrees of familiarity. Children whose families have immigrated from elsewhere may be just as baffled by how some Americans celebrate (or fail to celebrate) Halloween, Thanksgiving, or Christmas.

Even with relevant knowledge, cultural differences may limit the likelihood of that information being brought to bear during reading. Children become aware of gender roles by the time they are about three years old, and this knowledge is available to the typical elementary school age reader. However, Asian immigrants may be challenged by Western names. Which are boys and which are girls: Dorothy, Charlie, Alice, Madeline, Stuart, or Mike?

It is not that they cannot figure out these characters' genders from the texts, just that it is an added burden, something else they may have to work out rather than just knowing. These kinds of interpretive difference are not deficiencies. If your cultural background or upbringing did not grant you prior familiarity with Asian names, try reading texts with character names like Hajoon, Aiko, Hua, Bo, Lian, and Aoki. It is unlikely that you would recognize either the character's genders or ethnicities from the names alone.

All these kinds of knowledge are usually referred to as "prior knowledge" when it comes to reading comprehension. *Prior* is used to distinguish the knowledge that readers bring to a text from the knowledge they will gain from a text. Kintsch's theory that comprehension requires the building of a situation model connecting text information and reader knowledge is pertinent.[63] If readers have no relevant knowledge, then comprehension is nearly impossible. A reader may grasp some disconnected facts from such a text, but it would be very difficult to form a coherent situation model.

It is rare that readers have no relevant knowledge. When authors suspect such a gap may exist they often depend on analogies to facilitate reader understanding. With electricity, for instance, many authors turn to the idea of water running through a hose or pipe, an idea that may be more familiar. Another example of this would be a text that explains cricket matches in terms of their similarities and differences with American baseball. The trick for the author is to find a similar idea readers may already possess; the trick for a reader is to recognize the purpose of such an analogy and to use it to better understand the text.

It is important that teachers recognize the value of student knowledge in reading comprehension, that they appreciate that all students have some relevant prior knowledge, no matter their cultural backgrounds, and that there are powerful knowledge-related scaffolds that can make challenging texts more comprehensible. Research has revealed two somewhat overlapping approaches to knowledge scaffolding that may improve reading comprehension: knowledge activation and knowledge building.[64]

Knowledge activation refers to the idea of helping students make their knowledge maximally available during reading. Research shows that even when readers possess relevant knowledge they may fail to use it.[65] Teachers can guide students to call this knowledge up in ways that increase the likelihood of knowledge-based inference generation or the development of coherent text comprehension understanding.[66] One way to *activate* reader knowledge is by questioning students about what they know about a topic. This can take many forms. For instance, a teacher may have students brainstorm everything they know about a topic prior to reading. This may lead to a list of words or a word cloud of all the ideas the students generated (e.g., flower, garden, fruit, insects, soil, compost, fertilizer, rabbits, fence, trowel, spade, water). Another possibility is to fill out a K-W-L chart, listing what is already known about a subject, setting a goal as to what the readers want to find out, and—after the reading—detailing what was learned.[67] Still another possibility is for teachers to provide a preview to help students connect the text information with past experiences. "We're going to read about a family vacation. They went on a driving vacation, and they had to stay in motels along the way. This family confronted several problems on their trip." Then students may share their own travel experiences or generate predictions about what may happen in the story. Predictions of this type serve as text-relevant inferences drawn from background experience. Elaboration on such predictions can be useful: "You said they might get a flat tire. Then what might happen. Have you ever been driving with someone who had a flat? What happened then?"

However, knowledge may be a two-edged sword. When readers are misinformed, that is, when what they believe is wrong, this can negatively impact comprehension.[68] Good readers need be on the lookout not just for what a text says, but whether that information affirms or contradicts their own beliefs. These kinds of activities can reveal such misunderstandings, allowing the teacher to make students aware of this possibility.

Older readers can engage in these kinds of knowledge connecting activities profitably on their own, strategically increasing the availability of relevant knowledge for their impending reading. The same cannot be said for younger readers. With them, this kind of open-ended knowledge activation only works well when implemented as a group—which fits the directed reading situation nicely. The reason for this could be that the social interactions encourage younger students to more thoroughly consider available knowledge ("I didn't think of flowers until Billy said 'fruit.'") Or perhaps this kind of knowledge sharing in the reading group does more than activate existing knowledge; students may gain new relevant information from their classmates.

Teachers often engage students in these kinds of activities prior to reading. However, *prior* knowledge is used not only before reading, but during reading, and scaffolds that encourage its use throughout the reading of challenging text are a good idea. Dividing a text into shorter sections and then interleaving reading and discussion can accommodate access to knowledge. After students read a portion, the teacher may ask relevant inferential questions that require students to fill in gaps or make connections. This kind of questioning encourages students to infer, increasing their understanding of the text beyond what they, themselves, could do without such questioning. It also allows teachers to explain the need for inferences and to highlight the information readers used to fill the gap or make the connection.

Knowledge building may be necessary when students lack relevant knowledge. The text may require more than they have. Knowledge building as a preparation to reading has its place, though teachers must be careful not to fool themselves into thinking that they are supporting comprehension when they are really replacing it with something else. For instance, teachers who are certain their students will not understand a text because of a lack of relevant prior knowledge may tell the story or lecture on the topic prior to having students read the same information themselves. That approach makes the reading irrelevant.

One of the most interesting and powerful ways of scaffolding reading comprehension through knowledge building is to have students read multiple texts on the same topic.[69] Such text sets may address different aspects of a problem and may include texts at a variety of readability levels—easy and difficult. This approach allows students to scaffold their own comprehension by reading easier texts to increase knowledge which renders the harder texts more readable. Introducing new content through video prior to reading has also had positive results. In any event, whether the teacher is trying to activate relevant knowledge or to increase that knowledge prior to reading, these scaffolds can become tools readers can learn to activate themselves when dealing with challenging texts.

CONCLUSIONS

The instructional level idea requires that teachers place students in texts that they are almost certain to comprehend. Teachers then provide scaffolds to reading these texts (usually through the introduction of new vocabulary, prior knowledge sharing, or strategy teaching). If the texts are truly at students' instructional levels, then, for the most part, these supports are unnecessary, more likely to bore students than to help them. Pretending to use a strategy when it is not needed is not likely to increase one's reading ability.

Texts that students cannot easily comprehend on their own present obvious opportunities for learning, since any barrier to understanding can be a propitious target of instruction. The emphasis here has been on how one would scaffold the reading of such texts in ways that would allow students to comprehend them successfully. Unlike with instructional level teaching, the idea is to make sure that students confront authentic barriers to comprehension, rather than avoiding them. Directed or guided reading is then aimed at helping students to identify and surmount these barriers, ensuring comprehension through the students' own actions. This instruction has two goals: to enable students to conquer a formidable text and to develop a set of insights, skills, strategies, and abilities that will allow them to read other such texts successfully on their own in the future.

Maintaining Motivation

What role does text difficulty play in students' motivation and love of reading? Juliet Halladay, a professor of education at the University of Vermont, makes a useful distinction between cognitive and emotional frustration.[1] Cognitive frustration might lead to confusion and may, subsequently, suppress learning. Emotional frustration, on the other hand, may lead to feelings of incompetence, causing learners to withdraw or give up. This may interfere with later learning and could have long-term effects on students' attitudes toward reading. Instructional level theorists have not made this distinction. They label challenging texts as frustrating and leave it at that. Here we will consider both. Because affective variables were not addressed earlier, this chapter includes a brief examination of whether text complexity interferes with learning to read through any negative influences it may exercise on affective and behavioral factors. Then we will shift to contemplate motivation and other affective variables as potential outcomes of teaching reading with challenging text, and how teachers can maintain student motivation when teaching them with grade level texts.

The approaches described in the earlier chapters had strong research support. The specific practical recommendations here are necessarily more speculative. Most research on the affective impact of complex text has explored the issue in the context of brief text encounters in which older students read a few short texts. Even when more durable outcomes have been the subject of study, the role of text challenge has rarely been addressed.[2]

MOTIVATION, DIFFICULTY, AND LEARNING

It is worth considering the relationship between motivation and task difficulty. A basic premise of instructional level theory is that attempts to teach children to read with frustration texts will lead to failure and discouragement. This notion is supported by at least some empirical evidence. For instance, one study interviewed middle school students and found that if texts were difficult, student interest declined.[3] This could be important because more positive learning outcomes tend to be achieved when student interest is high.[4] Correlations among motivation and reading comprehension are consistently significant and positive. Much the same could be said about other affective and behavioral variables. Studies of undergraduate students report that higher perceptions of difficulty presage lower interest, more negative attitudes, and higher anxiety.[5]

Time on Task

One widely espoused claim about the instructional level is that it protects against classroom misbehavior. The theory is, basically, students get frustrated when struggling to read difficult text and so act out in the classroom. It appears that students placed in what for them is challenging text do exhibit more behavior problems.[6] This research is not especially convincing, however. A study of students (grades 3 through 5) reported more off-task behavior by students who had been placed in frustration level texts. Despite this, these students were learning as much as the students placed in easier texts, suggesting that the off-task behavior was inconsequential.[7] Another study with a similar pattern of results followed up by shifting the children's placements so that they were working with instructional level texts. This shift resulted in no improvement in behavior.[8] Lower-performing students exhibited more behavioral problems and time off-task, but these differences were evidently not attributable to text placements.

Many studies were aimed at showing that difficulty led to off-task behavior outside the context of the regular classroom. For instance, one study examined the reading instruction of eight first and second graders whom the researchers thought consistently performed at frustration levels in their classwork.[9] Five hours of instruction at each of the independent, instructional, and frustration levels was provided. Much of the time was spent in seatwork tasks. The researchers used separate criteria to determine the level of this seatwork. Students were observed for twenty minutes each day, observing more off-task behavior during frustration and independent level tasks. The text reading and seatwork variables were not separated, however, and off-task behaviors were poorly described. A replication study with three third graders found much the same thing.[10] In another single-subject-design study, four students with learning disabilities were shifted from frustration level text/task placements, and two of them saw improvements in how dutifully they performed.[11] From this, the researchers concluded that frustration level text placement had led to the problem behaviors—though this conclusion was not drawn from the study observations, which were decidedly mixed.

It is possible, however, that such attempts to link reading difficulty with behavioral aberrations may be overstated. In a very different kind of study, this one a qualitative examination of eight high school students in which the students and teachers were observed and interviewed, the researcher documented a tendency among teachers to confound low reading ability with behavioral problems, failing to distinguish them.[12] Low readers were thought to pose behavioral challenges for teachers whether there was misbehavior or not. This researcher concluded from her close-up analysis that the students' overly easy text and task placements were the *cause* of students' low enthusiasm and misbehavior. She, and some of the students themselves, thought the students could handle more challenging texts than the teachers were assigning.

Motivation

Other variables thought to be impacted by text placement include motivation, attitude toward reading, and interest in reading. There seems to be broad acceptance of the idea that "motivation affects learning behaviors and ultimately their learning outcomes."[13] If being taught from a challenging text undermines motive, attitude, or interest, it may harm learning downstream. In a survey study of 1,159 seventh graders, perceived text difficulty (a general feeling that instructional informational books are hard to comprehend) was negatively correlated with reading comprehension.[14] Similar results were obtained with German ninth graders: students who perceived the texts as difficult were less motivated to read those texts.[15] The directionality of this relationship—whether experience with challenging text suppressed comprehension or whether poor comprehension led to negative text evaluations—could not be determined. Nevertheless, the researchers interpreted the perception of text difficulty as an expression of "feelings of incompetence."

Other studies suggest this relationship to be less consistent and damaging. Tessa Roberts, a professor of education at the University of Manchester, tested the reading of 125 second and third graders from six schools and found that 57 percent of the students had been placed in frustration level texts for instruction.[16] Student attitudes towards reading were as positive as those of the "appropriately placed students." Perhaps this should not be surprising given the books students prefer reading when on their own. Even the best readers tend to choose books Betts would have deemed at frustration levels. The appeal of the content, sophistication of the harder texts, and the social cachet of the more challenging books seems to outweigh any discouragement the difficulty might impose.[17]

In a study of 514 fourth graders, researchers had them read fourteen short texts and examined their reactions: "The . . . difficult texts were more interesting for both, boys and girls. However, the relation between text difficulty and text-based interest was stronger for girls than for boys . . . Greater difficulty was associated with greater interest in this study; the more challenging text was more interesting to these fourth graders."[18]

Other researchers considered how interest and affect may be influenced by text placement during reading.[19] To test this hypothesis, sixth and seventh graders read texts at and above their reading levels, and interest and affect were measured immediately before and after each reading. There were variations with individual passages, but generally, this study found that better readers often began reading an instructional level text with interest, but this interest declined as they read. "Demanding tasks can hinder students' motivation resulting in higher negative affect . . . and lower interest and enjoyment."[20] However, the opposite was true when students were asked to read more challenging texts. With those, interest increased as the students read. These results are consistent with modern motivation theory which holds that academic challenge can exercise both positive and negative impacts on motivation.[21]

What is so interesting about these studies is the inconsistency and transiency of the responses. "Effective learning naturally involves challenge. The experience of challenge can lead to various, and sometimes conflicting emotional and motivational responses, which undergo changes as students engage in these tasks."[22] Negative emotions do not necessarily inhibit engagement, and positive ones may not facilitate it. Accordingly, the researchers decried the reluctance of teachers—in fear that challenge will "trigger resistance, disengagement and negative emotions"—to assign challenging reading.

These findings are reminiscent of other studies that have reported interest and other affective variables to be more situational or event-driven than generalized or person-centered.[23] "Contemporary views of engagement suggest that engagement can fluctuate during reading in ways that are sensitive to the context and features of the task."[24] Text difficulty can exert this effect, but so can text content, the novelty of the lesson, and other instructional variables, and these interact—dominating in some cases and compensating in others. Students may be negatively influenced by text difficulty in one instance (e.g., generating feelings of incompetence), and positively influenced by it in another (e.g., feelings of challenge and worthwhile accomplishment).

Mind Wandering

Similar conclusions can be drawn from research on mind wandering, a very different operationalization of time off task. Instead of observing how students behave when reading different kinds of texts, studies of mind wandering use reader reflection and self-report to reveal what may be going on in their minds during reading. Mind wandering studies have posited a U-shaped function, with especially easy and difficult tasks eliciting more daydreaming than moderate difficulty tasks.[25] A meta-analysis of twenty-five studies of mind wandering during reading have found that more mind wandering is related to lower comprehension.[26]

Nevertheless, these patterns are far from universal. Sometimes more difficult texts appear to diminish mind wandering.[27] Even when text difficulty has led to mind wandering, it did not necessarily reduce comprehension.[28] Sometimes it was even beneficial.[29] An important insight can be drawn from the mind-wandering literature. Several studies reported that students' interest, or their sense of the importance or value of the text tended to diminish the effects that the difficulty of the texts exerted on mind wandering.[30] Readers' interest in a difficult text reduces mind wandering. Reducing the amount of text students are required to read continuously, also has a positive impact.[31] Short passages seem to be less conducive to mind wandering. Readers also often compensate for the potentially deleterious effects of mind wandering by spending more time reading[32] or engaging in rereading.[33]

A fundamental problem with affective studies of task difficulty has been with what constitutes excessive struggle. These studies often focus on independent learning tasks, such as assigning students a series of math problems or English Language Arts (ELA) skills lessons.[34] If a student cannot complete a lesson, there is no alternative but to try harder or give up. For the most part, these studies have not considered the instructional level, per se. They consider *easy* versus *difficult*, with no thought as to a concept as specific as the instructional level. What is operationalized as difficult in these studies could be more in line with what is claimed to be the instructional level. Most studies concluded that moderate text placements would be most conducive to comprehension or learning, but without providing any operationalization of moderation. Another important consideration has to do with the variations in findings. Sometimes the harder texts were the ones students found most interesting, so their affective impacts were both positive and negative.

Also, in all these studies, students read passages independently, with no support. Harder texts either resulted in lower comprehension or greater student effort. Such situations may lead students to make unflattering judgments about the texts or themselves, judgments that would be less likely in a directed reading situation. Also, in these studies, the texts had no connection to student learning, so interest or engagement may have been particularly fragile.

Low comprehension of a text may be off-putting, but teachers can effectively mediate these feelings. Some studies showed that text difficulty provoked more effort, not less, and this improved comprehension.[35] Difficulty is also affected by the guidance, support, and scaffolding provided by teachers. This is probably why research shows that more learning accrues from direct instruction when the learning tasks are difficult.[36]

MOTIVATION AS AN OUTCOME

Challenging text may not consistently threaten learning, but perhaps it could undermine interest, motivation, persistence, attention, time on task, and self-concept. Unlike in previous chapters, the concern here is not with learning per se, but with the impact text difficulty may have on motivational or affective factors. Labeling hard books as frustrational encourages an emotional interpretation of their potential effects. I suspect that is why I often hear from teachers who express perplexity about my advocacy of challenging text. They sympathize with the children. They embrace the instructional level to avoid hurt feelings, discouragement, and the barrier they believe it poses for "a love of reading." They cannot understand why such a "nice man" would be so mean and uncaring.

The instructional level concept claims that there are particular levels of difficulty that will interfere with learning and lower the motivation or persistence of all students. However, research shows that individuals differ greatly in their ability to tolerate frustration.[37] Some individuals respond to difficulty with patience, while others may become distressed, displaying anger or withdrawal. That means that while most students are likely to do well while being taught in a grade level text regime, there are others who may react negatively. However, there are various ways that have been identified for relieving such anxiety. The best solution is not to reduce the demands of the curriculum, but to provide appropriate emotional supports that can both mitigate the difficulty in the short run and help these students to better persist in the face of frustration. Much as earlier chapters recommended ways to scaffold student learning of words, fluency, and comprehension, it is possible to scaffold more appropriate emotional responses to frustration.

Motivational theories that consider the role of difficulty tend to hypothesize a link with self-competency or self-efficacy. The basic idea is that if students find reading—or anything else—to be difficult, they may come to see themselves as less competent and will be less likely to engage in reading on their own or to persist when they confront difficulty.[38] It is thought that more competent readers—students who do not find reading difficult—will develop more adaptive behaviors which will allow them to deal with challenge when it does arise, and these students will be more likely to value reading and to enjoy it. At least that is the theory.

Results of empirical studies have not been quite so straightforward. Adolescents who struggle with reading express lower self-efficacy when confronted with grade level texts, and they feel like they have less control and may be anxious about their reading.[39] Generally, better readers express greater intrinsic motivation for reading as well.[40] These correlations, however, are not always this consistent. In some cases, it is the lower performing readers who express greater intrinsic motivation,[41] and there are individual differences in the degree of challenge students prefer.[42] This may be at least part of the reason why some studies report lower motivation for students when asked to read easier texts. They evaluate these texts as more boring or of less value.[43] Another complication is that difficulty and its motivational effects seem to be independent of how valuable students consider reading to be. The degree of reading challenge the texts pose seem irrelevant to their perceived utility or enjoyability.[44] Even struggling readers value reading, sometimes even more than better readers.[45]

It is important to consider the conditional nature of students' motivational responses. There is not only variance across students, but also within students. None of us are always driven by the same forces. We may prefer challenge at times, while other times avoiding it assiduously. That may be why even for those students who express less desire for reading difficult texts in school, there appears to be no relationship of this with their reading preferences and practices when on their own.[46]

Let's face it. Motivation is complicated. Students in a reading lesson may be driven by a desire to please parents, to identify with a teacher, to connect with peers, to seek competence, or to pursue interesting information from the text. These desires not only may reinforce or cancel each other out, but they may stimulate complex responses. Difficulty can lead to both withdrawal and intensification of effort. Motivation can vary minute to minute—students who are motivated early in a text may be less engaged by the end.

One could interpret—or misinterpret—these complexities and inconsistencies as being too unreliable to merit attention.[47] It seems more prudent to acknowledge that perceived difficulty plays a role in motivation, which means under some circumstances or with some students, a steady diet of difficult texts could have negative impacts on motivation. The science of human motivation reveals its negotiable nature. Negative impacts can be attenuated. If students find a text to be interesting, novel, or authentic, or if they have some choice in the matter, then difficulty does not matter or matters less.[48] Fostering adaptive, proactive behaviors, such as goal setting, also leads to fewer negative outcomes, and greater resiliency. Relaxation exercises may help, too.[49] Scaffolding provides beneficial social-emotional support to English language learners as well.[50]

There is a large body of motivational research on "locus of control."[51] Students who believe their success to be due to their own hard work—and not to native abilities like intelligence—are more adaptive, believing they can succeed and being unwilling to give up. The opposite is true as well. If students believe the reason for their struggle is their own incompetence, then maintaining interest or a positive attitude would be unlikely, since it seems to them that there is nothing they can do. Learning how to surmount comprehension barriers should prevent this sense of helplessness, leading to a greater sense of adaptability and competence.

One problem with instructional level theory is that it treats motivation simplistically. It assumes that difficulty alone matters and that if instruction is arranged so that students will find texts easy, then they will want to read and want to learn to read. Students may want to avoid difficulty, but they also may prefer to work with text better aligned with their maturity levels.[52] Assigning a fourth grader to a second-grade book may make reading easier and fool kids into thinking they are doing better, but it could also attenuate motivation. The embarrassment inherent in low group assignment has disheartened more than a few children. I suspect that a steady diet of such instruction does more to discourage personal reading than would ever result from working with grade level texts. Sadly, in far too many classrooms, students are not even allowed *to try* to read books on their own if they are not at "just the right" level,[53] enforcing a sense that "you are a low reader and there is nothing you can do to overcome the limits that imposes."

Instructional level theory holds that it is success in comprehension that has motivational power, and so its adherents assign relatively easy texts.

This ignores students' motivation to learn. The minimal nature of learning from a text one can already read well would make daily progress subtle, perhaps even imperceptible. Kids are not likely to have much sense of gain—except when advanced a level—and this success or failure is distinctly external in nature. If you make the difference between success and failure too subtle, then students will be unaware of their own progress. No one is likely to get too excited about a lesson in which they went from 94 percent accuracy to 97 percent accuracy, or 80 percent to 85 percent in comprehension. By contrast, starting with a text that one obviously cannot read well, and by the end of the lessons being able to, provides more credible evidence of success.

Even when teachers are scrupulous in their efforts to match texts to students, the matches will not always be apt. Sometimes the texts will be more difficult than anticipated. When that happens, both teachers and students may be frustrated. This is because teachers have few alternatives to turn to. That is why when mismatches occur, teachers so often end up reading the text to the students or telling them what it says. A positive sense of self-efficacy develops from accomplishment. It is hard to feel accomplishment in these situations. From existing data, there is no reason to think that learning to read with challenging texts—frustration level texts—would have long term negative consequences for reading motivation or interest.

MOTIVATIONAL SCAFFOLDS FOR WORKING WITH CHALLENGING TEXT

I do not claim that text difficulty may not have negative impacts on student affect, but rather that those effects when they do arise are likely to be transitory and malleable. Whatever the motivational effects of text difficulty may be, they can be offset by teacher guidance. Unfortunately, there is little research on the effectiveness of these kinds of motivational supports regarding text difficulty, though there are such studies in other learning venues.[54] Nevertheless, given the extensive scholarship on motivation, it is possible to make reasonable recommendations. The following suggestions are not exhaustive but should go a long way towards providing students with a positive and nurturing learning environment.

Apprise Students of the Situation

Motivation is heavily impacted by students' interpretations of their circumstances. If students think difficulty is due to task demands, they respond differently than if they attribute it to their own incompetency.[55] Let students know that you are intentionally placing them in texts they will not already be able to read well, and that your purpose—through a series of lessons—is to enable them to do so.

Motivational research emphasizes the importance of clear learning goals.[56] Knowing what is expected and what is to be accomplished shifts control to the students and helps support a positive, adaptive mind set when it comes to learning. When I explain this to students, I tell them about the instructional level and how I used to teach with books students would have little trouble with—and how little learning took place. I make sure they know that if I still taught like that, many of them would be placed in books a grade level or two below the other kids. I also tell them that I do not expect them to read this selection on their own. But with my assistance and their effort, their ability to handle this text will improve. I understand how hard the task is going to be and I trust and respect that they will strive to meet the challenge.

Sometimes students want to see for themselves how hard the text would be if they read it on their own. If so, let them give it a try. They can read it aloud or silently depending on the problems you think the text may pose. Have them write a short summary when they finish or answer some of your questions. You may expect this to be discouraging, but it tends to generate excitement. Sometimes they ask to try even harder texts. They feel challenged and respected, proud that their teacher believes they can successfully handle difficulty.

Scaffold Success

Ultimately, it is not difficulty that undermines motivation, but failure. Failure conveys a sense of incompetence.[57] "I know I'm stupid because I couldn't read that." The instructional level attempts to prevent such inadaptability by ensuring success. No one fails to comprehend. That kind of success can be pyrrhic, however. "I can read a baby text." If the challenge is insufficient, then any victory is meaningless.[58] Assigning students to challenging texts and making them successful—that is, making sure they can read and understand the text by the end of the lessons—is the key to raising reading achievement and to supporting attributions of value and competence.

Teachers must match the amount and type of scaffolding to the circumstance. If students are struggling to read a text fluently, then teaching words and guiding repeated reading makes sense. The same can be said for all other scaffolds. Preview the texts to try to anticipate problems—identifying words students may not know, sentences that might trip them up, and so on.

Likewise, tailor "comprehension questions" not to a scheme like Bloom's taxonomy, but to revealing likely failures to understand. When misunderstandings are uncovered, return to the text to guide efforts to figure it out.

Encourage students to keep a close watch on their own success, too. If they notice misunderstandings—including when they just feel lost—then it becomes possible for teachers to offer effective guidance. As far as that feeling of being lost, I recommend starting over; working through the text sentence by sentence or paragraph by paragraph to ensure a firm foothold as the basis for further reading.

Foster Improvement Awareness

Even when students are successful, they may fail to perceive success.[59] This happens when they lack appropriate goals. For instance, if students think they should be able to read a text perfectly with no mistakes, that is likely to be a dispositive goal when working with a text they can read with only 80 percent accuracy. It would be more reasonable to aim for an "instructional level"—90 to 95 percent accuracy.

How we talk to students about what they are doing and the implications of their efforts matter.[60] If you want students to develop an adaptability mindset, it helps to provide encouraging commentary. Emphasize success and the idea that success comes from informed effort. Make sure students see failure or difficulty as a temporary condition that can be overcome. Teaching with more challenging text provides heightened possibilities of student awareness of their own learning progress. Towards that end, it can be useful to set aside a small amount of time at the end of a lesson to have students appraise themselves and their progress. Asking "What were you able to do with this text at the end that you couldn't at the beginning?" is a good idea. If students are improving in something but not noticing, assurance should be provided. Teachers should provide specific examples of the improvement progress that is being made.

Be Positive and Encouraging

Recently, I took on a challenge that seemed beyond my ability. My wife, Cyndie, and I, both in our seventies, decided to go to the Himalayas to climb to Mt. Everest base camp at over 18,000 feet. We found it to be unbelievably hard. Everything about it was a challenge—the distances, the altitude, the rough terrain, the unfamiliar food, the need to drink great quantities of water, the cold, the lack of showers, the miserably hard beds, and so on. Our guides monitored our progress closely but were also unfailingly enthusiastic and encouraging. They did whatever they could to keep our heads in the game and to make sure that we were feeling as successful as possible, at times under brutal conditions.

Anyone who has ever run a 5K run or watched a kids' t-ball game has witnessed the frequent applause and cheering that is offered for almost any success, no matter how trivial or insignificant. When anyone is taking on something they find to be potentially discouraging, they benefit from enthusiastic reassurance. Smile. Pat kids on the back. Shake their hands. Nod profusely. Bump fists. Behaviorists refer to these actions as "positive reinforcement."[61] The tougher the challenge, the more of it that is needed.

However, the behaviorists did not go far enough. Modern day cognitive psychologists stress the need to make sure students not only know they did well, but also make them aware of what they did well and why it matters.[62] A teacher might say: "Remember when I was teaching you about how an author connects ideas across a text. The only way you could have gotten that question right is if you recognized that this . . . and this . . . were the same thing. That's why you knew that. . . . Good job." Feedback like that is both motivational *and* educative—students are rewarded for something specific which increases their understanding of why or how they succeeded.[63] This makes it more likely the student will rely on that behavior productively in the future, making them more adaptive and persistent.

Teach Texts Worth Reading

Text selection matters. More should go into that than just determining how difficult a text is likely to be. The content and its potential relationship to the readers matters, too. Interest can override difficulty when it comes to reading.[64] Readers who might be put off by a demanding text will often ignore difficulty if intrigued by what the text has to say. Think about all those low readers who have busted their tails to read *Harry Potter*!

Find out your students' interests. Ask them. But also, do some research. For decades, the International Literacy Association together with the Children's Book Council have identified what students in different age groups want to read and what they enjoy reading.[65] Such lists can be helpful in identifying specific books but also in providing guidance to topics and types of texts students like. Often, when a district is adopting new reading textbooks, they involve teachers in reviewing the books. It can be wise to involve students in a selection process, having them rate the selections in terms of their interest.[66] Another consideration in providing books that students would choose to read—beyond topical interest—is cultural representation; students often seek texts in which they can see themselves.[67]

Recognize the Power of Choice

The need for control plays an important role in motivation. People tend to be motivated when they feel that they have some autonomy or control over their situation. That is why motivation is believed to lead to more adaptive behaviors—greater proactivity, persistence, and resilience and less withdrawal and aggressive response. Giving students the chance to choose or to express preferences can mitigate the negative impacts of difficulty.[68] This may entail identifying two or three selections that could be the instructional focus for the week and allowing kids to weigh in on which texts they would prefer. Research shows that even such narrow choices can have a positive impact on the reading comprehension of difficult text. This approach can be taken if a teacher is willing to work with multiple groups, since expressing a preference and then having it stifled is not motivational. Kids are likely to differ over texts, so making sure everyone gets a top choice or one of their two top choices is important.

Choice is not always about which text to read or which topic to explore. Students might be given a choice over who they want to work with, where certain work will be completed within the classroom, or the sequence of events for the lesson. The point is to convey a sense of control and empowerment to the students dealing with difficulty, and choice can play an important part in that.[69]

Don't Overdo It—Not Every Text Must Be Challenging

Athletic training schedules have long championed the benefits of varying difficulty. Someone preparing to run a marathon must build up to twenty-six miles. This requires more than just running a lot each week. Proper training requires a constant variation in challenge levels—both up and down. One popular training plan calls for four runs each week with the first week including fifteen miles of total running (three miles, then four, three, five). The weekly totals increase each week: 15, 16, 17, 19, 21, 24, but the really interesting part is the daily variation: 3, 4, 6, 3, 4, 7, 3, 5, 3, 8, 3, 5, 3, 10, 4, 5, 4, 11. This increasing and decreasing degree of difficulty protects against injury, better conditions blood flow and skeletal musculature development, encourages better physical and psychological adaptation, and reduces the monotony of training.[70]

Athletic training and reading instruction are different animals, but such training variations also make sense with cognitive instruction. Varying the difficulty or intensity level of training has positive impacts on some cognitive learning[71] and on memory tasks more generally.[72] Minimizing challenge variation in instruction is a self-defeating approach. Students should be asked to read a lot at school, across English Language Arts, science, social studies and so on. Everyone agrees that the texts used for this should vary (e.g., fiction, non-fiction, narrative, exposition, genres, topics). Text should also differ in degree of challenge. If every text is super hard, training will be monotonous, and enthusiasm will flag.

I am reasoning by analogy here, but I think it makes sense to start with a relatively easy text (e.g., three miles), and then ramp up the difficulty. I want students to see the difference in a three-mile and an eight-mile text—that should allow them to attribute difficulty to the texts and not to their own competence. I also want them to see how much simpler that three-mile text is when it follows a much more challenging one. It makes sense to vary the amounts of scaffolding too, offering more assistance the tougher the course. It helps student confidence when a teacher will help as needed. Vary text lengths, as well: with relatively easy texts, provide longer and less supportive reads, shortening the distances and increasing assistance with harder texts, supporting both motivation and endurance.

These seven suggestions should help keep students engaged when taught with potentially frustrating texts. They also should help students to develop more adaptive mindsets for reading, recognizing the nature of text challenges, while developing the tools that allow for success in surmounting those barriers. Don't avoid potential frustration, but guide students to deal with it successfully.

CHAPTER 9

Conclusions and Answers to Practical Questions

What is a teacher to make of all this? You've now read this book, so what to do daily in the classroom? Because this book challenges conventional wisdom, there is not yet an extended body of research or teacher lore pertinent to the daily instructional decisions that teaching with challenging text requires. Existing research is sufficient for determining that exposure to more challenging text is beneficial, but not for providing detailed guidance for the best ways to implement it. Chapters 6, 7, and 8 repurposed well-studied instructional approaches to facilitate student learning from grade level text. That is as far as the research can be prudently stretched. Accordingly, this chapter offers responses to teacher questions based on experience, logic, and what I hope is intelligent guesswork. Relevant research is referenced where possible, but the density of endnotes and bibliographic references is markedly less than in earlier chapters.

After this practical catechism, the entire volume is summarized, and final conclusions are presented. According to the Merriam-Webster dictionary, the word *cogent* comes from the Latin verb *cogere*, meaning "to drive or force together." Something described as cogent fuses thoughts and ideas into a meaningful whole.[1] The purpose of this summary is to connect or "drive together" the distinct points made throughout the book to articulate a brief, coherent and, I hope, convincing argument for why grade level text is the best ground for reading instruction.

RESPONSES TO TEACHER QUESTIONS

How Do I Plan Lessons with Complex Text?

Start with the mindset that reading is the ability to make sense of text—and that readers must learn how to negotiate those text features that convey the meaning. Read the instructional texts before the students do. This seemingly obvious advice is essential if you are to identify potential barriers to understanding. Use the text features described in chapters 6, 7, and 8 as a list of possibilities to consider. It may help to take on one feature at a time. Your ability to spot these barriers will improve with experience. I often recommend that teachers do this together; conversation increases sensitivity. Then, when teaching these lessons, pay attention to how it turns out. There will be surprises both ways, features that cause unanticipated confusions, and those you thought would be barriers that turn out not to be.

Aim your questions at these potential barriers. Here is a brief passage from Robert Lawson's *Mr. Popper's Penguins* that may trip kids up—because of complex syntax and subtle cohesion: "Even when he was busiest smoothing down the paste on the wallpaper, or painting the outside of other people's houses, he would forget what he was doing. Once he had painted three sides of a kitchen green, and the other side yellow."[2] The grammar of the first sentence presents a premise and a consequent—when he was busy, he forgot what he was doing. What makes this hard is the memory effort it requires—readers must remember the premise while they consider two separate examples of it before the consequent is presented. The next sentence provides an example of a consequent without a restatement of the premise. Readers must stitch those ideas together to end up with a coherent understanding.

The simplest way to know for sure if this complexity is a barrier is to query students. A teacher might ask, "Why did he paint one side of the kitchen yellow?" If the students can answer the question, there is nothing more to do. However, for planning purposes, I would be ready to show how to break down this sentence and connect the ideas. If this is new to them, I would demonstrate how I would deal with it. If it has come up before, I would guide the students to break the sentence down themselves, assisting as little as necessary.

How Challenging Can a Text Be Before It Is No Longer Useful? Some Of My Students Are Far Behind Grade Level

There are two answers to this question—one theoretical, the other practical. The theoretical response is that there is no bridge too far, no challenge too great, and no text too complex. Theoretically, no matter how hard a text, it can be successfully scaffolded, and there is reason to think this is possible. Here I would consider an interesting case study. Grace Fernald, an influential educational psychologist, described her work with a thirteen-year-old who was a total non-reader.[3] She took him to the library and asked which book he would like to learn to read. He impishly chose the fattest encyclopedia volume he could find, what to him must have seemed like the hardest book in the world.

Dr. Fernald's response? "Sure, I'll teach you to read that."

The good doctor Fernald was the one who came up with tactile-kinesthetic approaches to teaching reading, with all the tracing of words and such. She literally took the first word in the book and wrote it down and had him tracing it. I can't remember how many years she worked with this student, but at the end of some length of time he could read the whole doggone book. Now that's scaffolding!

Theory tells us what is possible, and here it suggests that with sufficient scaffolding and support there is no chasm between student and text that cannot be overcome. The practical response is less rosy. We must consider how much lesson time there is, how different that student is from the other twenty-five kids in the class, his or her degree of motivation, and so on.

Scaffolding someone to read a difficult text takes time in real classrooms with real kids. There can be gulfs too wide to bridge successfully with available resources. In grades 4 and up, I think scaffolding across two years of difficulty is par for the course. If your fourth graders read at a second- or third-grade level, lessons from a fourth-grade science textbook will not present too much of a challenge. By middle school, three-year gaps can usually be effectively bridged with the approaches proposed earlier. If fluency practice with the texts is provided prior to the lesson, you might be able to guide students with even more challenging texts. The bigger the gaps, the more likely that fluency and word reading supports will be needed.

What Levels of Text Should Students Read for Independent Reading?

Betts made no effort to validate his independent level criteria. The independent level was more of a side effect of the instructional level. Since 98 percent accuracy was the highest indicator of instructional text, then the independent level had to be easier than that—more a logical offshoot than a set of empirical criteria. According to Betts, for students to make headway with a text, they must be able to read it nearly perfectly, with no assistance. Such texts can be read independently since kids will find them to be super easy. Neither Betts, nor anyone else, has said what independent leveled texts should deliver in terms of enjoyment, learning, sense of competence, and so on.

Not surprisingly, poor readers, when left to their own devices, select books above their supposed reading levels. That makes sense because their interests will usually outstrip their reading abilities. Interests are better aligned with age than reading levels. What is surprising is that this aspirational tendency is almost as evident with better readers.[4] About 70 percent of struggling readers choose books above level, and about 60 percent of the better readers do! Studies report no relationship between student enjoyment of books and the degree to which the books match independent reading levels, and students rarely refer to difficulty when they discuss their book selections.[5] Reading desires rarely correspond to independent level criteria.

Let kids read what they want to read on their own—or at least let them give it a try. Even instructional level advocates reject the idea of limiting kids' free reading to certain levels.[6] Often teachers and librarians limit children's reading to this figment-of-the-imagination "independent reading level," instilling a dread of reading and a fear of failure. Rather than sequestering the hard books and prohibiting children from trying to read books on the H shelves or in the L bins, it would be better to encourage them to take a chance. "Billy, that book on World War II may be hard for you but give it a try. If you find it too difficult, let me know and I'll help you find an easier one on that subject." Kids should learn there is nothing wrong with discontinuing a book in the middle or to read it more than once to get what it says. Perhaps let them check out two books—the desired one and a similar easier one. Reading independence is not a matter of text levels, but of desire and courage. Give kids a chance to explore both.

My Students Read at Different Speeds, Which Makes Directed Reading Lessons Hard to Manage. Any Suggestions?

The longer the text segment, the greater the disparities in time needed to read it. I find that shortening the text segments reduces disparities. This works, but it can work against the building of reading stamina—some of the time, we want kids to do longer reads and with practice, text segments should lengthen. Another possibility is to provide fluency practice for slower readers. Let's say that tomorrow you are going to provide a directed reading lesson with a challenging text. Then, today use the fluency instruction to have those slower readers practice the new text. That should bolster their participation in tomorrow's lesson, reducing the time disparities.

In My Class, the Better Readers Tend to Answer Most of the Questions. That Makes It Hard for Me to Determine How Well the Other Kids Are Doing. What Should I Do?

This is a common problem with reading discussions of any kind of text. Teachers use their questions to reveal comprehension breakdowns, but once a student answers the question, everyone else knows the answer, too. I prefer written responses. That slows things down a bit, but it allows every student to go on the record for each question. That supports a much better discussion and enables teachers to understand how their students are doing. Notebooks or white boards should be out during a reading lesson. These days electronic apps like *Poll Everywhere, Slido, Mentimeter, Kahoot,* and many others can make the opportunity for answering available to everyone simultaneously.

When some of the kids' answers reveal a text barrier, do not hesitate to explore the problem with the whole class. Guiding everyone through those barriers should help sensitize those who struggled as well as those who managed to deal with it this time. Often the kids who succeeded do not know why they did.

I'm Not Convinced That Students Don't Benefit from Small Group Instruction. Can Small Group Teaching Play a Role in Teaching with Complex Text?

Yes, it can. Unlike with the instructional level, however, the point of such groups is not to protect students from grade level books. For example, it is possible that only some of the boys and girls require fluency practice and word teaching prior to guided reading. The teacher might have those kids practicing reading the text orally, while the rest of the kids are engaged in seatwork. Another possibility is that some kids may not need to do any more with a text beyond the guided reading lesson, while others might benefit from some rereading. Perhaps a teacher wants to teach with only one text, but to vary the amount of scaffolding. One group may receive a more streamlined lesson than the more challenged group. Small group teaching should be a tool that helps the teacher to make sure all students learn the curriculum.

You Mentioned Repetition. How Much Rereading Should Students Do?

Rereading has not played a big role in past reading instruction. That makes sense when the texts are relatively easy. With harder texts, rereading has a bigger role to play. Rereading is valuable when a barrier has been discovered—you will want to take the students back into the text immediately to reread the portion that disrupted comprehension.

However, reading the text again after the directed reading lesson makes sense, too, giving students a chance to read the text with their new learning readily available. This should allow students to gain a fuller understanding and more coherent memory of the text content—increasing learning, while providing a more successful and coherent grade level reading experience. Rereading is less of a chore when students can see the difference in their success across readings. Sometimes later in the year, I like to take students back to an earlier text that presented a great challenge. Having them take another swing at such texts can make their progress especially apparent, while revisiting some barriers that may continue to interfere with their comprehension.

In Our School, the Pullout Reading Teacher Teaches the Struggling Students with Instructional Level Text. Should Intervention Teachers Teach with Complex Text, Too?

In a regular classroom, teachers are expected to deal with twenty to thirty kids, who often have widely disparate reading levels. They may try to limit this variability by working with small groups while managing the rest of the class, which can be a real challenge. Some classroom teachers may have advanced training in reading instruction; most don't. They are responsible for teaching not only all the aspects of the English Language Arts, but the other subjects, too. Regular classroom teachers may group for reading, but they rarely do that with science or social studies textbooks, texts that may be even more challenging than the grade level reading books.

Contrast those circumstances with a typical elementary reading intervention (Tier 2). Interventionists usually deal with fewer students, and they may be able to establish a schedule that narrows variations in ability. Interventionists rarely manage students they are not directly teaching. They typically have advanced training in reading instruction, and they almost never deal with other subjects. Despite these decidedly advantaged circumstances, interventionists often proudly teach students at their instructional reading levels.

Anyone should be able to see that more substantial scaffolding of challenging reading could be provided more easily in the intervention room than in the regular classroom. Third-grade teachers notice that some students are reading at a second-grade level, and this upends their ability to teach with the science or social studies textbooks. They refer those students for remediation. The intervention teacher spends the year teaching those kids to read second-grade text. The classroom teachers are dubious since the students still cannot read their classroom textbooks. To them, the intervention looks useless; its only benefit is getting those lower achievers out of the room for a while.

Struggling readers need more opportunities to read and reread grade level materials with support—such as taking on such texts in the intervention class and then reading them again in the classroom with less support. Kids will make more growth that way than in the upside-down approaches that we are now using (upside down in the sense that when maximum scaffolding is available we teach students with the easiest texts).

How Much Time in Reading Class Should Students Be Reading?

Research generally has found that kids do better in classes with more reading but has not identified any certain amounts that are optimum.[7] Students should read a lot in school. Here I am not talking about independent reading—reading kids do without instruction. Students need to read in reading class, and throughout the rest of the curriculum, too.

In a directed reading lesson, there should be a balance between the reading and the teaching and discussion. When students are working with text that is challenging, it is to be expected that they will read more slowly. Likewise, since there will be greater possibility of misunderstanding, the guided parts of the lessons—the part with teacher and student talk—may need to be more extended, too. That means that guided reading time will be longer than in the past, though the balance between talking and reading should remain. Devoting less time to teaching different books to different groups of children should free up sufficient time to make way for such teaching and reading.

Given the lack of empirical evidence on this question, I recommend that teachers experiment with a fifty-fifty split. In a thirty-minute guided reading lesson, the kids would be reading for fifteen minutes. Try that and adjust up or down based on progress.

Does Artificial Intelligence (AI) Have Any Potential Role in This Kind of Teaching?

It is probably too early to decide, but I have found some uses for it already. The large language models of AI make it handy for identifying lower frequency vocabulary, certain grammatical structures, or types of cohesive links.

If you have an electronic version of an instructional text, those kinds of analyses are easily accomplished. They are not perfect, but they can help identify potential barriers. Then teachers can closely examine these items to see which they think will be most likely to hinder their students' understanding. Likewise, AI can generate potential questions about parts of the text that can help uncover failures to comprehend. In the future, it may prove to be even more useful than this.

I Teach Many Multilingual Learners. Does Complex Text Make Sense with Them?

It does, but that depends on how much English they have. Sarah Lupo and her colleagues found that, with secondary students, the only ones who failed to read successfully with the scaffolds they provided were the lowest performing English language learners.[8] Much of the scaffolding recommended in the previous chapters takes advantage of the students' oral English, something that newcomers are unlikely to have. Once students have attained a reasonable amount of basic conversational English, then they can be quite successful with more complex English text, if there is sufficient and appropriate scaffolding.[9]

Many of the language scaffolds described in chapter 7 provide more explicit language teaching than is usually available in regular classrooms, which can be a real boon to Multilingual Learners. Of course, selecting texts that correspond well with their cultural knowledge and aspirations can be especially supportive.

When Teaching with Complex Text, How Do I Evaluate Success?

One way to monitor success is to evaluate student performance with rereading. Is their ability to handle those familiar texts improving? Perhaps for the past nine weeks, students have been reading and rereading grade level texts. Fashion a brief assessment with passages from some of those texts. How well can they read them now? Their reading of such texts—because of the work that they did with them—should have improved. It can also be useful to evaluate performance with comparable grade level texts that they have not yet tried. How is their fluency and comprehension with those? This is a higher standard, so I would expect clearer gains with the familiar texts.

Students' self-evaluations matter, too, not for grading and reports to parents, but in their own sense of progress. Returning to texts that earlier they had struggled with can provide them with a sense of their own learning. It can be very motivating to see that a text that seemed so hard before is now noticeably easier.

What Should We Do with the Texts in Content Area Classes?

Too often content area teachers—and elementary teachers who teach science and social studies—try to meet the challenges of demanding content textbooks through round robin reading, with kids reading snippets of text aloud and the teacher explaining the text meaning. Or the textbooks may sit on a shelf unused, the teacher providing key information through Powerpoint lectures or videos. These efforts avoid texts rather than making sure students can learn from them. This is a big mistake.

The scaffolding suggested for reading lessons makes as much sense with content texts. This is especially true as students advance through the grades, because the linguistic and text features of literature, mathematics, science, and social studies become more distinctive.[10] The sentences one finds in a high school science book are quite different from those in a comparable social studies book. There are more clauses and fewer phrases in science sentences, and verbs tend to come later in the sentences. Graphics play a different role, too. Human intentionality matters more in literature than science, so scaffolding character goals is valuable in the one and immaterial in the other. Directing student reading in the various content areas matters greatly in the development of awareness of these specialized disciplinary demands.[11]

You Suggest That We Should Vary the Difficulty of Texts. What Is the Best Way to Do This?

Varied difficulty has both cognitive and affective benefits. Unfortunately, we have nothing like the validated performance-enhancing schedules that athletes use to vary the difficulty of their exercise and training routines. But those routines suggest patterns we may consider. Earlier, I described a training schedule used to prepare marathon runners. I applied that template to text choices for third graders. The Common Core indicates that third graders should learn to read texts ranging from 520 Lexiles to 820 Lexiles; I simplified that to 500L to 800L. To match the marathon schedule, I treated 50L differences as the equivalent of one-mile differences. If a third grade used this preparation schedule, about 70 percent of their reading would be with texts at the lowest levels of the grade level span. Most of their instruction would be with texts ranging 500L to 600L. By the second semester, texts that easy would only appear about 15 percent of the time. Nevertheless, even late in the year, students might be asked to read something as easy as 500L.

Increases in difficulty from one text to another would vary as little as 50L and as much as 300L. The 50L shifts may not even be noticeable, but those in the 200L to 300L range certainly would be. Usually, these difficulty increases would be brief. If the increase was 200L, it would be followed immediately by a similar decrease. Occasionally, these would not be full retreats, and text difficulty would adjust down, just not as much as it had recently risen. Perhaps the increase would be 200L, but the backdown would only be 100L or 150L.

Remember, there is no science to this yet, but these ideas have some logic: lots of work at the lowest target levels of difficulty, some big jumps in difficulty, but not too many, some increases big enough to be daunting, increases followed by decreases, and gradual increases with the floor or the average text levels rising gradually over time. A plan that varies difficulty but that neither overdoes the challenging text demands nor makes the learning progression into an arduous and unremitting climb without relief makes a lot of sense.

What About Students Who Read Above Grade Level?

Let's consider some possibilities. One option is to do nothing special. Simply teach them along with everyone else. Their reading is not likely to improve much from that practice, but it would not be damaged by it either. That would be efficient, but it should offend the sensibilities of anyone committed to the success of all students. An attractive variation is to be especially careful that the content of these texts is interesting and worthwhile. That way, even if their reading makes no improvement, they will have a chance to gain valuable knowledge anyway.

Another idea is to exempt these students from some directed reading lessons, allowing them to read on their own or to work on the computer. This may deliver some modest reading benefits since the kids would likely choose more mature texts, and they may enjoy it. Nevertheless, too much of this can lead to feelings of isolation or exclusion. Some teachers may prefer to work with multiple groups. Teaching the kids who cannot yet read third-grade text well with the third-grade texts, and those who have already mastered that level with above grade texts. That way everyone has a chance to work with challenging texts with teacher supervision and guidance. Still another possibility is "walking reading," letting a third grader go to a fourth or fifth grade class for reading instruction.[12] If done right, this works.

Carol Connor and her colleagues found, at least with younger kids, that those who are reading at relatively high levels were the most able to work profitably on their own, away from a teacher.[13] That means it is possible to engage advanced readers in pedagogically meaningful activities, with less teacher attention during class time. Some semi-independent activities that make sense are Literature Circles,[14] Book Club,[15] and Project Based Instruction;[16] pretty much any pedagogical activity that involves collaborative inquiry or cooperative learning. For the most part, these are activities ordinarily carried out with direct teacher supervision and explicit instruction. The above grade readers should be able to gain from these activities with relatively less explicit teacher support.

SUMMARY AND LAST WORDS

Social scientists and historians have catalogued the essential pillars of a liberal society,[17] including a broad array of beliefs, cultural mores, and institutional characteristics. These lists describe fundamental freedoms (e.g., press, assembly, religion), limited or constrained government including equality and individual rights before the law, private property, separation of powers, independent judiciary with due process for all, checks and balances among governmental branches, multi-party systems, civilian control of the military, and commitments to pluralism and tolerance.

Any thoughtful consideration of any of these pillars reveals the essential role of education. If these ideals are to be vouchsafed, then education—both wide (for all) and deep (capable of enabling a high level of social, economic, and civic participation along with self- realization)—must be provided. As Thomas Jefferson famously wrote, “If a nation expects to be ignorant and free, in a state of civilization, it expects what never was and never will be.” Education, in a twenty-first century liberal society, must empower its citizens to read complex and subtle text thoughtfully and critically.

Although United Nations statistics report nearly 100 percent literacy in English speaking nations, those figures only tally the lowest levels of literacy attainment—the ability to read and write simple messages.[18] The Programme for International Student Assessment (PISA) provides a more nuanced description of the high-level literacy needed if the liberal vision of human society is to be realized:

> Tasks at this level typically require the reader to make multiple inferences, comparisons and contrasts that are both detailed and precise. They require demonstration of a full and detailed understanding of one or more texts and may involve integrating information from more than one text. Tasks

> may require the reader to deal with unfamiliar ideas, in the presence of prominent competing information, and to generate abstract categories for interpretations. Reflect and evaluate tasks may require the reader to hypothesise about or critically evaluate a complex text on an unfamiliar topic, taking into account multiple criteria or perspectives, and applying sophisticated understandings from beyond the text. A salient condition for access and retrieve tasks at this level is precision of analysis and fine attention to detail that is inconspicuous in the texts.[19]

That is their description of the highest levels of literacy reached by fifteen-year-olds around the world. More specifically, it indicates that to be fully literate students must be able to gain "a full and detailed understanding of a text whose content or form is unfamiliar," including "dealing with concepts that are contrary to expectations,"[20] and be able to "demonstrate an accurate understanding of long or complex texts whose content or form may be unfamiliar."[21]

Unfortunately, as has been documented here, the American system of education seems carefully designed to prevent most students from even gaining the opportunity to try to attain these levels of literacy. American youngsters who fall behind in the early years of their education may never catch up in a system that insists that they can only learn to read texts at their current literacy levels. The idea of expecting students to read long, complex, unfamiliar texts is foreign to American reading instruction, which has more often tried to shield students from such experiences. None of the instructional level schemes is solidly evidence-based, and all ensure that large numbers of children will be taught below the text levels that have been staircased to ensure that by high school graduation they will be able to participate productively in higher education, the workplace, or military service.

This pedagogical strategy has its historical roots in well-meaning efforts to make education attractive by making it easy, and to differentiate instruction to meet the needs of all students. These efforts have gained intellectual respectability by links—albeit superficial links—to widely respected psychological theories. As each theory went out of style, instructional level theory has been espoused on behalf of whatever thinking took its place. Nevertheless, an exhaustive examination of research aimed at evaluating the effectiveness of teaching students with such easy texts revealed that the approach provided little if any benefit, and often did more harm than good. Additional analyses revealed why this commonsensical approach failed—given the limitations of student testing, text leveling, and homogenously-grouped teaching.

It is important to remember that instructional level teaching works in the sense that most students taught with books at their instructional level make some learning progress. It is likely that most people reading these words were taught by that approach. The problem is not its total ineffectiveness, but the severe limits it places on the literacy attainment of large numbers of students who would do better if taught with more demanding texts.

Admittedly, teaching students to read—and to learn about the natural and social worlds from challenging texts—requires more on the part of teachers than current pedagogical practices. Teachers are not expected to do very much when reading is taught mainly by having students practice with book they can already read reasonably well. Instead of all the student testing aimed at determining reading levels, the management of leveled book collections, and the juggling of instructional groups, teacher efforts would better be expended towards anticipating barriers to understanding, recognizing failures to comprehend, and guiding students to surmount these barriers. We must turn those comprehension failures into opportunities to learn. They should be the basis of our teaching. Such work is challenging, of course, but to tell the truth it is also particularly rewarding. It is more heartening to teach students to read better than to observe their reading practice with texts that allow little room for improvement.

Any serious effort to increase literacy rates in the United States and other Western nations must pivot from these seemingly endless arguments over letters and sounds. Enhancing early literacy will not translate to higher literacy rates for high school graduates without a substantial recognition of and commitment to the importance and value of teaching students to read more complex texts.[22] This will only be accomplished when educators acknowledge the fruitlessness of teaching students with books they can already read. It is time that we dedicate ourselves to ensuring that every child has the greatest opportunity to accomplish the highest levels of literacy. It is time to throw off the ideological cloak that claims that matching texts to student reading levels maximizes literacy, and to don new pedagogical vestments more in line with a science of reading. Leveled reading instruction, indeed, levels lives.

Notes

To supplement the endnotes, a complete bibliography for each chapter is provided online at: https://hep.gse.harvard.edu/9798895570036/leveled-reading-leveled-lives/.

Introduction

1. A. J. Liebling, *The Road Back to Paris* (Literary Classics of the United States, 2008), 213.
2. National Center for Education Statistics, *National Assessment of Educational Progress (NAEP) 2022 Reading Assessment* (National Center for Education Statistics, Institute of Education Sciences, 2022).
3. Irwin S. Kirsch et al., *Adult Literacy in America*, 3rd ed. (US Department of Education, 2002).
4. Tom Krenzke et al., *Program for the International Assessment of Adult Competencies (PIAAC): State and County Estimation Methodology Report* (NCES 2020–225); US Department of Education, National Center for Education Statistics (US Government Printing Office, 2020); Jonathon Rothwell, *Assessing Economic Gains of Eradicating Illiteracy Nationally and Regionally in the United States* (Barbara Bush Foundation for Family Literacy, 2020).
5. Andrew Sum, *Literacy in the Labor Force* (US Department of Education, 1999).
6. Darren Dewalt and Michael P. Pignone, "The Role of Literacy in Health and Health Care," *American Family Physician* 72, no. 3 (August 2005): 387–88.
7. David Kaplan and Richard L. Venezky, *Literacy and Voting Behavior: A Statistical Analysis Based on the 1985 Young Adult Literacy Survey* (National Center on Adult Literacy, 1995); Kirsch et al., *Adult Literacy*.
8. Lester R. Collins, Jr. et al., "State-Wise Variation in Teenage Birth Rates in the United States: Role of Teenage Birth Prevention Policies," in *Child and Adolescent Health Yearbook 2014,* ed. Joav Merrick (Nova Biomedical Books, 2015); Kirsch et al., *Adult Literacy*; Zeinab Nemati, and Hossein Matlabi, "Assessing Behavioral Patterns of Internet Addiction and Drug Abuse Among High School Students," *Psychology Research and Behavior Management* 10, no. 7 (2017): 39–45; Margaret J. Snowling et al., "Levels of Literacy Among Juvenile Offenders: The Incidence of Specific Reading Difficulties," *Criminal Behaviour and Mental Health* 10, no. 4 (2000): 229–41.
9. Ina V. S. Mullis et al., *PIRLS (Progress in International Reading Literacy Study) 2021 International Results in Reading* (Boston College, Trends in International Mathematics and Science Study (TIMSS); PIRLS International Study Center, 2023).
10. Marilyn Jager Adams, "The Challenge of Advanced Texts: The Interdependence of Reading and Learning," in *Reading More, Reading Better: Are American Students Reading Enough of the Right Stuff?*, ed. Elfrieda H. Hiebert (Guilford, 2009), 163–89; Richard C. Anderson et al., *Becoming a Nation of Readers: The Report of the Commission on Reading.* (National Academy of Education, 1985); Jeanne S. Chall et al., *Should*

Textbooks Challenge Students? The Case for Easier or Harder Books (Teachers College Press, 1991); Jill Fitzgerald et al., "Has First-Grade Core Reading Program Text Complexity Changed Across Six Decades?" *Reading Research Quarterly* 51, no. 1 (January–February 2016): 7–28; David A. Gamson et al., "Challenging the Research Base of the Common Core State Standards: A Historical Reanalysis of Text Complexity," *Educational Researcher* 42, no. 7 (Oct 2013): 381–91.

11. Emmett A. Betts, *Foundations of Reading Instruction: With Emphasis on Differentiated Guidance* (American Book Co., 1946).
12. Edward E. Gickling, "Controlling Academic and Social Performance Using an Instructional Delivery Approach," in *Programming for the Emotionally Handicapped: Administrative Considerations* (Lexington, KY: Coordination Office for Regional Resource Centers, 1977), 46–55.
13. Marie M. Clay, *Becoming Literate: The Construction of Inner Control* (Heinemann, 1991).
14. Irene Fountas and Gay Su Pinnell, *Guided Reading* (Heinemann, 1996).
15. Lucy Calkins, *A Guide to the Reading Workshop: Intermediate Grades* (Heinemann, 2015).
16. Michael P. Ford and Michael F. Opitz, "A National Survey of Guided Reading Practices: What We Can Learn from Primary Teachers," *Literacy Research and Instruction* 47, no. 4 (2008): 309–31.
17. MRI-Simmons, *American Kids Survey* (Mediamark Research, 2006).
18. For example, Richard L. Allington et al., "What Research Says About Text Complexity and Learning to Read," *The Reading Teacher* 68, no. 7 (March 2015): 491–501.
19. The New Teacher Project (TNTP), "Paths of Opportunity: What It Will Take for All Young People to Thrive," TNTP, August 8, 2024, https://tntp.org/publication/paths-of-opportunity/; Jill Barshay, "The Habits of 7 Highly Effective Schools," *Hechinger Report,* September 30, 2024, https://hechingerreport.org/proof-points-tntp-effective-schools/.
20. US Department of Education, *National Assessment of Educational Progress 1990–2019 Mathematics and Reading Assessments* (Institute of Education Sciences, National Center for Statistics, 2019.)
21. I hope no one interprets this to mean that phonics and efforts to improve early reading are worthless. Nothing could be further from the truth. The point is not to cast aspersions on such efforts but to insist on comparable efforts to preserve and build upon the benefits they provide.
22. For instance, James W. Cunningham et al., "Investigating the Validity of Two Widely Used Quantitative Measures," *Reading and Writing* 31 (2018): 813–33.
23. David Griffith and Ann Duffett, *Reading and Writing Instruction in America's Schools* (Thomas Fordham Institute, 2018); Julia H. Kaufman et al., *What Teachers Know and Do in the Common Core Era: Findings from the 2015–2017 American Teacher Panel* (RAND Corporation, 2018).
24. New York State Education Department, *New York State Next Generation English Language Arts Learning Standards* (Albany: NY State Education Department, 2017).
25. Gallup, Inc. and Learning Heroes, *B-flation: How Good Grades Can Sideline Parents*, webinar, Gallup, 2023, https://www.gallup.com/learning/event/4395573/EventDetails.aspx.
26. Peter W. v. San Francisco Unified School District, 60 Cal. App. 3d 814 (1976).
27. Irene Fountas and Gay Su Pinnell, "Daily Learning Tip," Fountas and Pinnell Literacy Blog, August 23, 2021, https://fpblog.fountasandpinnell.com/daily-learning-tip-8-23-21.

28. Research Center, *Early Reading Instruction: Results of a National Survey* (Bethesda, MD: Education Projects in Education, 2019).
29. Irene Fountas and Gay Su Pinnell, *Guided Reading: Responsive Teaching Across the Grades* (Heinemann, 2016).
30. For example, Steve Amendum et al., "Does Text Complexity Matter in the Elementary Grades? A Research Synthesis of Text Difficulty and Elementary Students' Reading Fluency and Comprehension," *Educational Psychology Review* 30, no. 1 (March 2018): 121–51.
31. Maureen T. Hallinan and Aage B. Sørensen, "The Formation and Stability of Instructional Groups," *American Sociological Review* 48, no. 6 (December 1983): 838–51.

Chapter 1

1. Lawrence A. Cremin, American Education: The Colonial Experience, 1607–1783 (Harper & Row, 1970).
2. Eltjo Buringh and Jan Luiten Van Zanden, "Charting the 'Rise of the West': Manuscripts and Printed Books in Europe, a Long-Term Perspective from the Sixth Through Eighteenth Centuries," *Journal of Economic History* 69, no. 2 (2009): 409–45.
3. Stephen Tomkins, *The Journey to the Mayflower: God's Outlaws and the Invention of Freedom* (Pegasus Books, 2020).
4. Daniel Resnick and Lauren Resnick, "The Nature of Literacy: An Historical Exploration," *Harvard Educational Review* 47, no. 3 (1977): 370–85.
5. Benjamin Harris, *The New England Primer* (Boston, 1686).
6. Harris, *New England Primer.*
7. Noah Webster, *The American Speller* (Hartford, CT, 1783).
8. Joshua Kendall, *The Forgotten Founding Father* (Berkeley Books, 2010).
9. Thomas Dilworth, *A New Guide to the English Tongue* (London, 1740).
10. Kendall, *Forgotten Founding Father.*
11. Noah Webster, *An Introduction to English Grammar* (Hartford, CT, 1784).
12. Noah Webster, *A Grammatical Institute of the English Language . . . Part III. Containing the Necessary Rules of Reading and Speaking, and a Variety of Essays, Dialogues, etc.* (Hartford, CT, 1785).
13. Rudolph R. Reeder, *The Historical Development of School Readers and of Method in Teaching Reading* (Macmillan, 1900), 37.
14. Nila Banton Smith, *American Reading Instruction* (International Reading Association, 1965).
15. David B. Tyack, ed., *Turning Points in American Educational History* (Blaisdell Publishing, 1967).
16. Richard L. Venezky, "A History of the American Reading Textbook," *Elementary School Journal* 87, no. 3 (1987): 256.
17. Mann, Horace, *The Republic and the New School,* (New York: Teachers College, 1838; repr., 1957).
18. Tyack, *Turning Points*, 187.
19. Mann, *Republic*, 37–38.
20. Spring, Joel, *The American School, 1642–1985* (Longman, 1986), 132.
21. Cremin, Lawrence A., *American Education, the National Experience, 1783–1876* (Harper & Row, 1980): 85.
22. "Reading No. 4," *Connecticut Common School Journal* 3, no. 5 (1841): 65–66.
23. "Reading No. 4," *Connecticut Common School Journal.*

24. New England Journal of Education, "Methods of Teaching Reading," *New England Journal of Education* 4, no. 21 (1876): 244–45.
25. For example, Tyack, *Turning Points*, 156–64.
26. Allison Speicher, *Schooling Readers: Reading Common Schools in Nineteenth Century American Fiction* (University of Alabama Press, 2016).
27. Venezky, *History*, 261.
28. Lyman Cobb, *New Juvenile Readers* (Caleb Bartlett, 1943), preface.
29. Richard L. Venezky, "Steps Toward a Modern History of American Reading Instruction," *Review of Research in Education* 13, no. 1 (1986): 129–67.
30. David B. Tower, *The Gradual Readers* (New York: 1843).
31. William H. McGuffey, *The Eclectic Readers* (Cincinnati, OH: 1838).
32. Stanley W. Lindberg, *The Annotated McGuffey: Selections from the McGuffey Eclectic Readers, 1836–1920* (Van Nostrand Reinhold, 1976).
33. William H. DuBay, *Unlocking Language: The Classic Readability Studies* (Impact Information, 2007), iv.
34. Venezky, *History*, 256.
35. Cremin, *American Education*, 398.
36. Gray, William S., "Value of Informal Tests of Reading Accomplishment," *Journal of Educational Research* 1 (1920): 103–11.
37. George C. Kyte, "Calibrating Reading Materials," *Elementary School Journal* 25, no. 7 (March 1925): 533–46.
38. Bertha A. Lively and Sidney L. Pressey, "A Method for Measuring the 'Vocabulary Burden' of Textbooks," *Educational Administration and Supervision* 9 (1923): 389–98.
39. Eva D. Kellogg, ed., *Primary Reading: Teaching Reading in Ten Cities* (Educational Publishing Co, 1900), 2.
40. W. W. Theisen, "Provisions for Individual Differences in the Teaching of Reading," *Journal of Educational Research* 2, no. 2 (1920): 560–71.
41. E. B. Sherman and A. A. Reed, *Essentials of Teaching Reading* (Chicago: University Publishing, 1909), 130.
42. Joseph S. Taylor, *Principles and Methods of Teaching Reading* (Macmillan, 1912), 94.
43. Laura Zirbes, "Diagnostic Measurement as a Basis for Procedure," *Elementary School Journal* 18, no. 7 (March 2018): 505–22.
44. Harriet M. Barthelmess and Philip A. Boyer, "An Evaluation of Ability Grouping," *Journal of Educational Research* 26, no. 4 (1932): 284–94.
45. Edward L. Thorndike, *The Teacher's Word Book* (Teachers College Press, 1921).
46. For example, William S. Gray and Bernice E. Leary, *What Makes a Book Readable* (University of Chicago Press, 1935).
47. Smith, *American Reading Instruction*.
48. John M. Bradley and Wilbur S. Ames, "Readability Parameters of Basal Readers," *Journal of Literacy Research* 9, no. 2 (June 1977): 175–83.
49. "Albany Plan of Primary School Organization," *Elementary School Journal* 36, (1936): 413–16.
50. Anna Wieking, "A Flexible Reading Program," *The National Elementary Principal: Newer Practices in Reading in the Elementary School: Seventeenth Yearbook* (Department of Elementary School Principals, National Education Association, 1938), 530–31.
51. Myrtle L. Kaufman, "First-Grade Promotion Plan," *Journal of Educational Research* 10, (December 1924): 369–74.

52. Edward R. McCann, "A Study of the Effectiveness of Teaching Reading by Grouping According to Reading Level in Grades Five and Six" (unpublished master's thesis, Canisius College, 1941).
53. Mary B. O'Bannion, "An Experiment with Homogeneous Grouping in Reading," *The National Elementary Principal: Newer Practices in Reading in the Elementary School: Seventeenth Yearbook* (Department of Elementary School Principals, National Education Association, 1938), 533–38.
54. Edward L. Thorndike, "Improving the Ability to Read (Concluded)," *Teachers College Record* 37, no. 3 (1934): 230.
55. Barthelmess and Boyer, "Evaluation of Ability Grouping."
56. Emmett A. Betts, *Foundations of Reading Instruction: With Emphasis on Differentiated Guidance* (American Book Co., 1946).
57. Emmet A. Betts, Mabel Everett, and Frances Rodewald, "Remedial Reading: Based on First-Teaching," *Exceptional Children* 2, no. 4 (1936): 88–91, https://www.readinghalloffame.org/emmett-betts.
58. Carl F. Kaestle et al., *Literacy in the United States: Readers and Reading Since 1880* (Yale University Press, 1993).
59. Mary C. Austin and Coleman Morrison, *The First R: The Harvard Report on Reading in Elementary Schools* (Macmillan, 1963); James F. Baumann et al., "The First R Yesterday and Today: U.S. Elementary Reading Instruction Practices Reported by Teachers and Administrators," *Reading Research Quarterly* 35, no. 3 (July 2000): 338–77; David Griffith and Ann Duffett, *Reading and Writing Instruction in America's Schools* (Thomas Fordham Institute, 2018); Julia H. Kaufman et al., *What Teachers Know and Do in the Common Core Era: Findings from the 2015–2017 American Teacher Panel* (RAND Corporation, 2018); Timothy Shanahan and Ann Duffett, *Common Core in the Schools: A First Look at Reading Assignments* (Thomas B. Fordham Institute, 2013).
60. Mabel O'Donnell, *Alice and Jerry Readers* (Rowe, Peterson & Co., 1957).
61. William S. Gray and Zena Sharp, *Curriculum Foundations Program* (Scott, Foresman & Company, 1927).
62. For example, Rudolph Flesch, *Why Johnny Can't Read* (Harper & Bros., 1955); Arthur S. Trace, *What Ivan Knows that Johnny Doesn't* (Random House, 1965).
63. Elfrieda H. Hiebert and Taffy E. Raphael, "Psychological Perspectives on Literacy and Extensions to Educational Practice," in *Handbook of Educational Psychology*, ed. David C. Berliner and Robert C. Calfee (Macmillan Library Reference USA; Prentice Hall International, 1996); Steve Amendum et al., "Does Text Complexity Matter in the Elementary Grades? A Research Synthesis of Text Difficulty and Elementary Students' Reading Fluency and Comprehension," *Educational Psychology Review* 30, no. 1 (March 2018): 121–51.
64. Kenneth S. Goodman et al., *Report Card on Basal Readers* (Richard C. Owen, 1987); Yetta M. Goodman, "Roots of the Whole-Language Movement," *Elementary School Journal* 90, no. 2 (1989): 113–27; Michael A. Tulley and Roger Farr, "Textbook Adoption: Insight, Impact, and Potential," *Book Research Quarterly* 1, no. 2 (June 1985): 4–11.
65. Elfrieda H. Hiebert and Charles W. Fisher, "Whole Language: Three Themes of the Future," *Educational Leadership* 47, no. 6 (1990): 62–64.
66. California State Department of Education, *California English-Language Arts Framework* (Sacramento, CA: California State Department of Education, 1987).

67. Elfrieda H. Hiebert, "State Reform Policies and the Task Textbooks Pose for First-Grade Readers," *Elementary School Journal* 105 (2005): 443–60.
68. Elfrieda H. Hiebert, "Changing Readers, Changing Texts: Beginning Reading Texts from 1960 to 2010," *Journal of Education* 195, no. 3 (2015): 1–13.
69. Eugene H. Owen and Ina Mullis, *Reading In and Out of School* (Institute of Educational Sciences, National Center for Educational Statistics, 1992).
70. Nicholas Lemann, "The Reading Wars," *Atlantic* 230, no. 5 (1997): 128–34.
71. Irene Fountas and Gay Su Pinnell, *Guided Reading: Good First Teaching for All Children*, 1st ed. (Heinemann, 1996).
72. Irene Fountas and Gay Su Pinnell, *Leveled Book List K-8* (Heinemann, 2005).

Chapter 2

1. Stephen Pinker, *Rationality: What It Is, Why It Seems Scarce, Why It Matters* (Viking, 2021).
2. Loren J. Chapman, "Illusory Correlation in Observational Report," *Journal of Verbal Learning & Verbal Behavior* 6, no. 1 (1967): 151–55.
3. Leon Festinger, *The Theory of Cognitive Dissonance* (Stanford University Press, 1957).
4. Frederic Weitzman and Ben Harris, "Arnold Gesell: The Maturationist," in *Portraits of Pioneers in Developmental Psychology*, ed. Wade Pickren, Donald A. Dewsbury, and Michael Wertheimer (Taylor & Francis Group, 2011), 13.
5. Patricia K. Kuhl, "Brain Mechanisms in Early Language Acquisition," *Neuron* 67, no. 5 (September 9, 2010): 713–27.
6. Stanka A. Fitneva and Tomoko Matsui, "The Emergence and Development of Language Across Cultures," in *The Oxford Handbook of Human Development and Culture: An Interdisciplinary Perspective,* ed. Lene Arnett Jensen (Oxford University Press, 2014).
7. G. Stanley Hall, *The Contents of Children's Minds on Entering School* (New York, 1893).
8. Mabel Vogel Morphett and Carleton Washburne, "When Should Children Begin to Read?" *Elementary School Journal* 32, no. 7 (March 1931): 496–503.
9. Jerome Bruner, *The Process of Education* (Harvard University Press, 1960), 33.
10. The point here is not that there are no developmental limits on how early instruction can begin, though programs like, *Teach Your Baby to Read*, may misleadingly suggest that. There are many practical limits on when we might begin to teach something, including value (do two-year-olds need to learn to read?), degree of difficulty (for developmental reasons, toddlers have very brief attention spans), and practicality (the financial cost of establishing a system of education aimed at teaching reading to infants and toddlers).
11. Dorothy Ross, *G. Stanley Hall, the Psychologist as Prophet* (University of Chicago Press, 1972).
12. James M. Cattell, "Mental Tests and Measurements," *Mind* 15, no. 1 (July 1890): 373–81, 375.
13. Arthur R. Jensen, *Understanding Readiness: An Occasional Paper* (Washington, DC: Office of Education, Bureau of Research, 1969).
14. Sigmund Freud, *Three Essays on Sexuality: The Standard Edition of the Complete Psychological Works of Sigmund Freud* (Vol. IV). (London: The Hogarth Press and the Institute of Psychoanalysis, 1953).
15. Everett E. Davis, "Reading Frustration Level as Indicated by the Polygraph," *Journal of Educational Psychology* 68, no. 8 (April 1975): 286–88; Eldon E. Ekwall, "Informal Reading Inventories: The Instructional Level," *The Reading Teacher* 29, no. 7 (April 1975): 662–65.

16. Abram Amsel, "Frustration Theory: Many Years Later," *Psychological Bulletin* 112, no. 3 (1992): 396–99; Peter R. Killeen, "Frustration: Theory and Practice," *Psychonomic Bulletin & Review* 1, no. 3 (1994): 323–26.
17. Ryan S. J. D. Baker et al., "Better to Be Frustrated Than Bored: The Incidence, Persistence, and Impact of Learners' Cognitive–Affective States During Interactions with Three Different Computer-Based Learning Environments," *International Journal of Human-Computer Studies* 68, no. 4 (2010), 223–41; R. M. Yerkes and J. D. Dodson, "The Relation of Strength of Stimulus to Rapidity of Habit Formation," *Journal of Comparative Neurology & Psychology* 18 (1908): 459–82.
18. H. O. Beldin, "Informal Reading Testing: Historical Review and Review of the Research," in *Reading Difficulties: Diagnosis, Correction, and Remediation,* ed. William K. Durr (International Reading Association, 1970); William S. Gray, *Improving Instruction in Reading*, Supplementary Educational Monographs, no. 40 (University of Chicago Press, 1933).
19. William R. Powell, "Reappraising the Criteria for Interpreting Informal Inventories," in *Reading Diagnosis and Evaluation*, ed. D. L. DeBoer (International Reading Association, 1968).
20. Everett E. Davis, "Reading Frustration Level as Indicated by the Polygraph," *Journal of Educational Research* 68, no. 7 (2014): 286–88; Eldon E. Ekwall, "Should Repetitions Be Counted as Errors?," *The Reading Teacher* 27, no. 4 (1974): 365–67.
21. David A. Lieberman, *Human Learning and Memory* (Cambridge University Press, 2012).
22. Edward L. Thorndike, *The Elements of Psychology* (A. G. Seiler, 1905).
23. *Encyclopedia Britannica*, "Programmed Learning," last updated January 25, 2018, https://www.britannica.com/topic/programmed-learning.
24. B. F. Skinner, "'Superstition' in the Pigeon," *Journal of Experimental Psychology* 38, no. 2 (1948): 168–72.
25. *Encyclopedia Britannica*, "Programmed Learning."
26. Robert T. Ackland, "Informal Reading Inventories," in *Literacy Assessment and Instructional Strategies*, ed. Kathy B. Grant, Sandra E. Golden, and Nance S. Wilson (SAGE Publications, 2015).
27. Ackland, "Informal Reading Inventories"; James V. Hoffman, "What If 'Just Right' Is Just Wrong? The Unintended Consequences of Leveling Readers," *The Reading Teacher* 71, no. 3, (June 2017): 265–73; Robert S. Pehrsson, "Challenging Frustration Level," *Reading & Writing Quarterly: Overcoming Learning Difficulties* 10, no. 3 (1994): 201–08.
28. Yuriy V. Karpov, "The Vygotskian Notion of Mediation as the Major Determinant of Children's Learning and Development," in *Vygotsky for Educators,* ed. Yuriy V. Karpov (Cambridge University Press, 2014); Joseph C. Campione et al., "The Zone of Proximal Development: Implications for Individual Differences and Learning," *New Directions for Child Development* 23, (1984): 77–91; Fred Newman and Lois Holzman, *Lev Vygotsky: Revolutionary Scientist* (Routledge, 1993); Rene van der Veer and Jaan Valsiner, *Understanding Vygotsky: A Quest for Synthesis* (Blackwell, 1991).
29. Karpov, "Vygotskian Notion."
30. Ann C. Kruger and Michael Tomasello, "Cultural Learning and Learning Culture," in *The Handbook of Education and Human Development*, ed. David R. Olson and Nancy Torrance (Blackwell, 1998), 368.
31. Lisbeth A. Dixon et al., "Emergent Reading Levels in Expository and Narrative Materials," Paper presented at the annual meeting of the National Reading Conference, Austin, TX, 1983.

32. Ackland, "Informal Reading Inventories," 240.
33. John P. Helfeldt and William A. Heck, "Operationalizing the Instructional Range: An Extension and Clarification of an Informal Reading Inventory Tradition," *Journal of Correctional Education* 35, no. 1 (March 1984), 5–7.

Chapter 3

1. For example, H. Lee Swanson and Maureen Hoskyn, "Experimental Intervention Research on Students with Learning Disabilities: A Meta-Analysis of Treatment Outcomes," *Review of Educational Research* 68, no. 3 (1998): 277–321; James Van Patten et al., "A Review of Strategies for Sequencing and Synthesizing Instruction," *Review of Educational Research* 56, no. 4 (1986): 437–71.
2. Swanson and Hoskyn, "Experimental Intervention Research," 277–321.
3. Richard A. Schmidt and Robert A. Bjork, "New Conceptualizations of Practice: Common Principles in Three Paradigms Suggest New Concepts for Training," *Psychological Science* 3, no. 4 (July 1992): 207–17; Robert A. Bjork, "Being Suspicious of the Sense of Ease and Undeterred by the Sense of Difficulty," *Perspectives on Psychological Science* 13, no. 2 (March 2018): 146–48.
4. For example, Danielle S. McNamara et al., "Are Good Texts Always Better? Interactions of Text Coherence, Background Knowledge, and Levels of Understanding in Learning from Text," *Cognition and Instruction* 14, no. 1 (1996): 1–43.
5. Danielle S. McNamara, "Reading Both High-Coherence and Low-Coherence Texts: Effects of Text Sequence and Prior Knowledge," *Canadian Journal of Experimental Psychology* 55, no. 1 (March 2001): 51–62.
6. Emmett A. Betts, *Foundations of Reading Instruction: With Emphasis on Differentiated Guidance* (American Book Co., 1946).
7. Patsy Aloysius Killgallon, "A Study of Relationships Among Certain Pupil Adjustments in Language Situations" (unpublished PhD diss., Pennsylvania State University, 1942).
8. Timothy Shanahan, "A Critique of P. A. Killgallon's Study: A Study of Relationships Among Certain Pupil Adjustments in Reading Situations," in *Reading Research Revisited*, eds. Lance Gentile, Michael L. Kamil, and Jay Blanchard (Merrill, 1983).
9. Emma M. Bolenius, *Teacher's Manual of Silent and Oral Reading* (Houghton Mifflin, 1919); Donald D. Durrell, "Individual Differences and Their Implications with Respect to Instruction in Reading," in *Teaching of Reading: A Second Report, 36th Yearbook of the National Society for the Study of Education* (Public School Publishing Co., 1937); Edward L. Thorndike, "Improving the Ability to Read," *Teachers College Record* 36, (October–December 1934): 229–41.
10. H. O. Beldin, "Informal Reading Testing: Historical Review and Review of the Research," in *Reading Difficulties: Diagnosis, Correction, and Remediation,* ed. William K. Durr (International Reading Association, 1970).
11. Jerry Johns, "Speaking my Mind: The Common Core State Standards and Matching Students with Materials They Can Read," *Colorado Reading Journal* 24, (2013): 35–37; Darrell Morris et al., "Reading Instructional Level from a Print-Processing Perspective," *Reading & Writing Quarterly* 35, no. 6 (2019): 556–71.
12. William R. Powell, "Reappraising the Criteria for Interpreting Informal Inventories," in *Reading Diagnosis and Evaluation*, ed. D. L. DeBoer (International Reading Association, 1968).
13. Powell, "Interpreting Informal Inventories."

14. William R. Powell, *Measuring Reading Performance Informally*, paper presented at the annual meeting of the International Reading Association (ERIC 155 589), 1978.
15. Susan P. Homan and Janell P. Klesius, "A Re-Examination of the IRI: Word Recognition Criteria," *Reading Horizons* 26, no. 1 (1985): 53–61.
16. Homan and Klesius, "Re-Examination of the IRI," 60.
17. Jerry L. Johns and Anne Marie Magliari, "Informal Reading Inventories: Are the Betts Criteria the Best Criteria?," *Reading Improvement* 26, no. 2 (1989): 124–32, 124.
18. This is also true of both Gickling's and Clay's versions of the instructional level.
19. Beldin, "Informal Reading Testing."
20. Richard L. Allington, *What Really Matters for Struggling Readers: Designing Research-Based Programs*, 3rd ed. (Pearson, 2011); Irene Fountas and Gay Su Pinnell, *Guided Reading: Good First Teaching for All Children*, 1st ed. (Heinemann, 1996); Johns, "Speaking My Mind"; Morris et al., "Reading Instruction Level."
21. Jerry Johns and Beth Johns, *Basic Reading Inventory: Kindergarten through Grade Twelve and Early Literacy Assessments* (Kendall-Hunt Publishing, 2016); Lauren Leslie and JoAnne S. Caldwell, *Qualitative Reading Inventory* (Pearson, 2010); Mary Lynn Woods and Alden Moe, *Analytical Reading Inventory: Comprehensive Standards-Based Assessment for All Students Including Gifted and Remedial* (Pearson, 2014).
22. Mary C. Austin and Coleman Morrison, *The First R: The Harvard Report on Reading in Elementary Schools* (Macmillan, 1963); James F. Baumann et al., "The First R Yesterday and Today: U.S. Elementary Reading Instruction Practices Reported by Teachers and Administrators," *Reading Research Quarterly* 35, no. 3 (July 2000): 338–77; Julia H. Kaufman et al., *What Teachers Know and Do in the Common Core Era: Findings from the 2015–2017 American Teacher Panel* (RAND Corporation, 2018); Timothy Shanahan and Ann Duffett, *Common Core in the Schools: A First Look at Reading Assignments* (Thomas B. Fordham Institute, 2013).
23. J. Louis Cooper, "The Effect of Adjustment of Basal Reading Materials in Reading Achievement" (unpublished PhD diss., Boston University, 1952).
24. Cooper, *Effect of Adjustment*, 108.
25. Linda M. Anderson et al., "An Experimental Study of Effective Teaching in First-Grade Reading Groups," *Elementary School Journal* 79, no. 4 (1979): 193–223; David C. Berliner, "Academic Learning Time and Reading Achievement," in *Comprehension and Teaching: Research Reviews*, ed. John T. Guthrie (International Reading Association, 1981).
26. Berliner, "Academic Learning Time," 210.
27. Gerald W. Jorgenson et al., "Achievement and Behavioral Correlates of Matched Levels of Student Ability and Materials Difficulty," *Journal of Educational Research* 71, no. 2 (1977): 100–03.
28. Susan P. Homan et al., "An Investigation of Varying Reading Level Placement on Reading Achievement of Chapter I Students," *Reading Research and Instruction* 33, no. 1: (2010): 29–38.
29. William R. Powell and Colin G. Dunkeld, "Validity of the IRI Reading Levels," *Elementary English* 48, no. 6 (October 1971): 637–42.
30. Steve A. Stahl and Kathleen M. Heubach, "Fluency-Oriented Reading Instruction," *Journal of Literacy Research* 37, no. 1 (2005): 25–60.
31. For example, Richard L. Allington et al., "What Research Says About Text Complexity and Learning to Read," *The Reading Teacher* 68, no. 7 (March 2015): 491–501.

32. Linnea C. Ehri et al., “Reading Rescue: An Effective Tutoring Intervention Model for Language-Minority Students Who Are Struggling Readers in First Grade,” *American Educational Research Journal* 44, no. 2 (2007): 414–48.
33. Ehri et al., “Reading Rescue.”
34. Thomas C. Lovitt and Cheryl L. Hansen, “Round One—Placing the Child in the Right Reader,” *Journal of Learning Disabilities* 9, no. 6 (1976): 18–24.
35. K. A. Neufeld, and Ogden R. Lindsley, “Charting to Compare Children’s Learning at Four Different Performance Levels,” *Journal of Precision Testing* 1 (1980): 9–17.
36. John Scott, Jr., “Learning Rates for Oral Reading at Instructional and Frustration Levels by Elementary Students with Mild Learning Problems” (unpublished PhD diss., University of Florida, 1988).
37. Patricia G. Mathes, and Lynn S. Fuchs, “Peer-Mediated Reading Instruction in Special Education Resource Rooms,” *Learning Disabilities Research & Practice* 8, no. 4 (1993): 233–43.
38. Stahl and Heubach, “Fluency-Oriented Reading Instruction”; Niles V. Stanley, “A Concurrent Validity Study of the Emergent Reading Level” (unpublished PhD diss., University of Florida, 1986).
39. Cara Jean Cahalan, “Reading Fluency and Optimal Difficulty Level in a Literature-Based Reading Curriculum” (unpublished PhD diss., Fordham University, 2003).
40. Sharon Vaughn et al., *Providing Reading Interventions for Students in Grades 4–9*, National Center for Education Evaluation and Regional Assistance (NCEE), Institute of Education Sciences, US Department of Education, 2022: 3.
41. Michael F. Hock et al., “The Effects of a Comprehensive Reading Program on Reading Outcomes for Middle School Students with Disabilities,” *Journal of Learning Disabilities* 51, no. 2 (2017): 195–212; Sharon Vaughn et al., “Effects from a Randomized Control Trial Comparing Researcher and School-implemented Treatments with Fourth Graders with Significant Reading Difficulties,” *Journal of Research on Educational Effectiveness* 9, no. S1 (2016): 23–44; Sharon Vaughn et al., Efficacy of a Word- and Text Based Intervention for Students with Significant Reading Difficulties,” *Journal of Learning Disabilities* 52, no. 1 (2019): 31–44.
42. Yusra Ahmed et al., “Structure Altering Effects of a Multicomponent Reading Intervention: An Application of the Direct and Inferential Mediation (DIME) Model of Reading Comprehension in Upper Elementary Grades,” *Journal of Learning Disabilities* 55, no. 1 (2022): 58–78; Garrett J. Roberts et al., “Examining the Effects of Afterschool Reading Interventions for Upper Elementary Struggling Readers,” *Remedial and Special Education* 39, no. 3 (May 2018) 131–43; Stacy Lynn Smith, “Will Raising the Bar Result in Greater Reading Growth” (unpublished PhD dissertation, Ball State University, 2019).
43. Henry May et al., “The Effects of Bookworms Literacy Curriculum on Student Achievement in Grades 2–5,” *Scientific Studies of Reading* 28, no. 3 (2024): 321–44; Sharon Walpole et al., “The Promise of a Literacy Reform Effort in the Upper Elementary Grades,” *The Elementary School Journal* 118, no. 2 (December 2017): 257–80.
44. David D. Paige and William H. Rupley, “Revisiting Complex Text Instruction: A Study of 11th-Grade History Students,” *Psychology in the Schools* 6, no. 9 (September 2023): 3633–47.
45. Matthew K. Burns, “Assessing an Instructional Level During Reading Fluency Interventions: A Meta-Analysis of the Effects of Reading,” *Assessment for Effective Intervention*, (2024): 1–11.

46. Mariola Moeyaert, "Meta-Analysis of Single-Case Experimental Designs: An Overview on Current Synthesis Methods," webinar, February 7, 2023, by Campbell Collaborative, https://ktdrr.org/training/webcasts/webcast81/webcast81-020723-508.pdf; Mariola Moeyaert et al., "Single-Case Design Meta-Analyses in Education and Psychology: A Systematic Review of Methodology," *Frontiers in Research Metrics and Analytics* 8 (2023): 1190362; Maaike Ugille et al., "Multilevel Meta-Analysis of Single-Subject Experimental Designs: A Simulation Study," *Behavior Research Methods* 44, no. 4 (2012): 1244–54.
47. Scott P. Ardoin et al., "Promoting Generalization of Reading: A Comparison of Two Fluency-Based Interventions for Improving General Education Student's Oral Reading Rate," *Journal of Behavioral Education* 17 (2008): 237–52.
48. Alisa Morgan et al., "Effect of Difficulty Levels on Second-Grade Delayed Readers Using Dyad Reading," *Journal of Educational Research* 94, no. 2 (2000): 113–19, 119.
49. Lisa Trottier Brown et al., "The Effects of Reading and Text Difficulty on Third-Graders' Reading Achievement," *Journal of Educational Research* 111, no. 5 (2017): 541–53.
50. Melanie R. Kuhn and Steven S. Stahl, "Fluency: A Review of Developmental and Remedial Practices," *Journal of Educational Psychology* 95, no. 1 (2003): 3–21.
51. Allington et al., "What Research Says."
52. Melanie R. Kuhn et al., "Teaching Children to Become Fluent and Automatic Readers," *Journal of Literacy Research* 38, no. 4 (2006): 357–87.
53. Kuhn et al., "Teaching Children," 380.
54. Rollanda E. O'Connor et al., "Teaching Reading to Poor Readers in the Intermediate Grades: A Comparison of Text Difficulty," *Journal of Educational Psychology* 94, no. 3 (2002): 474–85; Rollanda E. O'Connor et al., "Improvement in Reading Rate Under Independent and Difficult Text Levels: Influences on Word and Comprehension Skills," *Journal of Educational Psychology* 102, no. 1 (2010): 1–19.
55. O'Connor et al., "Improvement in Reading Rate."
56. Michael L. Kamil and W. Christine Rauscher, "Effects of Grouping and Difficulty of Materials on Reading Achievement," *National Reading Conference Yearbook* 39 (1990): 121–27.
57. Kamil and Rauscher, "Effects of Grouping," 122.
58. Kamil and Rauscher, "Effects of Grouping," 127.
59. Sarah M. Lupo et al., "An Exploration of Text Difficulty and Knowledge Support on Adolescents' Comprehension," *Reading Research Quarterly* 54, no. 4 (October–December 2019): 457–79.
60. Lupo et al., "Exploration of Text Difficulty," 476.
61. This is not to say that there is no evidence with first graders. For example, one study of 140 first graders found that those who were reading with 95% accuracy made faster book level growth than those with 85% accuracy. However, these gains were confounded with the students' abilities. Robert H. Kelly, "Investigating the Role of Accuracy and Self-Correction in the Progress of Struggling First-Grade Readers Participating in a Literacy Intervention" (unpublished PhD diss., Ohio State University, 2017).
62. Lupo et al., "Exploration of Text Difficulty."
63. Jill Fitzgerald et al., "Important Text Characteristics for Early-Grades Text Complexity," *Journal of Educational Psychology* 107, no. 1 (2015): 4–29; Elfrieda H. Hiebert, "Text Matters in Learning to Read," *The Reading Teacher* 52, no. 6 (March 1999): 552–66;

Elfrieda H. Hiebert and Misty Sailors, eds., *Finding the Right Text: What Works for Beginning and Struggling Readers* (Guilford Press, 2009), 203–26.

64. Kuhn et al., "Teaching Children"; Morgan et al., "Effect of Difficulty Levels"; Brown et al., "Effects of Reading."

Chapter 4

1. Emmett A. Betts, *Foundations of Reading Instruction: With Emphasis on Differentiated Guidance* (American Book Co., 1946).
2. Edward E. Gickling and John F. Havertape, "Curriculum Based Assessment," in *Non-Test Based Assessment,* ed. J. A. Tucker (The National School Psychology Inservice Network, University of Minnesota, 1981).
3. Mary Abbott et al., "The Relationship of Error Rate and Comprehension in Second and Third Grade Oral Reading Fluency," *Reading Psychology* 33, no. 1–2 (2012): 104–32; Matthew K. Burns et al., "Minimum Reading Fluency Rate Necessary for Comprehension: A Potential Criterion for Curriculum-Based Assessments," *Assessment for Effective Intervention* 28, no. 1 (2002), 1–7; Amanda M. Vanderheyden and Benjamin G. Solomon, "Valid Outcomes for Screening and Progress Monitoring: Fluency Is Superior to Accuracy in Curriculum-Based Measurement," *School Psychology* 38, no. 3 (2023): 160–72.
4. Edward E. Gickling and David L. Armstrong, "Levels of Instructional Difficulty as Related to On-Task Behavior, Task Completion, and Comprehension," *Journal of Learning Disabilities* 11, no. 9 (1978): 559–66.
5. Matthew K. Burns, "Assessing an Instructional Level During Reading Fluency Interventions: A Meta-Analysis of the Effects of Reading." *Assessment for Effective Intervention* (2024): 1–11; Matthew K. Burns et al., "Minimum Reading Fluency Necessary for Comprehension among Second-Grade Students," *Psychology in the Schools* 48, no. 2 (2011): 124–32.
6. Irene C. Fountas and Gay Su Pinnell, *Fountas and Pinnell Benchmark Assessment Systems* (Heineman, 2022).
7. Michael P. Ford and Michael F. Opitz, "A National Survey of Guided Reading Practices: What We Can Learn from Primary Teachers," *Literacy Research and Instruction* 47, no. 4 (2008): 309–31.
8. Tamara J. Arthaud et al., "Reading Assessment and Instructional Practices in Special Education," *Diagnostique* 25, no. 3 (2000): 205–27.
9. Education Week Research Center, *Early Reading Instruction: Results of a National Survey.* (Bethesda, MD: Education Projects in Education, 2019).
10. Theresa A. Deeney, and Minsuk K. Shim, "Teachers' and Students' Views of Reading Fluency: Issues of Consequential Validity in Adopting One-Minute Reading Fluency Assessments," *Assessment for Effective Intervention* 41, no. 2 (March 2016): 109–26.
11. Mary D. Austin and Coleman Morrison, *The First R: The Harvard Report on Reading in the Elementary School* (Macmillan, 1963); Patrick J. Groff, "A Survey of Basal Reading Group Practices," *The Reading Teacher* 15, no. 4 (January 1962): 232–35; Ford and Opitz, "National Survey"; Michael L. Hawkins, "Mobility of Students in Reading Groups," *The Reading Teacher* 20, no. 2 (November 1966): 136–40; Beth Maloch et al., "Portraits of Practice: A Cross-Case Analysis of Two First-Grade Teachers and Their Grouping Practices," *Research in the Teaching of English* 47, no. 3 (February 2013): 277–312; Ray C. Rist, "Student Social Class and Teacher Expectations: The Self-Fulfilling Prophecy in Ghetto Education," *Harvard Educational Review* 40, no. 3 (1970): 411–51; Rhona S. Weinstein, "Reading Group Membership in First Grade: Teacher Behaviors and

Pupil Experience Over Time," *Journal of Educational Psychology* 68, no. 1 (February 1976): 103–16.

12. For example, Douglas Fuchs et al., "Performance Instability: An Identifying Characteristic of Learning Disabled Children?," *Learning Disabilities Quarterly* 8, no. 1 (1985): 19–26; Valerie A. Helgren-Lempesis and Charles T. Mangrum, "An Analysis of Alternate-Form Reliability of Three Commercially-Prepared Informal Reading Inventories," *Reading Research Quarterly* 21, no. 2 (Spring 1986): 209–15; Nina L. Nilsson, "The Reliability of Informal Reading Inventories: What Has Changed?," *Reading & Writing Quarterly* 29, no. 3 (2013): 208–30; Janet E. Spector, "How Reliable are Informal Reading Inventories?," *Psychology in the Schools* 42, no. 6 (July 2005): 593–603.
13. Spector, "Informal Reading Inventories?"
14. For example, Matthew K. Burns et al., "Interscorer, Alternate-Form, Internal Consistency, and Test-Retest Reliability of Gickling's Model of Curriculum-Based Assessment for Reading," *Journal of Psychoeducational Assessment* 18, no. 4 (2000): 353–60.
15. John M. Hintze et al., "An Investigation of the Effects of Passage Difficulty Level on Outcomes of Oral Reading Fluency Progress Monitoring, *School Psychology Review* 27, no. 3 (1998): 433–45.
16. Marie M. Clay, "Emergent Reading Behavior" (unpublished PhD diss., University of Auckland, 1966); Carolyn A. Denton et al., "Text-Processing Differences in Adolescent Adequate and Poor Comprehenders Reading Accessible and Challenging Narrative and Informational Text," *Reading Research Quarterly* 50, no. 4 (2015): 393–416.
17. Jerome V. D'Agostino et al., "The Generalizability of Running Record Accuracy and Self-Correction Scores," *Reading Psychology* 42, no. 2 (2021): 111–30; Parker C. Fawson et al., "Examining the Reliability of Running Records: Attaining Generalizable Results," *Journal of Educational Research* 100, no. 2 (2006): 113–26.
18. Gregg Bieber et al., "An Independent Evaluation of the Technical Features of the Basic Reading Inventory," *Journal of Psychoeducational Assessment* 33, no. 3 (2015): 199–209.
19. Darrell Morris et al., "The Simple View, Instructional Level, and the Plight of Struggling Fifth-/Sixth-Grade Readers," *Reading & Writing Quarterly* 33, no. 3 (2017): 278–89.
20. Patrick R. McCabe et al., "The Consistency of Reading Disabled Students' Instructional Levels As Determined by the Metropolitan Achievement Test and the Ekwall Informal Reading Inventory," *Reading Research and Instruction* 30, no. 3 (1991): 53–62.
21. Spector, "Informal Reading Inventory?," 598.
22. Joe Peterson et al., "Assessing Instructional Placement with the IRI: The Effectiveness of Comprehension Questions," *Journal of Educational Research* 71, no. 5 (1978): 247–50.
23. Peterson et al., "Assessing Instructional Placement," 248.
24. Scott P. Ardoin and Theodore J. Christ, "Curriculum-Based Measurement of Oral Reading: Standard Errors Associated with Progress Monitoring Outcomes from DIBELS, AIMSweb, and an Experimental Passage Set," *School Psychology Review* 38, no. 2 (2009): 266–83; Theodore J. Christ and Benjamin Silberglitt, "Curriculum-Based Measurement of Oral Reading Fluency: The Standard Error of Measurement," *School Psychology Review* 36, no. 1 (2007): 130–46; Erin K. Dunn and Tanya L. Eckert, "Curriculum-Based Measurement in Reading: A Comparison of Similar Versus Challenging Material," *School Psychology Quarterly* 17, no. 1 (2002): 24–46, 41; David J. Francis et al., "Form Effects on the Estimation of Students' Oral Reading Fluency Using DIBELS," *Journal of School Psychology* 46, no. 3 (2008): 315–42; Michael Stoolmiller et al., "Measurement Properties of DIBELS Oral Reading Fluency in Grade 2: Implications

for Equating Studies," *Assessment for Effective Intervention* 38, no. 2 (March 2013): 76–90.

25. Richard L. Allington, "Teacher Ability in Recording Oral Reading Performance," *Academic Theory* 14 (1978): 1871–91; J. Harvey Littrell, "Teacher Estimates Versus Reading Test Results," *Journal of Reading* 12, no. 1 (October 1968): 18–23, William D. Page and Kenneth L. Carlson, "The Process of Observing Oral Reading Scores," *Reading Horizons* 15, no. 3 (April 1975): 147–50; Elaine Wunderlich and Mary Bradtmueller, "Teacher Estimates of Reading Levels Compared with IRPI Instructional Level Scores," *Journal of Reading* 14, no. 5 (February 1971): 303–08.
26. Bieber et al., "Independent Evaluation"; Matthew K. Burns, "Reading at the Instructional Level with Children Identified as Learning Disabled: Potential Implications for Response-to-Intervention," *School Psychology Quarterly* 22, no. 3 (2007): 297–313; Katurah Cramer and Sylvia Rosenfield, "Effect of Degree of Challenge on Reading Performance," *Reading & Writing Quarterly: Overcoming Learning Difficulties* 24, no. 1: 119–37; Douglas B. Marston, "A Curriculum-Based Measurement Approach to Assessing Academic Performance: What It Is and Why Do It," in *Curriculum-Based Measurement: Assessing Special Children*, ed. Mark R. Shinn (Guilford Press, 1989); Darrell Morris et al., "Validating Craft Knowledge: An Empirical Examination of Elementary-Grade Students' Performance on an Informal Reading Assessment," *Elementary School Journal* 112, no. 2 (2011): 205–33; Nilsson, "What Has Changed?"; David C. Parker et al., "A Brief Report of the Diagnostic Accuracy of Oral Reading Fluency and Reading Inventory Levels for Reading Failure Risk Among Second- and Third-Grade Students," *Reading & Writing Quarterly* 31, no. 1 (2015): 56–67; Spector, "Informal Reading Inventory?"
27. The "car" pronunciation is common among many New Englanders, the "cold" pronunciation is drawn from Black English Vernacular, the "here" pronunciation is common in the American south, and the "out" variation is Canadian and is common in the upper Midwest (and this latter pronunciation is my own).
28. Edward E. Gickling, "Controlling Academic and Social Performance Using an Instructional Delivery Approach," in *Programming for the Emotionally Handicapped: Administrative Considerations* (Lexington, KY: Coordination Office for Regional Resource Centers, 1977), 47.
29. Betts, Foundations, 447.
30. Matthew K. Burns et al., "Accuracy of Student Performance While Reading Leveled Books Rated at their Instructional Level by a Reading Inventory," *Journal of School Psychology* 53, no. 6 (2015): 437–45, 441–42; Fethi Calisir and Zafer Gurel, "Influence of Text Structure and Prior Knowledge of the Learner on Reading Comprehension, Browsing and Perceived Control," *Computers in Human Behavior* 19, no. 2 (2003): 135–45; Theodore J. Christ et al., "Curriculum Based Measurement of Reading: Consistency and Validity Across Best, Fastest, and Question Reading Conditions," *School Psychology Review* 42, no. 4 (2013): 415–36; Elfrieda H. Hiebert and P. David Pearson, *An Examination of Current Text Difficulty Indices with Early Reading Texts* (TextProject, 2010).
31. Susan S. Homan, and Janell P. Klesius, "A Re-Examination of the IRI: Word Recognition Criteria," *Reading Horizons* 26, no. 1 (1985).
32. John J. Pikulski and Timothy Shanahan, "Informal Reading Inventories: A Critical Analysis," in *Approaches to the Informal Evaluation of Reading*, ed. John J. Pikulski and Timothy Shanahan (International Reading Association, 1982).

33. Sheila W. Valencia et al., "Oral Reading Fluency Assessment: Issues of Construct, Criterion, and Consequential Validity," *Reading Research Quarterly* 45, no. 3 (July–September 2010): 270–91.
34. Francis et al., "Form Effects."
35. Douglas Fuchs et al., "Reliability and Validity of Curriculum-Based Informal Reading Inventories," *Reading Research Quarterly* 18, no. 1 (1982), 6–26.
36. Fuchs and Deno, "Performance Instability," 9.
37. Steve Amendum, Kristin Conradi, and Elfrieda H. Hiebert, "Does Text Complexity Matter in the Elementary Grades? A Research Synthesis of Text Difficulty and Elementary Students' Reading Fluency and Comprehension," *Educational Psychology Review* 30, no. 1 (March 2018): 121–51.
38. Betts, *Foundations*, 449–50, 457.
39. R. D. Brecht, "Testing Format and Instructional Level with the Informal Reading Inventory," *The Reading Teacher* 31, no. 1 (October 1977): 57–59.
40. Robert E. Lowell, "Problems in Identifying Reading Levels with Informal Reading Inventories," in *Reading Difficulties: Diagnosis, Correction, and Remediation*, ed. William Durr (International Reading Association, 1970).
41. Phillip C. Gonzalez and David Elijah, "Stability of Error Patterns on the Informal Reading Inventory," *Reading Improvement* 15, no. 4 (Winter 1978): 279–88.
42. Phillip C. Gonzalez, "The Effect of Repeated Oral Readings at Instructional and Frustration Levels on Reading Performance in Third Grade Developmental Readers" (unpublished PhD diss., New Mexico Highlands University); Edward J. Daly, III et al., "The Effects of Instructional Match and Content Overlap on Generalized Reading Performance," *Journal of Applied Behavior Analysis* 29, no. 4 (1996): 507–18.
43. Matthew K. Burns et al., "Comparison of the Effectiveness and Efficiency of Text Previewing and Preteaching Keywords as Small-Group Reading Comprehension Strategies with Middle-School Students," *Literacy Research and Instruction* 50 (2011): 241–52.
44. Valencia et al., "Oral Reading Fluency Assessment."
45. John T. Guthrie, "Learnability Versus Readability of Texts," *Journal of Educational Research* 65, no. 6 (1972): 273–80.
46. Aristotle, *Poetics*, trans. Malcolm Heath (Penguin Classics, 1997).
47. Bertha A. Lively and Sidney L. Pressey, "A Method for Measuring the Vocabulary Burden of Textbooks," *Educational Administration and Supervision* 9 (1923): 389–98.
48. Kathleen C. Stevens, "Readability Formulae and McCall-Crabbs Standard Test Lessons in Reading," *Reading Teacher* 33, no. 4 (January 1980): 413–15, 413.
49. William S. Gray and Beverly E. Leary, *What Makes a Book Readable* (University of Chicago Press, 1935).
50. Tiffany Gallagher et al., "Comparison of Readability in Science-Based Texts: Implications for Elementary Teachers," *Canadian Journal of Education* 40, no. 1 (2017): 1–29; Yukie Toyama, Elfrieda H. Hiebert, and P. David Pearson, "An Analysis of the Text Complexity of Leveled Passages in Four Popular Classroom Reading Assessments," *Educational Assessment* 22, no. 3 (2017): 139–70.
51. Gallagher et al., "Comparison of Readability."
52. Heidi Anne E. Mesmer, *Tools for Matching Readers to Texts* (Guilford Press, 2008), 38.
53. Elfrieda H. Hiebert and P. David Pearson, *An Examination of Current Text Difficulty Indices with Early Reading Texts* (TextProject, 2010).
54. Toyama et al., "Popular Reading Assessments," 161.

55. Alice Davison and Robert N. Kantor, "On the Failure of Readability Formulas to Define Readable Texts: A Case Study from Adaptations," *Reading Research Quarterly* 17, no. 2 (1982), 187–209; Mesmer, *Tools for Matching Readers.*
56. Alice Davison and Georgia M. Green, eds. *Linguistic Complexity and Text Comprehension: Readability Issues Reconsidered* (Lawrence Erlbaum, 1988); Davison and Kantor, "Failure of Readability Formulas"; P. David Pearson, "The Effects of Grammatical Complexity on Children's Comprehension, Recall, and Conception of Certain Semantic Relations," *Reading Research Quarterly* 10, no. 2 (1974): 153–92.
57. Ludivine Javourey-Drevet et al., "Simplification of Literary and Scientific Texts to Improve Reading Fluency and Comprehension in Beginning Readers of French," *Applied Psycholinguistics* 43, no. 2 (2022): 485–512.
58. Isabel L. Beck et al., "Revising Social Studies Text from a Text-Processing Perspective: Evidence of Improved Comprehensibility," *Reading Research Quarterly* 26, no. 3 (1991): 251–76.
59. Mark A. McDaniel et al., "When Text Difficulty Benefits Less-Skilled Readers," *Journal of Memory and Language* 46, no. 3 (2020), 544–61.
60. John M. Bradley and Wilbur S. Ames, "The Influence of Intrabook Readability Variation on Oral Reading Performance," *Journal of Educational Research* 70, no. 2 (1976): 101–05.
61. For example, Gallagher et al., "Comparison of Readability"; Sheida White and John Clement, *Assessing the Lexile Framework: Results of a Panel Meeting* (U.S. Department of Education, National Center for Education Statistics, 2001).
62. A. Jackson Stenner et al., "How Accurate are Lexile Text Measures?," *Journal of Applied Measurement* 7, no. 3 (2006): 307–22.
63. Elfrieda H. Hiebert, "Beyond Single Readability Measures: Using Multiple Sources of Information in Establishing Text Complexity," *Journal of Education* 191, no. 2 (April 2011): 33–42, 35.
64. American Educational Research Association, American Psychological Association, and National Council on Measurement in Education, *Standards for Educational and Psychological Testing* (National Council on Measurement in Education, 2014), 11.
65. James W. Cunningham and Heidi Anne E. Mesmer, "Quantitative Measurement of Text Difficulty," *Elementary School Journal* 115, no. 2 (December 2014): 255–69, 259.
66. Cunningham and Mesmer, "Quantitative Measurement," 262.
67. Council of Chief State School Officers and National Governors Association, *Supplemental Information for Appendix A of Common Core State Standards for English Language Arts & Literacy: New Research on Text Complexity* (Washington, DC: Council of Chief State School Officers and National Governors Association, n.d.).
68. For example, James W. Cunningham et al., "Investigating the Instructional Supportiveness of Leveled Texts," *Reading Research Quarterly* 40, no. 4 (2005): 410–27; Heidi Anne E. Mesmer, "Text-Reader Matching: Meeting the Needs of Struggling Readers," in *Finding the Right Texts*, Elfrieda H. Hiebert and Misty Sailors (Guilford Press, 2009).
69. Council of Chief State School Officers and National Governors Association, n.d.
70. Heidi Anne E. Mesmer, *Tools for Matching Readers to Texts* (Guilford Press, 2008).
71. P. David Pearson and Elfrieda H. Hiebert, "The State of the Field: Qualitative Analyses of Text Complexity," *Elementary School Journal* 115, no. 2 (December 2014): 161–83.
72. B. L. Peterson, "Selecting Books for Beginning Readers," in *Bridges to Literacy: Learning from Reading Recovery*, ed. Diane E. DeFord, Carol A. Lyons, and Gay Su Pinnell (Heineman, 1991).

73. Irene C. Fountas and Gay Su Pinnell, *The F & P Text Level Gradient: Revision to Recommended Grade-Level Goals* (Heinemann, 2012).
74. Kath Glasswell and Michael Ford, "Let's Start Leveling about Leveling," *Language Arts* 88, no. 3 (January 2011): 208–16, 212.
75. Brandy Pitcher and Zhihui Fang, "Can We Trust Levelled Texts? An Examination of Their Reliability and Quality from a Linguistic Perspective," *Literacy* 41, no. 1 (April 2007): 43–51, 46.
76. Peter J. Hatcher, "Predictors of Reading Recovery Book Levels," *Journal of Research in Reading* 23, no. 1 (2000): 67–77.
77. James V. Hoffman et al., "Test Leveling and 'Little Books' in First-Grade Reading," *Journal of Literacy Research* 33, no. 3 (September 2001): 507–28.
78. Pearson and Hiebert, "State of the Field."
79. Fountas and Pinnell, *F & P Text.*
80. Pitcher and Fang, "Linguistic Perspective," 50.
81. Glasswell and Ford, "Let's Start Leveling."
82. Karin Berendes et al., "Reading Demands in Secondary School: Does the Linguistic Complexity of Textbooks Increase with Grade Level and the Academic Orientation of the School Track?," *Journal of Educational Psychology* 110, no. 4 (2018): 518–43; Arthur C. Graesser et al., "Coh-Metrix: Providing Multilevel Analyses of Text Characteristics," *Educational Researcher* 40, no. 5 (2011): 223–34; Elfrieda H. Hiebert, "Beyond Single Readability Measures: Using Multiple Sources of Information in Establishing Text Complexity," *Journal of Education* 191, no. 2 (April 2011): 33–42.
83. Scott A. Crossley et al., "Predicting Text Comprehension, Processing, and Familiarity in Adult Readers: New Approaches to Readability Formulas," *Discourse Processes* 54, no. 5–6 (2017): 340–59.
84. Graesser et al., "Coh-Metrix."
85. Thomas K. Landauer et al., "Word Maturity: A New Metric for Word Knowledge," *Scientific Studies of Reading* 15, no. 1 (2011): 92–108.
86. Kathleen M. Sheehan et al., "The TextEvaluator Tool: Helping Teachers and Test Developers Select Texts for Use in Instruction and Assessment," *Elementary School Journal* 115, no. 2 (December 2014): 184–209.
87. Graesser et al., "Coh-Metrix."
88. Aage B. Sørensen and Maureen T. Hallinan, "Effects of Ability Grouping on Growth in Academic Achievement," *American Educational Research Journal* 23, no. 4 (Winter 1986): 519–42, 537.
89. Elfrieda H. Hiebert, "The Context of Instruction and Student Learning: An Examination of Slavin's Assumptions," *Review of Educational Research* 57, no. 3 (Autumn 1987): 337–40, 337.
90. David C. Berliner and Bruce J. Biddle, *The Manufactured Crisis: Myths, Fraud, and the Attack on America's Public Schools* (Perseus Books, 1995), 321.
91. Jeanne S. Schumm et al., "Grouping for Reading Instruction: Does One Size Fit All?," *Journal of Learning Disabilities* 33, no. 5 (September 2000): 477–88.
92. Elfrieda H. Hiebert, "An Examination of Ability Grouping for Reading Instruction," *Reading Research Quarterly* 18, no. 2 (Winter 1983): 231–55.
93. Rebecca Barr and Robert Dreeben, *How Schools Work* (University of Chicago Press, 1983); Barbara Fink Chorzempa and Steve Graham, "Primary-Grade Teachers' Use of Within-Class Ability Grouping in Reading," *Journal of Educational Psychology* 98, no. 3 (2006): 529–41; Ford and Opitz, "National Survey."

94. Hilda Borko and Jerome Niles, "Factors Contributing to Teachers' Judgments about Students and Decisions about Grouping Students for Reading Instruction," *Journal of Reading Behavior* 14, no. 2 (1982): 127–40; Hallinan and Sørensen, "Effects of Ability Grouping"; Ron Haskins et al., "Teacher and Student Behavior in High- and Low-Ability Groups," *Journal of Educational Psychology* 75, no. 6 (1983): 865–76.
95. Emil J. Haller, "Pupil Race and Elementary School Ability Grouping: Are Teachers Biased Against Black Children?," *American Educational Research Journal* 22, no. 2 (1985): 465–83.
96. Cathy M. Roller, "Teacher–Student Interaction During Oral Reading and Rereading," *Journal of Reading Behavior* 26, no. 2 (June 1994): 191–209, 207.
97. Anthony Buttaro Jr. et al., "An Organizational Perspective on the Origins of Instructional Segregation: School Composition and Use of Within-Class Ability Grouping in American Kindergartens," *Teachers College Record* 112, no. 5 (2010): 1300–37; Chorzempa and Graham, "Primary-Grade"; Dennis J. Condron, "An Early Start: Skill Grouping and Unequal Reading Gains in the Elementary Years," *Sociological Quarterly* 49, no. 2 (2008): 363–94; Dennis J. Condron, "Stratification and Educational Sorting: Explaining Ascriptive Inequalities in Early Childhood Reading Group Placement," *Social Problems* 54, no. 1 (2007): 139–60; Diane Felmlee and Donna Eder, "Contextual Effects in the Classroom: The Impact of Ability Groups on Student Attention," *Sociology of Education* 56, no. 2 (1983): 77–87; Grant and Rothenberg, "Social Enhancement"; Haskins et al., "Teacher and Student Behavior."
98. Laura Northrop and Sean Kelly. "Who Gets to Read What? Tracking, Instructional Practices, and Text Complexity for Middle School Struggling Readers," *Reading Research Quarterly* 54, no. 3 (July–September 2019): 339–61.
99. For example, Sally Watson Moody et al., "Grouping Suggestions for the Classroom: What Do Our Basal Reading Series Tell Us?," *Reading Research and Instruction* 38, no. 4 (1999): 319–31.
100. A. H. Turney, "The Status of Ability Grouping," *Educational Administration and Supervision* 17 (1931): 21–42, 110–27.
101. Chorzempa and Graham, "Primary-Grade."
102. Ford and Opitz, "National Survey."
103. Carol McDonald Connor et al., "Beyond the Reading Wars: Exploring the Effect of Child-Instruction Interactions on Growth in Early Reading," *Scientific Studies of Reading* 8, no. 4 (2004): 305–36; Carol McDonald Connor et al., "A Second Chance in Second Grade: The Independent and Cumulative Impact of First- and Second-Grade Reading Instruction and Students' Letter-Word Reading Skill Growth," *Scientific Studies of Reading* 11, no. 3 (2007): 199–233; Carol McDonald Connor et al., "A Longitudinal Cluster-Randomized Controlled Study on the Accumulating Effects of Individualized Literacy Instruction on Students' Reading from First through Third Grade," *Psychological Science* 24, no. 8 (August 2013): 1408–19.
104. Joseph P. Robinson, "Evidence of a Differential Effect of Ability Grouping on the Reading Achievement Growth of Language-Minority Hispanics," *Educational Evaluation and Policy Analysis* 30, no. 2 (2008): 141–80.
105. Sørenson and Hallinan, "Effects of Ability Grouping"; Guanglei Hong and Yihua Hong, "Reading Instruction Time and Homogeneous Grouping in Kindergarten: An Application of Marginal Mean Weighting Through Stratification," *Educational Evaluation and Policy Analysis* 31, no. 1 (2009): 54–81.
106. Haller, "Pupil Race."

107. Barr and Dreeben, *How Schools Work*; Hallinan and Sørenson, "Effects of Ability Grouping."
108. Neena Banerjee, "Student–Teacher Ethno-Racial Matching and Reading Ability Group Placement in Early Grades," *Education and Urban Society* 51, no. 3 (2019): 395–422; James D. Jones et al., "Individual and Organizational Predictors of High School Track Placement," *Sociology of Education* 68, no. 4 (October 1995): 287–300; Jeannie Oakes, *Keeping Track: How Schools Structure Inequality* (Yale University Press, 1985); James E. Rosenbaum, "Track Misperceptions and Frustrated College Plans: An Analysis of the Effects of Tracks and Track Perceptions in the National Longitudinal Survey," *Sociology of Education* 53 (April 1980): 74–88; Elizabeth L. Useem, "Middle Schools and Math Groups: Parents' Involvement in Children's Placement," *Sociology of Education* 65, no. 4 (1992): 263–79.
109. Robert E. Slavin, "Ability Grouping in Elementary Schools: Do We Really Know Nothing Until We Know Everything?," *Review of Educational Research* 57, no. 3 (Fall 1987b): 347–50.
110. Michael L. Kamil and W. Christine Rauscher, "Effects of Grouping and Difficulty of Materials on Reading Achievement," *National Reading Conference Yearbook* 39 (1990): 121–27.
111. Anthony Buttaro Jr. and Sophia Catsambis, "Ability Grouping in the Early Grades: Long-Term Consequences for Educational Equity in the United States," *Teachers College Record* 121, no. 2 (2019): 1–50; Adam Gamoran, "Instructional and Institutional Effects of Ability Grouping," *Sociology of Education* 59, no. 4 (1986): 185–98; Maureen T. Hallinan and Aage B. Sørensen, "The Formation and Stability of Instructional Groups," *American Sociological Review* 48, no. 6 (December 1983): 838–51; Hong and Hong, "Reading Instruction Time"; Aaron M. Pallas et al., "Ability-Group Effects: Instructional, Social, or Institutional?," *Sociology of Education* 67, no. 1 (1994): 27–46; Elfrieda H. Hiebert, "The Context of Instruction and Student Learning: An Examination of Slavin's Assumptions," *Review of Educational Research* 57, no. 3 (Autumn 1987): 337–40; Robert E. Slavin, "Ability Grouping and Student Achievement in Elementary Schools: A Best-Evidence Synthesis," *Review of Educational Research* 57, no. 3 (Fall 1987): 293–336; Slavin, "Until We Know Everything"; Robert E. Slavin, "Ability Grouping in the Middle Grades: Achievement Effects and Alternatives," *The Elementary School Journal* 93, no. 5 (May 1993): 535–52.
112. Jill L. Adelson and Brittany D. Carpenter, "Grouping for Achievement Gains: For Whom Does Achievement Grouping Increase Kindergarten Reading Growth?," *Gifted Child Quarterly* 55, no. 4 (2011): 265–78; Batya Elbaum et al., "Grouping Practices and Reading Outcomes for Students with Disabilities," *Exceptional Children* 65, no. 3 (1999): 399–415; Richard H. Hart, "The Effectiveness of an Approach to the Problem of Varying Abilities in Teaching Reading," *Journal of Educational Research* 52, no. 6 (1959): 228–31; Yiping Lou et al., "Within-Class Grouping: A Meta-Analysis," *Review of Educational Research* 66, no. 4 (Winter 1996): 423–58; D. Betsy McCoach et al., "Ability Grouping Across Kindergarten Using an Early Childhood Longitudinal Study," *Journal of Educational Research* 99, no. 6 (July–August 2006): 339–46; Susan Kemper Patrick, "Homogeneous Grouping in Early Elementary Reading Instruction: The Challenge of Identifying Appropriate Comparisons and Examining Differential Associations Between Grouping and Reading Growth," *Elementary School Journal* 120, no. 4 (June 2020): 611–35.
113. Steven J. Amendum et al., "Which Reading Lesson Instruction Characteristics Matter for Early Reading Achievement?," *Reading Psychology* 30, no. 2 (2009): 119–47; Mitchell M.

Berkun et al., "An Experiment on Homogeneous Grouping for Reading in Elementary Classes," *Journal of Educational Research* 59, no. 9 (1966): 413–14; Hallinan and Sørenson, "Formation and Stability"; Hong and Hong, "Reading Instruction Time."

114. Steven J. Amendum et al., "Which Reading Lesson Instruction Characteristics Matter for Early Reading Achievement?," *Reading Psychology* 30, no. 2 (2009): 119–47, 141.

115. Amendum et al., "Which Reading Lesson"; Condron, "Early Start"; Felmlee and Eder, "Contextual Effects"; Hallinan and Sørenson, "Formation and Stability"; Northrop and Kelly, "Who Gets to Read"; Patrick, "Homogeneous Grouping"; Sørenson and Hallinan, "Effects of Ability Grouping,"1986).

116. Buttaro and Catsambis, "Ability Grouping"; James Collins, "Discourse Style, Classroom Interaction and Differential Treatment," *Journal of Reading Behavior* 14, no. 4 (1982): 429–37; Condron, "Stratification and Educational Sorting."

117. Jere E. Brophy, "Teacher Behavior and Student Learning;" *Educational Leadership* 37 (1979): 33–38; Bonnie W. Camp and Sara G. Zimet, "Classroom Behavior During Reading Instruction," *Exceptional Children* 42, no. 2 (October 1975): 109–10; Donna Eder, "Differences in Communicative Styles Across Ability Groups," in *Communicating in the Classroom*, ed. Louise Cherry Wilkinson (Academic, 1982), 245–64; Linda Grant and James Rothenberg, "The Social Enhancement of Ability Differences: Teacher-Student Interactions in First- and Second-Grade Reading Groups," *The Elementary School Journal* 87, no. 1 (1986): 29–49; Ray C. Rist, "Student Social Class and Teacher Expectations: The Self-Fulfilling Prophecy in Ghetto Education," *Harvard Educational Review* 40, no. 3 (September 1970): 411–51.

118. Richard L. Allington, "Teacher Interruption Behaviors During Primary-Grade Oral Reading," *Journal of Educational Psychology* 73, no. 7 (1980): 371–77; Richard L. Allington, "The Reading Instruction Provided Readers of Differing Ability," *Elementary School Journal* 83, no. 5 (1983): 255–65.

119. Linda B. Gambrell et al., "Classroom Observations of Task-Attending Behaviors of Good and Poor Readers," *Journal of Educational Research* 74, no. 6 (1981): 400–404.

120. Judith L. Alpert, "Teacher Behavior Across Ability Groups: A Consideration of the Mediation of Pygmalion Effects," *Journal of Educational Psychology* 66, no. 3 (1974): 348–53; Barr and Dreeben, *How Schools Work*; Rhona S. Weinstein, "Reading Group Membership in the First Grade: Teacher Behaviors and Pupil Experience over Time," *Journal of Educational Psychology* 68, no. 1 (February 1976): 103–16.

121. Christy Lleras and Claudia Rangel, "Ability Grouping Practices in Elementary School and African American/Hispanic Achievement," *American Journal of Education* 115, no. 2 (2009): 279–304.

122. Banerjee, "Student–Teacher Ethno-Racial Matching."

123. Condron, "Stratification and Educational Sorting."

124. Condron, "Stratification and Educational Sorting."

125. Sørenson and Hallinan, "Effects of Ability Grouping," 540.

126. Dorothy P. Hall and Patricia M. Cunningham, "Reading Without Ability Grouping: Issues in First-Grade Instruction," *National Reading Conference Yearbook* 41 (1992): 235–41.

127. P. Karen Murphy et al., "Exploring the Influence of Homogeneous Versus Heterogeneous Grouping on Students' Text-Based Discussions and Comprehension," *Contemporary Educational Psychology* 51 (2017): 336–55.

128. Alisa Morgan et al., "Effect of Difficulty Levels on Second-Grade Delayed Readers Using Dyad Reading," *Journal of Educational Research* 94, no. 2 (2000): 113–19, 119.

129. Heidi Anne E. Mesmer and Elfrieda H. Hiebert, "Third Graders' Reading Proficiency Reading Texts Varying in Complexity and Length: Reponses of Students in an Urban, High-Needs School," *Journal of Literacy Research* 47, no. 4 (2016): 473–504.
130. Douglas Fisher and Nancy Frey, "Scaffolded Reading Instruction of Content-Area Texts," *The Reading Teacher* 67, no. 5 (February 2014): 347–51.

Chapter 5

1. Anthony Buttaro Jr. and Sophia Catsambis, "Ability Grouping in the Early Grades: Long-Term Consequences for Educational Equity in the United States," *Teachers College Record* 121, no. 2 (2019): 1–50; Aage B. Sørensen and Maureen T. Hallinan, "Effects of Ability Grouping on Growth in Academic Achievement," *American Educational Research Journal* 23, no. 4 (Winter 1986): 519–42.
2. Kath Glasswell and Michael Ford, "Let's Start Leveling about Leveling," *Language Arts* 88, no. 3 (January 2011): 208–16; James V. Hoffman, "What If "Just Right" Is Just Wrong? The Unintended Consequences of Leveling Readers," *The Reading Teacher* 71, no. 3 (June 2017): 265–73.
3. Irene C. Fountas and Gay Su Pinnell, *Guided Reading*, 2nd ed. (Heinemann, 2016).
4. Morton Wiener and Ward Cromer, "Reading and Reading Difficulty: A Conceptual Analysis," *Harvard Educational Review* 37, no. 4 (December 1967): 620–43.
5. Wiener and Cromer, "Reading and Reading Difficulty," 621.
6. For example, Catherine E. Snow and the RAND Reading Study Group, *Reading for Understanding: Toward an R&D Program in Reading Comprehension* (RAND, 2002).
7. Philip B. Gough and William E. Tunmer, "Decoding, Reading, and Reading Disability," *Remedial and Special Education* 7, no.1 (January–February 1986): 6–10.
8. For example, Hollis S. Scarborough, "Connecting Early Language and Literacy to Later Reading (Dis)abilities: Evidence, Theory, and Practice," in *Handbook for Research in Early Literacy*, ed. Susan B. Neuman and David K. Dickinson (Guilford Press, 2001).
9. Nell K. Duke, and Kelly B. Cartwright, "The Science of Reading Progresses: Communicating Advances Beyond the Simple View of Reading," *Reading Research Quarterly* 56, no. S1 (2021): S25–S44.
10. E. D. Hirsch Jr., *Validity in Interpretation* (Yale University Press, 1967).
11. Garry Wills, *Lincoln at Gettysburg* (Simon & Schuster, 1992).
12. Wills, *Lincoln at Gettysburg.*
13. American College Testing, *Reading Between the Lines* (American College Testing, 2006).
14. For example, National Reading Panel (U.S.) and National Institute of Child Health and Human Development (U.S.), *Report of the National Reading Panel: Teaching Children to Read: An Evidence-based Assessment of the Scientific Research Literature on Reading and Its Implications for Reading Instruction* (Bethesda, MD.: U.S. Dept. of Health and Human Services, Public Health Service, National Institutes of Health, National Institute of Child Health and Human Development, 2000).
15. Daniel T. Willingham, "Beyond Comprehension," *Educational Leadership* 81, no. 4 (2023). https://ascd.org/el/articles/beyond-comprehension.
16. Marie M. Clay, *Reading Recovery: A Guidebook for Teachers in Training* (Heinemann, 1993).
17. Irene C. Fountas and Gay Su Pinnell, *Guided Reading*, 2nd ed. (Heinemann, 2016).
18. David L. Share and Keith E. Stanovich, "Cognitive Processes in Early Reading Development: Accommodating Individual Differences into a Model of Acquisition," *Issues in Education: Contributions from Educational Psychology* 1, (1995): 1–57.

19. National Governors Association Center for Best Practices and Council of Chief State School Officers, *Common Core State Standards for English Language Arts & Literacy in History/Social Studies, Science, and Technical Subjects (with Appendices A & B)* (Washington, DC: National Governors Association Center for Best Practices and Council of Chief State School Officers, 2010).
20. Elfrieda H. Hiebert, "The Common Core's Staircase of Text Complexity: Getting the Size of the First Step Right," *Reading Today* 1, no. 3 (2011–2012): 26–28.
21. James W. Cunningham et al., "Investigating the Validity of Two Widely Used Quantitative Measures," *Reading and Writing* 31 (2018): 813–33; James W. Cunningham et al., "Investigating the Instructional Supportiveness of Leveled Texts," *Reading Research Quarterly* 40, no. 4 (2005): 410–27; Heidi Anne E. Mesmer, "Text-Reader Matching: Meeting the Needs of Struggling Readers," in *Finding the Right Texts*, ed. Elfrieda H. Hiebert and Misty Sailors (Guilford Press, 2009), 149–76; Heidi Anne E. Mesmer and Elfrieda H. Hiebert, "Third Graders' Reading Proficiency Reading Texts Varying in Complexity and Length: Responses of Students in an Urban, High-Needs School," *Journal of Literacy Research* 47, no. 4 (2015): 473–504.
22. Sheila W. Valencia et al., "Putting Text Complexity in Context: Refocusing on Comprehension of Complex Text," *The Elementary School Journal* 115, no. 2 (2014): 270–89; Susan R. Goldman and Carol D. Lee, "Text Complexity: State of the Art and the Conundrums it Raises," *The Elementary School Journal* 115, no. 2 (2014): 290–300.
23. David C. Parker and Matthew K. Burns, "Using the Instructional Level as a Criterion to Target Reading Interventions," *Reading & Writing Quarterly* 30, no. 1 (November 2013): 79–94.
24. Karen K. Wixson, "Vocabulary Instruction and Children's Comprehension of Basal Stories," *Reading Research Quarterly* 21, no. 3 (Summer 1986): 317–29.
25. Chase Young et al., "Read Like Me: An Intervention for Struggling Readers," *Education Sciences* 10, no. 3 (March 2020): 57–68.
26. Matthew K. Burns, "Reading at the Instructional Level with Children Identified as Learning Disabled: Potential Implications for Response-to-Intervention," *School Psychology Quarterly* 22, no. 3 (2007): 297–313.
27. Stacy Lynn Smith, "Will Raising the Bar Result in Greater Reading Growth" (unpublished PhD diss., Ball State University, 2019).
28. Cunningham et al., "Investigating the Instructional"; Pearson and Hiebert, "The State of the Field: Qualitative Analyses of Text Complexity," *Elementary School Journal* 115, no. 2 (December 2014): 161–83, https://doi.org/10.1086/678297.
29. John D. Bransford et al., "Anchored Instruction: Why We Need It and How Technology Can Help," in *Cognition, Education and Multimedia*, ed. Don Nix and Rand Sprio (Erlbaum Associates, 1990), 111–28.
30. For example, Cailbhe Doherty et al., "An Evaluation of the Training Determinants of Marathon Performance: A Meta-Analysis with Meta-Regression," *Journal of Science and Sports Medicine* 23, no. 2 (2019): 182–88.
31. John A. C. Hattie, 2008, *Visible Learning: A Synthesis of Over 800 Meta-Analyses Relating to Achievement* (Routledge, 2008).
32. Linnea C. Ehri et al., "Reading Rescue: An Effective Tutoring Intervention Model for Language-Minority Students Who Are Struggling Readers in First Grade," *American Educational Research Journal*, 44, no. 2 (2007): 414–48.
33. MRI-Simmons, *American Kids Survey* (Mediamark Research, 2006).
34. Hiebert, "The Common Core's Staircase of Text."

Chapter 6

1. Richard L. Venezky, *The American Way of Spelling* (Guilford Press, 2000), 135–40.
2. Richard L. Venezky, "English Orthography: Its Graphical Structure and Its Relation to Sound," *Reading Research Quarterly* 2, no. 3 (Spring 1967): 75–105.
3. Rebecca Barr, "The Effect of Instruction on Pupil Reading Strategies," *Reading Research Quarterly* 10, no. 4 (1974–1975): 555–82; Andrew Biemiller, "The Development of the Use of Graphic and Contextual Information as Children Learn to Read," *Reading Research Quarterly* 6, no. 1 (Autumn 1970): 75–96.
4. Linnea Ehri, "Orthographic Mapping in the Acquisition of Sight Word Reading, Spelling Memory, and Vocabulary Learning," *Scientific Studies of Reading* 18, no. 1 (2014): 5–21.
5. Marilyn J. Adams, "Decodable Text: Why, When, and How?" in *Finding the Right Texts: What Works for Beginning and Struggling Readers,* ed. Elfrieda H. Hiebert and Misty Sailors (Guilford Press, 2009), 23–46, 23.
6. Elfrieda H. Hiebert and Leigh Ann Martin, "Changes in the Texts of Reading Instruction During the Past Fifty Years," in *Research Based Practices for Teaching Common Core Literacy*, ed. P. David Pearson and Elfrieda H. Hiebert (Teachers College Press, 2015); Jill Fitzgerald et al., "Has First-Grade Core Reading Program Text Complexity Changed Across Six Decades?," *Reading Research Quarterly* 51, no. 1 (January–February 2016): 7–28.
7. Elfrieda H. Hiebert, "Unpacking Automaticity: Scaffolded Texts and Comprehension," *Journal of Adolescent and Adult Literacy* (forthcoming).
8. Leonard Bloomfield and Clarence L. Burkhardt, *Let's Read: A Linguistic Approach* (Wayne State University Press), 1961.
9. Guy L. Bond and Robert Dykstra, "The Co-Operative Research Program in First Grade Reading Instruction," *Reading Research Quarterly* 2, no. 2 (Summer 1967): 5–142.
10. Connie Juel and Diane Roper-Schneider, "The Influence of Basal Readers on First Grade Reading," *Reading Research Quarterly* 20, no. 2 (Winter 1985): 134–52.
11. Heidi Anne Mesmer, "Text Decodability and the First-Grade Reader," *Reading & Writing Quarterly* 21, no. 1 (2005): 61–85.
12. For example, Benita A. Blachman et al., "Effects of Intensive Reading Remediation for Second and Third Graders and a 1-Year Follow-Up," *Journal of Educational Psychology* 96, no. 3 (2004): 444–61; Hank Fine et al., "An Examination of the Efficacy of a Multitiered Intervention on Early Reading Outcomes for First Grade Students at Risk for Reading Difficulties," *Journal of Learning Disabilities* 48, no. 6 (2015): 602–21.
13. Joseph R. Jenkins, Julia A. Peyton, Elizabeth A. Sanders, and Patricia F. Vadasy, "Effects of Reading Decodable Texts in Supplemental First-Grade Tutoring," *Scientific Studies of Reading* 8, no. 1 (2004): 53–85.
14. Alia Pugh et al., "Text Types and Their Relations to Efficacy in Beginning Reading Instruction," *Reading Research Quarterly* 58, no. 4 (2023): 710–32.
15. Adams, "Decodable Text"; Leanne Doreen (Clarke) Bier, *Texts and Beginning Readers*, unpublished paper, University of Delaware, 2007; Rachel Birch et al., *A Systematic Literature Review of Decodable and Levelled Reading Books for Reading Instruction in Primary School Contexts: An Evaluation of Quality Research Evidence* (University of Newcastle, 2022); Jennifer Cheatham and Jill H. Allor, "The Influence of Decodability in Early Reading Text on Reading Achievement: A Review of the Evidence," *Reading and*

Writing: An Interdisciplinary Journal 25, no. 9 (2012): 2223–46; Heidi Anne E. Mesmer, "Decodable Text: A Review of What We Know," *Reading Research and Instruction* 40, no, 2 (2001): 121–42.

16. Mesmer, "Decodable Text," 134–136.
17. Eleanor J. Gibson and Harry Levin, *The Psychology of Reading* (The MIT Press, 1975), 72–73.
18. Kelly B. Cartwright et al., "Executive Function in the Classroom: Cognitive Flexibility Supports Reading Fluency for Typical Readers and Teacher-Identified Low-Achieving Readers," *Research in Developmental Disabilities* 88, (2019): 49–52.
19. Mark Seidenberg, *Language at the Speed of Sight* (Basic Books, 2017), 113.
20. Richard L. Venezky and Dale Johnson, "Development of Two Letter-Sound Patterns in Grades One and Three," *Journal of Educational Psychology* 64, no. 1 (1973), 109–15.
21. Elfrieda H. Hiebert. "Enhancing Opportunities for Decoding and Knowledge Building through Beginning Texts," *The Reading Teacher* 77, no. 6 (May–June 2024): 965–74.
22. Barbara R. Foorman et al., "Variability in Text Features in Six Grade 1 Basal Reading Programs," *Scientific Studies of Reading* 8, no. 2 (2004): 192.
23. Jeffrey Bowers and Peter Bowers, "Beyond Phonics: The Case for Teaching Children the Logic of the English Spelling System," *Educational Psychologist* 52, no. 2 (2017): 124–41; Joanne F. Carlisle, "Effects of Instruction in Morphological Awareness on Literacy Achievement: An Integrative Review," *Reading Research Quarterly* 45, no. 4 (2010): 464–87; Donald R. Bear et al., *Words Their Way: Word Study for Phonics, Vocabulary, and Spelling Instruction* (Pearson, 2020).
24. Matthew K. Burns, "Reading at the Instructional Level with Children Identified as Learning Disabled: Potential Implications for Response-to-Intervention," *School Psychology Quarterly* 22, no. 3 (2007): 297–313; Matthew K. Burns et al., "Preteaching Unknown Key Words with Incremental Rehearsal to Improve Reading Fluency and Comprehension with Children Identified as Reading Disabled," *Journal of School Psychology* 42, no. 4 (2004): 303–14; Matthew K. Burns et al., "Comparison of the Effectiveness and Efficiency of Text Previewing and Preteaching Keywords as Small-Group Reading Comprehension Strategies with Middle-School Students," *Literacy Research and Instruction* 50 (2011): 241–52.
25. National Reading Panel, *Report of the National Reading Panel: Teaching Children to Read: Reports of the Subgroups* (U.S. Government Printing Office, 2000).
26. Melanie R. Kuhn and Steven S. Stahl, "Fluency: A Review of Developmental and Remedial Practices," *Journal of Educational Psychology* 95, no. 1 (2003): 3–21.
27. National Reading Panel, *Report of the National Reading Panel: Teaching Children to Read: Reports of the Subgroups* (U.S. Government Printing Office, 2000).
28. Alisa Morgan et al., "Effect of Difficulty Levels on Second-Grade Delayed Readers Using Dyad Reading," *Journal of Educational Research* 94, no. 2 (2000): 113–19; Lisa Trottier Brown et al., "The Effects of Reading and Text Difficulty on Third-Graders' Reading Achievement," *Journal of Educational Research* 111, no. 5 (2017): 541–553; Melanie R. Kuhn et al., "Teaching Children to Become Fluent and Automatic Readers," *Journal of Literacy Research* 38, no. 4, (2006): 357–87.
29. Here are a few examples of those studies. The complete list is included in the online bibliography for this book. Gwendolyn Schultz Ashley, "The Effects of Great Leaps Reading on the Reading Fluency of Elementary Students with Reading and Behavioral Deficits" (unpublished PhD diss., University of Louisville, 2021); Christine M. Bonfiglio et al., "An Experimental Analysis of the Effects of Reading Interventions in a Small Group Reading

Instruction Context," *Journal of Behavioral Education* 15, no. 2 (2006): 93–109; Tanya L. Eckert et al., "Empirically Evaluating the Effectiveness of Reading Interventions: The Use of Brief Experimental Analysis and Single-Case Designs," *Psychology in the Schools* 37, no. 5 (2000): 463–74; Heather J. Faulkner and Betty Ann Levy, "How Text Difficulty and Reader Skill Interact to Produce Differential Reliance on Word and Content Overlap in Reading Transfer," *Journal of Experimental Child Psychology* 58, no. 1 (1994): 1–24; Elfrieda H. Hiebert, "The Effects of Text Difficulty on Second Graders' Fluency Development," *Reading Psychology* 26 (2005): 183–209.

Chapter 7

1. Keith E. Stanovich, "The Interactive-Compensatory Model of Reading: A Confluence of Developmental, Experimental, and Educational Psychology," *Remedial and Special Education* 5, no. 3 (1984): 11–19.
2. Walter Kintsch, *Comprehension: A Paradigm for Cognition* (Cambridge University Press, 1998).
3. Michael J. Kieffer et al., "Is the Whole Greater Than the Sum of Its Parts? Modeling the Contributions of Language Comprehension Skills to Reading Comprehension in the Upper Elementary Grades," *Scientific Studies of Reading* 20, no. 6 (2016): 436–54; National Early Literacy Panel, *Developing Early Literacy: Report of the National Literacy Panel* (National Institute of Literacy, 2008).
4. Rebecca D. Silverman et al., "Beyond Decoding: A Meta-Analysis of the Effects of Language Comprehension Interventions on K–5 Students' Language and Literacy Outcomes," *Reading Research Quarterly* 55 (September 2020): S207–S233.
5. Susan B. Neuman and Tanya Wright, "The Magic of Words," *American Educator* (Summer, 2014): 4–12.
6. Steven A. Stahl and Marilyn M. Fairbanks, "The Effects of Vocabulary Instruction: A Model-Based Meta-Analysis." *Review of Educational Research* 56, no. 1 (1986): 72–110.
7. John J. Carney et al., "Preteaching Vocabulary and the Comprehension of Social Studies Materials by Elementary School Children," *Social Education* 48, no. 3 (1984): 195–96; Leslie Scott Cowell, "Pre-Teaching Vocabulary to Improve Comprehension of a Narrative Text" (unpublished PhD diss., Auburn University, 2012); Richard E. Mayer et al., "Techniques that Help Readers Build Mental Models from Scientific Text: Definitions Pretraining and Signaling," *Journal of Educational Psychology* 76, no. 6 (December 1984): 1089–1105; Karen K. Wixson, "Vocabulary Instruction and Children's Comprehension of Basal Stories," *Reading Research Quarterly* 21, no. 3 (Summer 1986): 317–29.
8. Audrey J. Fowler, "Effects of Two Prereading Activities on Comprehending Science Text: Reading Abridged Text and Learning Vocabulary Words" (unpublished PhD diss., City University of New York, 2016).
9. Kevin A. Koury, "The Impact of Preteaching Science Content Vocabulary using Integrated Media for Knowledge Acquisition in a Collaborative Classroom," *Journal of Computing in Childhood Education* 7, no. 3–4 (1996): 179–97.
10. Diana Dee-Lucas and Jill H. Larkin, "Novice Rules for Assessing Importance in Scientific Texts," *Journal of Memory and Language* 27, no. 3 (June 1988): 288–308.
11. R. G. Fukkink and K. de Glopper, "Effects of Instruction in Deriving Word Meaning from Context: A Meta-Analysis," *Review of Educational Research* 68, no. 4 (January 1998): 450–69.
12. Catherine E. Snow and the RAND Reading Study Group, *Reading for Understanding: Toward an R&D Program in Reading Comprehension* (RAND Corporation, 2002), 94–96.

13. Danielle Brimo et al., "Examining the Contributions of Syntactic Awareness and Syntactic Knowledge to Reading Comprehension," *Journal of Research in Reading* 40, no. 1 (2017): 57–74; Kate Cain, "Syntactic Awareness and Reading Ability: Is There Any Evidence for a Special Relationship?," *Applied Psycholinguistics* 28 (2007): 679–94; Kate Cain and Jane Oakhill, "Profiles of Children with Specific Reading Comprehension Difficulties," *British Journal of Educational Psychology* 76, no. 4 (December, 2006): 683–96; Laurie E. Cutting and Hollis S. Scarborough, "Prediction of Reading Comprehension: Relative Contributions of Word Recognition, Language Proficiency, and Other Cognitive Skills Can Depend on How Comprehension Is Measured," *Scientific Studies of Reading* 10, no. 3 (2006): 277–99; S. Hélène Deacon and Michael Kieffer, "Understanding How Syntactic Awareness Contributes to Reading Comprehension: Evidence from Mediation and Longitudinal Models," *Journal of Educational Psychology* 110, no. 1 (2018): 72–86; Amanda P. Goodwin et al., "Unraveling Adolescent Language & Reading Comprehension: The Monster's Data," *Scientific Studies of Reading* 26, no. 4 (2021): 305–26; Elizabeth MacKay et al., "Informing the Science of Reading: Students' Awareness of Sentence-Level Information is Important for Reading Comprehension," *Reading Research Quarterly* 56, no. 5 (May 2021): S221–S230; Marilyn A. Nippold, "Reading Comprehension Deficits in Adolescents: Addressing Underlying Language Abilities," *Language, Speech, and Hearing Services in Schools* 48, no. 2 (2017): 125–31; Patsy Nomvete and Susan R. Easterbrooks, "Phrase-Reading Mediates Between Words and Syntax in Struggling Adolescent Readers," *Communication Disorders Quarterly* 41, no.3 (2020): 162–75; Mads Poulsen et al., "Remembering Sentences Is Not All about Memory: Convergent and Discriminant Validity of Syntactic Knowledge and Its Relationship with Reading Comprehension," *Journal of Child Language* 49, no. 2 (2022): 349–65; Cheryl M. Scott and Catherine Balthazar, "The Role of Complex Sentence Knowledge in Children with Reading and Writing Difficulties," *Perspectives on Literacy and Language* 39, no. 3 (2013): 18–30; Tamara Sorenson Duncan et al., "Not All Sentences Are Created Equal: Evaluating the Relation Between Children's Understanding of Basic and Difficult Sentences and Their Reading Comprehension," *Journal of Educational Psychology* 113, no. 2 (2021): 268–78; Xiuhong Tong and Catherine McBride, "A Reciprocal Relationship Between Syntactic Awareness and Reading Comprehension," *Learning and Individual Differences* 57 (July 2015): 33–44.
14. Arthur C. Graesser et al., "Coh-Metrix: Providing Multilevel Analyses of Text Characteristics," *Educational Researcher* 40, no. 5 (2011): 223–34; A. Jack Stenner et al., *The Lexile Framework for Reading Technical Report* (MetaMetrics, Inc., 2007).
15. Sorenson Duncan et al., "Not All Sentences."
16. MacKay et al., "Informing the Science."
17. Donald D. Neville and Evelyn F. Searls, "A Meta-Analytic Review of the Effect of Sentence-Combining on Reading Comprehension, *Reading Research and Instruction* 31, no. 1 (1991): 63–76; Phyllis A. Wilkinson and Del Patty, "The Effects of Sentence Combining on the Reading Comprehension of Fourth-Grade Students," *Research in the Teaching of English* 27, no. 1 (1993): 104–25.
18. Elizabeth A. Stevens et al., "The Effects of a Paraphrasing and Text Structure Intervention on the Main Idea Generation and Reading Comprehension of Students with Reading Disabilities in Grades 4 and 5," *Scientific Studies of Reading* 24, no. 5 (2020): 365–79.
19. Scott and Balthazar, "The Role of Complex Sentence Knowledge.

20. Kathleen, C. Stevens, "Chunking Material as an Aid to Reading Comprehension," *Journal of Reading* 25, no. 2 (November 1981): 126–29.
21. Susan Dara Rozen, "Sentence Disambiguation Using Syntactic Awareness as a Reading Comprehension Strategy for High School Students" (unpublished PhD diss., Boston University, 2005).
22. M. A. K. Halliday and Ruqaiya Hasan, *Cohesion in English* (Longman, 1976).
23. Graesser et al., "Analyses of Text Characteristics"; Arthur C. Graesser et al., "Coh-Metrix Measures Text Characteristics at Multiple Levels of Language and Discourse," *Elementary School Journal* 115, no. 2 (2014): 210–29.
24. Nicholas D. Duran et al., "Using Temporal Cohesion to Predict Temporal Coherence in Narrative and Expository Texts," *Behavior Research Methods* 39, no. 2 (2007): 212–23; Alexandra Gasparinatou and Maria Grigoriadou, "Exploring the Effect of Background Knowledge and Text Cohesion on Learning from Texts in Computer Science," *Educational Psychology* 33, no. 6 (2013): 645–70; Anke Schmitz et al., "Students' Genre Expectations and the Effects of Text Cohesion on Reading Comprehension," *Reading and Writing: An Interdisciplinary Journal* 30, no. 5 (2017): 1115–35.
25. Halliday and Hasan, *Cohesion in English*, 227.
26. Graesser et al., "Analyses of Text Characteristics"; Graesser et al., "Coh-Metrix Measures."
27. Peter Freebody and Richard C. Anderson, "Effects of Vocabulary Difficulty, Text Cohesion, and Schema Availability on Reading Comprehension," *Reading Research Quarterly* 18, no. 3 (April 1983): 277–94; Marianne Rice and Kausalai (Kay) Wijekumar, "Inference Skills for Reading: A Meta-Analysis of Instructional Practices," *Journal of Educational Psychology* 116, no. 4 (May 2024): 569–89.
28. Peter W. Foltz et al., "The Measurement of Textual Coherence with Latent Semantic Analysis," *Discourse Processes* 25, no. 2–3 (1998): 285–307; Janice M. Keenan, "Development of Microstructure Processes in Children's Reading Comprehension: Effect of Number of Different Arguments," *Journal of Experimental Psychology: Learning, Memory, and Cognition* 12, no. 4 (October 1986): 614–22.
29. Isabel L. Beck et al., "Revising Social Studies Text from a Text-Processing Perspective: Evidence of Improved Comprehensibility," *Reading Research Quarterly* 26, no. 3 (1991): 251–76; Susan A. Duffy et al., "The Effect of Encoding Task on Memory for Sentence Pairs Varying in Causal Relatedness," *Journal of Memory and Language* 29, no. 1 (February 1990): 27–42; Janice M. Keenan et al., "The Effects of Causal Cohesion on Comprehension and Memory," *Journal of Verbal Learning & Verbal Behavior* 23, no. 2 (Apr 1984): 115–26; Pascale Maury and Amélie Teisserenc, "The Role of Connectives in Science Text Comprehension and Memory," *Language and Cognitive Processes* 20, no. 3 (March 2005): 489–512; Keith K. Millis et al., "Causal Connectives Increase Inference Generation," *Discourse Processes* 20, no. 1 (July–August 1995): 29–49; Murray Singer and Michael Halldorson, "Constructing and Validating Motive Bridging Inferences," *Cognitive Psychology* 30, no. 1 (February 1996): 1–38.
30. Murray and Halldorson, "Constructing and Validating."
31. Tom Trabasso et al., "Causal Cohesion and Story Coherence," in *Learning and Comprehension of Text*, ed. Heinz Mandl, Nancy L. Stein, and Tom Trabasso (Erlbaum, 1984), 83–111.
32. Maury and Teisserenc, "Role of Connectives"; Keith K. Millis et al., "The Impact of Connectives on the Memory for Expository Texts," *Applied Cognitive Psychology* 7, no. 4 (August 1993): 317–39; John D. Murray, "Logical Connectives and Local Coherence," in *Sources of Coherence in Reading*, ed. Robert F. Lorch and Edward J. O'Brien

(Lawrence Erlbaum Associates, 1995), 107–26; Murray Singer and Gordon O'Connell, "Robust Inference Processes in Expository Text Comprehension," *European Journal of Cognitive Psychology* 15, no. 4 (2003): 607–31.

33. Leon Manelis and Frank R. Yekovich, "Repetitions of Propositional Arguments in Sentences," *Journal of Verbal Learning & Verbal Behavior* 15, no. 3 (June 1976): 301–12.
34. Gordon H. Bower et al., "Scripts in Memory for Text," *Cognitive Psychology* 11, no. 2 (April 1979): 177–220.
35. Rice and Wijekumar, "Inference Skills for Reading."
36. J. M. Barrie, *Peter and Wendy* (Grosset & Dunlap, 1911), 202–203.
37. Colby Hall et al., "The Effects of Inference Instruction on the Reading Comprehension of English Learners with Reading Comprehension Difficulties," *Remedial and Special Education* 41, no. 5 (September 2020): 259–70; Louis Maguet McKenna et al., "Improving Children's Reading Comprehension by Teaching Inferences," *Reading Psychology* 42, no. 3 (April 2021): 264–80; Kristen L. McMaster et al., Paul van den Broek, "Making the Right Connections: Differential Effects of Reading Intervention for Subgroups of Comprehenders," *Learning and Individual Differences* 22, no. 1 (February 2012): 100–11; Rice and Wijekumar, "Inference Skills for Reading"; Philip H. Winne et al., "A Model of Poor Readers' Text-Based Inferencing: Effects of Explanatory Feedback," *Reading Research Quarterly* 28, no. 1 (January 1993): 53–66.
38. Elaine Scott, *When Is a Planet Not a Planet: The Story of Pluto* (Houghton Mifflin Harcourt, 2007), 23.
39. Beck et al., "Revising Social Studies Text"; Isabel L. Beck et al., "Improving the Comprehensibility of Stories: The Effects of Revisions that Improve Coherence," *Reading Research Quarterly* 19, no. 3 (April 1984): 263–77; Bruce K. Britton and Sami Gülgöz, "Using Kintsch's Computational Model to Improve Instructional Text: Effects of Repairing Inference Calls on Recall and Cognitive Structures," *Journal of Educational Psychology* 83, no. 3 (September 1991): 329–45; Marie-France Erlich et al., "Processing of Anaphoric Devices in Young Skilled and Less Skilled Comprehenders: Differences in Metacognitive Monitoring," *Reading and Writing: An Interdisciplinary Journal* 11, no. 1 (February 1999): 29–63; Juan A. García-Madruga et al., "Executive Functions and the Improvement of Thinking Abilities: The Intervention in Reading Comprehension," *Frontiers in Psychology* 7 (February 4, 2016): 15.
40. Amy M. Elleman, "Examining the Impact of Inference Instruction on the Literal and Inferential Comprehension of Skilled and Less Skilled Readers: A Meta-Analytic Review," *Journal of Educational Psychology* 109, no. 6 (August 2017): 761–81; Colby S. Hall, "Inference Instruction for Struggling Readers: A Synthesis of Intervention Research," *Educational Psychology Review* 28, no. 1 (March 2016): 1–22; Hall et al., "Effects of Inference Instruction"; Rice and Wijekumar, "Inference Skills for Reading."
41. Carolyn A. Denton et al., "An Investigation of an Intervention to Promote Inference Generation by Adolescent Poor Comprehenders," *Learning Disabilities Research & Practice* 32, no. 2 (May 2017): 85–98.
42. Most research on argument structure explores the issue from the perspective of writing instruction rather than comprehension or learning. There are exceptions, such as Michelle M. Buehl et al., "Profiling Persuasion: The Role of Beliefs, Knowledge, and Interest in the Processing of Persuasive Texts that Vary by Argument Structure," *Journal of Literacy Research* 33, no. 2 (June 2001): 269–301, or Marilyn J. Chambliss and P. K.

Murphy, "Fourth and Fifth Graders Representing the Argument Structure in Written Texts," *Discourse Processes* 34, no. 1 (July 2002): 91–115. These studies suggest that argument structure instruction within reading instruction would improve comprehension.

43. For example, Tom Trabasso et al., "Children's Knowledge of Events: A Causal Analysis of Story Structure," *Psychology of Learning and Motivation* 15 (1981): 237–82.
44. Bonnie J. F. Meyer, *The Organization of Prose and Its Effects on Memory* (North-Holland Publishing Company, 1975).
45. National Reading Panel, *Report of the National Reading Panel: Teaching Children to Read: Reports of the Subgroups* (U.S. Government Printing Office, 2000), 4–42.
46. Goksel Cure et al., "Effectiveness of the Story-Mapping Strategy in Students with Disabilities: Meta-Analysis of Single-Case Experimental Design Studies," *Reading & Writing Quarterly: Overcoming Learning Difficulties* 37, no. 6 (2021): 513–34.
47. Suzanne Bogaerds-Hazenberg et al., "A Meta-Analysis on the Effects of Text Structure Instruction on Reading Comprehension in the Upper Elementary Grades," *Reading Research Quarterly* 56, no. 3 (July 2021): 435–62, 454.
48. Michael Hebert et al., "The Effects of Text Structure Instruction on Expository Reading Comprehension: A Meta-Analysis," *Journal of Educational Psychology* 108, no. 5 (July 2016): 609–29, 622.
49. Nicole Pyle et al., "Effects of Expository Text Structure Interventions on Comprehension: A Meta-Analysis," *Reading Research Quarterly* 52, no. 4 (October 2017): 469–501, 497; Menahem Yeari et al., "Meta-Strategic Learning of Structure Strategies in Reading Comprehension of Expository Texts," *Reading Psychology* 45, no. 1 (2024): 56–77.
50. Pyle et al., "Effects of Expository Text."
51. National Reading Panel, *Report of the National Reading Panel*, 4–39.
52. National Reading Panel, *Report of the National Reading Panel*.
53. Elleman, "Examining the Impact"; Russell Gersten et al., "Teaching Reading Comprehension Strategies to Students with Learning Disabilities: A Review of Research," *Review of Educational Research* 71, no, 2 (2001): 279–320; Sun Hee Lee and Shu-Fei Tsai, "Experimental Intervention Research on Students with Specific Poor Comprehension: A Systematic Review of Treatment Outcomes," *Reading and Writing* 30 (October 2016): 917–43; Peng Peng et al., "The Active Ingredient in Reading Comprehension Strategy Intervention for Struggling Readers: A Bayesian Network Meta-Analysis," *Review of Educational Research* 9, no. 2 (2023), 228–67; Michael Pressley et al., "Beyond Direct Explanation: Transactional Instruction of Reading Comprehension Strategies," *Elementary School Journal* 10, no. 5 (May 1992): 513–42; Barak Rosenshine and Carla Meister, "Reciprocal Teaching: A Review of the Research," *Review of Educational Research* 64, no. 4 (January–March 1994): 479–530; Barak Rosenshine et al., "Teaching Students to Generate Questions: A Review of the Intervention Studies," *Review of Educational Research* 66, no. 2 (July–September 1996): 181–221; Elizabeth Talbott et al., "Effects of Reading Comprehension Interventions for Students with Learning Disabilities," *Learning Disability Quarterly* 17, no. 3 (Summer 1994): 223–32.
54. Michael Pressley et al., "Beyond Direct Explanation."
55. Nell K. Duke and P. David Pearson, "Effective Practices for Developing Reading Comprehension," in *What Research Has to Say about Reading Comprehension*, ed. Alan E. Farstrup and S. J. Samuels (International Reading Association, 2002).
56. Timothy Shanahan et al., *Improving Reading Comprehension in Kindergarten through 3rd Grade: A Practice Guide* (NCEE 2010–4038); National Center for Education

Evaluation and Regional Assistance, Institute of Education Sciences, U.S. Department of Education, 2010.

57. Frederic Charles Bartlett, *Remembering: A Study in Experimental and Social Psychology* (Cambridge University Press, 1932); David P. Ausubel, *The Psychology of Meaningful Verbal Learning* (Grune & Stratton, 1963); John D. Bransford and Marcia K. Johnson, "Contextual Prerequisites for Understanding: Some Investigations of Comprehension and Recall," *Journal of Verbal Learning & Verbal Behavior* 11, no. 6 (1972): 717–26; Richard C. Anderson and P. David Pearson, "A Schema-Theoretic View of Basic Processes in Reading Comprehension," in *Handbook of Reading Research*, ed. P. David Pearson, Rebecca Barr, Michael L. Kamil, and Peter Mosenthal (Longman, 1984); Keith E. Stanovich, "Matthew Effects in Reading: Some Consequences of Individual Differences in the Acquisition of Literacy," *Reading Research Quarterly* 21, no. 4 (Autumn 1986): 360–407, Arthur C. Graesser et al., "Constructing Inferences During Narrative Text Comprehension," *Psychological Review* 101, no. 3 (1994): 371–95; Kintsch, *Comprehension*.
58. Michael B. W. Wolfe et al., "Learning from Text: Matching Readers and Texts by Latent Semantic Analysis," *Discourse Processes* 25, no. 2–3 (1998): 309–36.
59. Courtney Hattan et al., "Leveraging What Students Know to Make Sense of Texts: What the Research Says about Prior Knowledge Activation," *Review of Educational Research* 94, no. 1 (February 2024): 73–111.
60. Fergus I. Craik and Robert S. Lockhart, "Levels of Processing: A Framework for Memory Research," *Journal of Verbal Learning & Verbal Behavior* 11, no. 6 (1972): 671–84.
61. Joanne M. Golden and John T. Guthrie, "Convergence and Divergence in Reader Response to Literature," *Reading Research Quarterly* 21, no. 4 (Autumn 1986): 408–21.
62. Bartlett, *Remembering*.
63. Kintsch, *Comprehension*.
64. Hattan et al., "Leveraging what Students Know."
65. Kate Cain et al., "Comprehension Skill, Inference-Making Ability, and Their Relation to Knowledge," *Memory & Cognition* 29 (2001): 850–59.
66. Carsten Elbro, "Knowledge-Based Inference Making for Reading Comprehension: What to Teach and What Not," *Bulletin of Educational Psychology* 49, no. 4 (June 2018): 701–13.
67. Donna M. Ogle, "K-W-L: A Teaching Model That Develops Active Reading of Expository Text," *The Reading Teacher* 39, no. 6 (February 1986): 564–70.
68. Donna E. Alvermann and Cynthia R. Hynd, "Effects of Prior Knowledge Activation Modes and Text Structure on Nonscience Majors' Comprehension of Physics," *Journal of Educational Research* 83, no. 2 (1989): 97–102.
69. James S. Kim et al., "A Longitudinal Randomized Trial of a Sustained Content Literacy Intervention for First to Second Grade: Transfer Effects on Students' Reading Comprehension," *Journal of Educational Psychology* 115, no. 1 (January 2023): 73–98.

Chapter 8

1. Juliet L. Halladay, "Revisiting Key Assumptions of the Reading Level Framework," *The Reading Teacher* 66, no. 1 (September 2012): 53–62.
2. For example, John T. Guthrie et al., "Increasing Reading Comprehension and Engagement through Concept-Oriented Reading Instruction," *Journal of Educational Psychology* 96, no. 3 (September 2004): 403–23.
3. Suzanne E. Wade, "Research on Importance and Interest: Implications for Curriculum Development and Future Research," *Educational Psychology Review* 13, no. 3 (2001): 243–61.

4. For example, Suzanne Hidi, "Interest and Its Contribution as a Mental Resource for Learning," *Review of Educational Research* 60, no. 4 (Winter 1990): 49–71; Ulrich Schiefele, "Topic Interest, Text Representation, and Quality of Experience," *Contemporary Educational Psychology* 21, no. 1 (January 1996): 3–18.
5. Amanda M. Durik and Kristina L. Matarazzo, "Revved Up or Turned Off? How Domain Knowledge Changes the Relationship Between Perceived Task Complexity and Task Interest," *Learning and Individual Differences* 19, no. 1 (2009): 155–59.
6. Linda B. Gambrell et al., "Classroom Observations of Task-Attending Behaviors of Good and Poor Readers," *Journal of Educational Research* 74, no. 6 (1981): 400–404; Edward E. Gickling and David L. Armstrong, "Levels of Instructional Difficulty as Related to On-Task Behavior, Task Completion, and Comprehension," *Journal of Learning Disabilities* 11, no. 9 (1978): 559–66; Gerald W. Jorgenson et al., "Achievement and Behavioral Correlates of Matched Levels of Student Ability and Materials Difficulty," *Journal of Educational Research* 71, no. 2 (1977): 100–103; Amanda K. Sanford and Robert H. Horner, "Effects of Matching Instruction Difficulty to Reading Level for Students with Escape-Maintained Problem Behavior," *Journal of Positive Behavior Interventions* 15, no. 2 (April 2012): 79–89.
7. Jorgenson et al., "Achievement and Behavioral Correlates."
8. Gambrell et al., "Classroom Observations."
9. Gickling and Armstrong, "Levels of Instructional Difficulty."
10. Megan A. Treptow et al., "Reading at the Frustration, Instructional, and Independent Levels: The Effects on Students' Reading Comprehension and Time on Task," *School Psychology Review* 36, no. 1 (2007): 159–66.
11. Sanford and Horner, "Effects of Matching Behavior."
12. Julie E. Learned, "'The Behavior Kids': Examining the Conflation of Youth Reading Difficulty and Behavior Problem Positioning Among School Institutional Contexts," *American Educational Research Journal* 53, no. 5 (2016): 1271–1309.
13. Jizhi Zhang et al., *Reading Motivation, Reading Achievement, and Reading Achievement Gaps: Evidence from the NAEP 2015 Reading Assessment* (American Institutes for Research, 2020), i.
14. John T. Guthrie et al., "Modeling the Relationships Among Reading Instruction, Motivation, Engagement, and Achievement for Adolescents," *Reading Research Quarterly* 48, no. 1 (January–March 2013): 9–26.
15. Franziska M. Locher et al., "The Relation Between Students' Intrinsic Reading Motivation and Book Reading in Recreational and School Contexts," *AERA Open* 5, no. 2 (2019).
16. Tessa Roberts, "'Frustration Level' Reading in the Infant School," *Education Research* 19, no. 1 (1976): 41–44.
17. Carol A. Donovan et al., "Beyond the Independent-Level Text: Considering the Reader-Text Match in First Graders' Self-Selections During Recreational Reading," *Psychology* 21, no. 4 (2000): 309–33; Mary Jo Fresch, "Self-Selection of Early Literacy Learners," *The Reading Teacher* 49, no. 3 (November 1995): 220–27; Halladay, "Revisiting Key Assumptions."
18. Chantal Lepper et al., "Gender Differences in Reading: Examining Text-Based Interest in Relation to Text Characteristics and Reading Comprehension," *Learning and Instruction* 82 (2022): 1–11, 3.
19. Sara M. Fulmer and Maria Tulis, "Changes in Interest and Affect During a Difficult Reading Task: Relationships with Perceived Difficulty and Reading Fluency," *Learning and Instruction* 27 (October 2013): 11–20; Maria Tulis and Mary Ainley, "Interest,

Enjoyment and Pride After Failure Experiences? Predictors of Students' State-Emotions After Success and Failure During Learning Mathematics," *Educational Psychology* 31, no. 7 (2011): 779–807; Maria Tulis and Sarah M. Fulmer, "Students' Motivational and Emotional Experiences and Their Relationship to Persistence During Academic Challenge in Mathematics and Reading," *Learning and Individual Differences* 27, (October 2013): 35–46.

20. Fulmer and Tulis, "Changes in Interest," 13.
21. Mihaly Csikszentmihalyi, *Flow: The Psychology of Optimal Experience* (Harper Perennial, 1991); Edward L. Deci and Richard M. Ryan, *Intrinsic Motivation and Self-Determination in Human Behavior* (Plenum Press, 1985).
22. Tulis and Fulmer, "Challenge in Mathematics and Reading," 44.
23. Suzanne Hidi and K. Ann Renninger, "The Four-Phase Model of Interest Development," *Educational Psychologist* 41, no. 2 (2006): 111–27.
24. Sara M. Fulmer et al., "Interest-Based Text Preference Moderates the Effect of Text Difficulty on Engagement and Learning," *Contemporary Educational Psychology* 41, no. 6 (2015): 91–110.
25. Alexander Soemer et al., "Mind Wandering and Reading Comprehension in Secondary School Children," *Learning and Individual Differences* 75 (October 2019): 11; Nash Unsworth and Brittany D. McMillan, "Mind Wandering and Reading Comprehension: Examining the Roles of Working Memory Capacity, Interest, Motivation, and Topic Experience," *Journal of Experimental Psychology: Learning, Memory, and Cognition* 39, no. 3 (2013): 832–42.
26. Paola Bonifacci et al., "The Relationship Between Mind Wandering and Reading Comprehension: A Meta-Analysis," *Psychonomic Bulletin & Review* 30, no 1 (2023): 40–59.
27. Myrthe Faber et al., "The Effect of Disfluency on Mind Wandering During Text Comprehension," *Psychonomic Bulletin & Review* 24, no. 3 (2017): 914–19.
28. Teresa Schurer et al., "Concurrent Prospective Memory Task Increases Mind Wandering During Online Reading for Difficult but Not Easy Texts," *Memory & Cognition* 51, no. 1–2 (January 2023): 221–33.
29. Alexander Soemer et al., "Mind Wandering May Both Promote and Impair Learning," *Memory & Cognition* 52, no. 2 (2023): 373–89; Sarah Bro Trasmundi and Juan Toro, "Mind Wandering in Reading: An Embodied Approach," *Frontiers in Human Neuroscience* 17 (March 1, 2023): 15.
30. Rebecca Kahmann et al., "Mind Wandering Increases Linearly with Text Difficulty," *Psychological Research* 86, no. 1 (2022): 284–93; Caitlin Mills et al., "The Influence of Consequence Value and Text Difficulty on Affect, Attention, and Learning While Reading Instructional Texts," *Learning and Instruction* 40, (December 2015): 9–20; Emily Q. Rosenzweig and Allan Wigfield, "What If Reading Is Easy but Unimportant? How Students' Patterns of Affirming and Undermining Motivation for Reading Information Texts Predict Different Reading Outcomes," *Contemporary Educational Psychology* 48 (January 2017): 133–48.
31. Noah D. Forrin et al., "On the Relation Between Reading Difficulty and Mind-Wandering: A Section-Length Account," *Psychological Research* 83, no. 3 (April 2019): 485–97.
32. Schurer et al., "Concurrent Prospective Memory Task."
33. Trish Varao-Sousa et al., "Re-Reading After Mind Wandering," *Canadian Journal of Experimental Psychology/Revue Canadienne De Psychologie Expérimentale* 71, no. 3 (September 2017): 203–11.

34. Matthew K. Burns and Vincent J. Dean, "Effect of Acquisition Rates on Off-Task Behavior with Children Identified as Having Learning Disabilities, *Learning Disability Quarterly* 28, no. 4 (2005): 273–81; Matthew K. Burns et al., "Assessing the Instructional Level for Mathematics: A Comparison of Methods," *School Psychology Review* 35, no. 3 (2006): 401–18.
35. For example, Mark A. McDaniel et al., "When Text Difficulty Benefits Less-Skilled Readers," *Journal of Memory and Language* 46, no. 3 (2002): 544–61; Danielle S. McNamara and Walter Kintsch, "Learning from Texts: Effects of Prior Knowledge and Text Coherence," *Discourse Processes* 22, no. 3 (1996): 247–88.
36. Evelyn W. Francis, "Grade Level and Task Difficulty in Learning by Discovery and Verbal Reception Methods," *Journal of Educational Psychology* 67, no.1 (1975): 146–50.
37. Jenny Nordman and Justin Adcock, "Addressing Low Frustration Tolerance in Students with Learning Disabilities," *Behavior Management* 59, no. 2 (2022): 133–37.
38. Albert Bandura, *Self-Efficacy: The Exercise of Control* (W. H. Freeman, 1997); Alan Wigfield and Jacquelynne S. Eccles, "Expectancy-Value Theory of Achievement Motivation," *Contemporary Educational Psychology* 25 (2000): 68–81.
39. Susan L. Klauda et al., "Struggling Readers' Information Text Comprehension and Motivation in Early Adolescence," in *Adolescents' Engagement in Academic Literacy*, ed. John T. Guthrie, Alan Wigfield, and Susan L. Klauda (Corwin Press, 2012); Christopher A. Wolters et al., "Adolescents' Motivation for Reading: Group Differences and Relation to Standardized Achievement," *Reading and Writing* 27, no. 3 (2014): 503–33.
40. Cordula Artelt et al., *Learners for Life: Student Approaches to Learning: Results from PISA 2000* (Paris: Organisation for Economic Co-operation and Development, 2003); Kit-ling Lau and David W. Chan, "Reading Strategy Use and Motivation Among Chinese Good and Poor Readers in Hong Kong," *Journal of Research in Reading* 26, no. 2 (2003): 177–90; McGeown, 2012.
41. Klauda et al., "Struggling Readers' Information Text."
42. Seokhee Cho et al., "For Challenging Tasks: The Critical Factor on Late Academic Achievement and Creative Problem Solving Ability," *KEDI Journal of Educational Policy* 2, no. 2 (2005): 57–78; Ann K. Boggiano et al., "Children's Preference for Challenge: The Role of Perceived Competence and Control," *Journal of Personality and Social Psychology* 54, no. 1, (1988): 134–41; Oliver Fisher and Daphna Oyserman, "Assessing Interpretations of Experienced Ease and Difficulty as Motivational Constructs," *Motivation Science* 3, no. 2 (2017): 133–63; Ellen A. Skinner and Jennifer R. Pitzer, "Developmental Dynamics of Student Engagement, Coping, and Everyday Resilience," in *Handbook of Research on Student Engagement,* ed. Sandra L. Christenson, Amy L. Reschly, and Cathy Wylie (Springer, 2012), 21–44; Michael J. Sulik et al., "Moving Beyond Executive Functions: Challenge Preference as a Predictor of Academic Achievement in Elementary School," *Journal of Experimental Child Psychology* 198 (2020), n.p.
43. Rosenzweig and Wigfield, "Different Reading Outcomes."
44. Wigfield and Eccles, "Expectancy-Value Theory"; Paul R. Pintrich and Dale H. Schunk, *Motivation in Education: Theory, Research, and Applications* (Merrill Prentice Hall, 2002).
45. Rosenzweig and Wigfield, "Different Reading Outcomes."
46. Locher et al., "School Contexts."
47. Roberta J. Goldberg et al., "Predictors of Success in Individuals with Learning Disabilities: A Qualitative Analysis of a 20-Year Longitudinal Study," *Learning Disabilities Research & Practice* 18, no. 4 (2003), 222–36.

48. Mary Ainley et al., "Interest, Learning, and the Psychological Processes that Mediate Their Relationship," *Journal of Educational Psychology* 94, no. 3 (2002): 545–61; Shi Feng et al., "Mind Wandering While Reading Easy and Difficult Texts," *Psychonomic Bulletin & Review* 20, no. 3 (June 2013): 586–92; Noah D. Forrin et al., "On the Relation Between Reading Difficulty and Mind-Wandering: A Section-Length Account, *Psychological Research* 83, no. 3 (2019): 485–97; Sara M. Fulmer and Jan C. Frijters, "Motivation During an Excessively Challenging Reading Task: The Buffering Role of Relative Topic Interest," *Journal of Experimental Education* 79, no. 2 (2011), 185–208; Sara M. Fulmer and Maria Tulis, "Changes in Interest;" *Learning and Instruction* 27, (2013): 11–20; James S. Kim et al., "Engaging Struggling Adolescent Readers to Improve Reading Skills, *Reading Research Quarterly* 53, no. 2, (2016): 357–82; Miriam McBreen and Robert Savage, "The Impact of Motivational Reading Instruction on the Reading Achievement and Motivation of Students: A Systematic Review and Meta-Analysis," *Educational Psychology Review* 33, no. 3 (2020): 1125–63; Caitlan Mills et al., "The Influence of Consequence Value and Text Difficulty on Affect, Attention, and Learning While Reading Instructional Texts," *Learning and Instruction* 40, (2015): 9–20; Caitlin Mills et al., "Cognitive Coupling During Reading," *Journal of Experimental Psychology: General* 146 (2017): 872–83; Rosenzweig and Wigfield, "Different Reading Outcomes"; Ulrich Schiefele and Andreas Krapp, "Topic Interest and Free Recall of Expository Text," *Learning and Individual Differences* 8, no. 2 (1996): 141–60; Soemer et al., "Mind Wandering and Reading Comprehension."
49. John L. Carter and Harold L. Russell, "Relationship Between Reading Frustration and Muscle Tension Levels in Children with Reading Disabilities," *American Journal of Clinical Biofeedback* 2, no. 2 (1979): 60–62.
50. Christine M. Leighton et al., "Engaging Second-Grade English Learners in Complex Texts, Topics, and Tasks," *Literacy Research and Instruction* 58, no. 4 (2019): 272–94.
51. Jacquelynne S. Eccles and Allan Wigfield, "From Expectancy-Value Theory to Situated Expectancy-Value Theory: A Developmental, Social Cognitive, and Sociocultural Perspective on Motivation," *Contemporary Educational Psychology* 61 (2020), https://www.sciencedirect.com/science/article/pii/S0361476X20300242.
52. Lupo et al., "Exploration of Text Difficulty."
53. Kath Glasswell and Michael Ford, "Let's Start Leveling about Leveling," *Language Arts* 88, no. 3 (January 2011): 208–16; James V. Hoffman, "What If 'Just Right' Is Just Wrong? The Unintended Consequences of Leveling Readers," *The Reading Teacher* 71, no. 3, (June 2017): 265–73.
54. William J. Knaus, "Frustration Tolerance Training for Children," in *Rational Emotive Behavioral Approaches to Childhood Disorders: Theory, Practice and Research*, ed. Albert Ellis and Michael E. Bernard (Springer Science, 2006).
55. Eccles and Wigfield, "From Expectancy-Value Theory"; Louise David et al., "The Relation Between Perceived Mental Effort, Monitoring Judgments, and Learning Outcomes: A Meta-Analysis," *Educational Psychology Review* 36, no. 3 (2024): Article 66.
56. Elke Baten et al., "How Can the Blow of Math Difficulty on Elementary School Children's Motivational, Cognitive, and Affective Experiences Be Dampened? The Critical Role of Autonomy-Supportive Instructions," *Journal of Educational Psychology* 112, no. 8 (2020): 1490–1505.
57. Boggiano et al., "Children's Preference."

58. Rosenzweig and Wigfield, "Different Reading Outcomes."
59. Oliver Fisher and Daphna Oyserman, "Assessing Interpretations of Experienced Ease and Difficulty as Motivational Constructs," *Motivation Science* 3, no. 2 (2017): 133–63.
60. Grace Bennett-Pierre et al., "'This is Hard!' Children's and Parents' Talk about Difficulty During Dyadic Interactions," *Developmental Psychology* 59, no. 7 (July 2023): 1268–82.
61. B. F. Skinner, "Reinforcement Today," *American Psychologist* 13, no. 3 (March 1958): 94–99.
62. Vicki L. Lee, "Behavior as a Constituent of Conduct," *Behaviorism* 11, no. 2 (October–December 1983): 199–224.
63. Jeffrey Liew et al., "Pathways to Reading Competence: Emotional Self-Regulation, Literacy Contexts, and Embodied Learning Processes," *Reading Psychology* 41, no. 7 (2020): 633–59.
64. Fulmer and Tulis, "Changes in Interest"; McBreen and Savage, "Impact of Motivational Reading."
65. Originally, those reports were referred to as "Children's Choices"; now they are labeled "Favorites." (See International Literacy Association (ILA), "Choices Reading Lists," ILA website, https://www.literacyworldwide.org/get-resources/reading-lists.)
66. Lauren A. Sosniak, "If Children Chose Textbooks," *Journal of Research in Childhood Education* 5, no. 1 (1990): 47–59.
67. Alfred W. Tatum, *Teaching Black Boys in the Elementary Grades* (Teachers College Press, 2021); Junko Yokota, "Issues in Selecting Multicultural Children's Literature," *Language Arts* 70, no. 3 (March 1993): 156–67.
68. Fulmer et al., "Interest-Based Text Preference."
69. Boggiano et al., "Children's Preference."
70. Thomas Haugen et al., "The Training Characteristics of World-Class Distance Runners: An Integration of Scientific Literature and Results-Proven Practice," *Sports Medicine* 8, no. 46 (April 2022).
71. Vivian I. Schneider et al., "Effects of Difficulty, Specificity, and Variability on Training to Follow Navigation Instructions," *Psychonomic Bulletin & Review* 22, no. 3 (June 2015): 856–62.
72. Kristin E. Flegal et al., "Adaptive Task Difficulty Influences Neural Plasticity and Transfer of Training," *Neuroimage* (March 2019): 111–21, https://doi.org/10.1016/j.neuroimage.2018.12.003.

Chapter 9

1. Merriam-Webster, "Word of the Day: Cogent," *Merriam-Webster Online*, July 16, 2023, https://www.merriam-webster.com/word-of-the-day/cogent-2023-07-16#:~:text=Cogent%20comes%20from%20the%20Latin,it%20is%20clear%20and%20pertinent.
2. Richard Atwater and Florence Atwater, *Mr. Popper's Penguins* (Little Brown, 1992), 5.
3. Grace M. Fernald, *Remedial Techniques in Basic School Subjects* (McGraw-Hill, 1943).
4. Carol A. Donovan et al., "Beyond the Independent-Level Text: Considering the Reader-Text Match in First Graders' Self-Selections During Recreational Reading," *Psychology* 21, no. 4 (2000): 309–33.
5. Juliet L. Halladay, "Difficult Texts and the Students Who Choose Them: The Role of Text Difficulty in Second Graders' Text Choices and Independent Reading Experiences" (unpublished PhD diss., Michigan State University, 2008).

6. Kiera Parrott, "Fountas and Pinnell Say Librarians Should Guide Readers by Interest, Not Level," *School Library Journal*, October 12, 2017, https://www.slj.com/story/fountas-pinnell-say-librarians-guide-readers-interest-not-level. This position suggests that it is okay for students to deal with challenging text when they are on their own with little possibility of assistance, but that it is harmful to allow students to study such books under the close supervision of a teacher, an illogical inconsistency at best.
7. Barbara M. Taylor et al., "Effective Schools and Accomplished Teachers: Lessons about Primary-Grade Reading Instruction in Low-Income Schools," in *Teaching Reading: Effective Schools, Accomplished Teachers*, ed. Barbara M. Taylor and P. David Pearson (Lawrence Erlbaum Associates Publishers, 2002).
8. Sarah Lupo et al., "An Exploration of Text Difficulty and Knowledge Support on Adolescents' Comprehension," *Reading Research Quarterly* 54, no. 4 (October–December 2019): 457–79.
9. Christine M. Leighton et al., "Engaging Second-Grade English Learners in Complex Texts, Topics, and Tasks," *Literacy Research and Instruction* 58, no. 4 (2019): 272–94.
10. Douglas Biber and Bethany Gray, *Grammatical Complexity in Academic English* (Cambridge University Press, 2016).
11. Timothy Shanahan and Cynthia R. Shanahan, "Teaching Disciplinary Literacy to Adolescents: Rethinking Content-Area Literacy," *Harvard Educational Review* 78, no. 1, (2008): 40–59; Cynthia R. Shanahan and Timothy Shanahan, "Disciplinary Literacy," in *The SAT® Suite and Classroom Practice: English Language Arts/Literacy*, ed. James Patterson (College Board, 2020).
12. Roberto Gutiérrez and Robert E. Slavin, "Achievement Effects of the Nongraded Elementary School: A Best-Evidence Synthesis," *Review of Educational Research* 62, no. 4 (1992): 333–76.
13. Carol McDonald Connor et al.,"Testing the Impact of Child Characteristics X Instruction Interactions on Third Graders' Reading Comprehension by Differentiating Literacy Instruction," *Reading Research Quarterly* 46, no. 3, (July–September 2011): 189–221.
14. Chase Young and Kathleen A. J. Mohr, "Exploring Factors that Influence Quality Literature Circles." *Literacy Research and Instruction* 57, no. 1 (January 2018): 44–58.
15. Virginia J. Goatley et al., "Diverse Learners Participating in Regular Education 'Book Clubs.'" *Reading Research Quarterly* 30, no. 3 (July–August 1995): 352–80.
16. Nell K. Duke et al., "Putting PjBL to the Test: The Impact of Project-Based Learning on Second Graders' Social Studies and Literacy Learning and Motivation in Low-SES School Settings," *American Educational Research Journal* 58, no. 1 (2021): 160–200; Angela Imbaquingo and Jorge Cárdenas, "Project-Based Learning as a Methodology to Improve Reading and Comprehension Skills in the English Language," *Education Science* 13 (2023): 587.
17. For example, Samuel P. Huntington, *The Clash of Civilizations and the Remaking of the World Order* (Simon & Schuster, 2011); Pierre Manent, *An Intellectual History of Liberalism,* trans. Rebecca Balinski (Princeton University Press, 1996).
18. United Nations Educational, Scientific and Cultural Organization (UNESCO) Institute for Statistics, "Literacy," UNESCO website, last updated September 7, 2019, https://uis.unesco.org/en/topic/literacy.
19. Organization for Economic Co-operation and Development (OECD), "PISA for Development Assessment and Analytical Framework: Reading, Mathematics and Science" (OECD Publishing, 2018), 39.
20. OECD, "PISA for Development Assessment," 39.

21. OECD, "PISA for Development Assessment," 39.
22. Supporting this point are the long-term trend assessment results from the National Assessment of Educational Progress. These have shown relatively stable eighth grade scores over roughly a forty-year period, despite periodic increases or declines in fourth grade reading. Raising early reading scores has not translated to later improvements. See the NAEP's Long-Term Trend Assessment Results page at https://www.nationsreportcard.gov/ltt/?age=9.

About the Author

Timothy Shanahan is Distinguished Professor Emeritus at the University of Illinois at Chicago, where he founded the UIC Center for Literacy. He has served as director of reading for the Chicago Public Schools and was Visiting Research Professor at Queens University, Belfast, Northern Ireland. He has studied and taught reading for more than fifty-five years. He is past president of the International Literacy Association, served on the Advisory Board of the National Institute for Literacy under Presidents George W. Bush and Barack Obama, and has led several federal research review panels on reading education. Dr. Shanahan was inducted to the Reading Hall of Fame in 2007, and he has been recognized with numerous awards for research, teaching, and public service. He is a former first-grade teacher.

Tim and his wife, Cyndie, have pursued many adventures, including climbing to Base Camp at Mount Everest, bicycling across Europe, cruising Antarctica, running a marathon, and helping with their nine grandchildren.

About the Author

Index